FISHERMEN, RANDIES AND FRAUDSTERS

Also by Malcolm Archibald:

POWERSTONE
WHALES FOR THE WIZARD
THE DARKEST WALK
A SINK OF ATROCITY
GLASGOW: THE REAL MEAN CITY
WHISKY WARS, RIOTS AND MURDERS

FISHERMEN, RANDIES AND FRAUDSTERS

Crime in Nineteenth-century
Aberdeen and the North-east

Malcolm Archibald

BLACK & WHITE PUBLISHING

First published 2014
by Black & White Publishing Ltd
29 Ocean Drive, Edinburgh EH6 6JL

1 3 5 7 9 10 8 6 4 2   14 15 16 17

ISBN: 978 1 84502 744 5

Copyright © Malcolm Archibald 2014

The right of Malcolm Archibald to be identified as the author of this work has been asserted
by him in accordance with the Copyright, Designs and Patents Act 1988.

All rights reserved. No part of this publication may be reproduced, stored in a retrieval
system, or transmitted in any form, or by any means, electronic, mechanical, photocopying,
recording or otherwise, without permission in writing from the publisher.

A CIP catalogue record for this book is available from the British Library.

Typeset by RefineCatch Limited, Bungay, Suffolk
Printed and bound by Grafica Veneta S. p. A.

FOR CATHY

Contents

It is long since the calendar of crime in Aberdeen presented such a fearful aspect – there now being no fewer than four individuals charged with murder.

— Aberdeen Weekly Journal, 18 July 1849

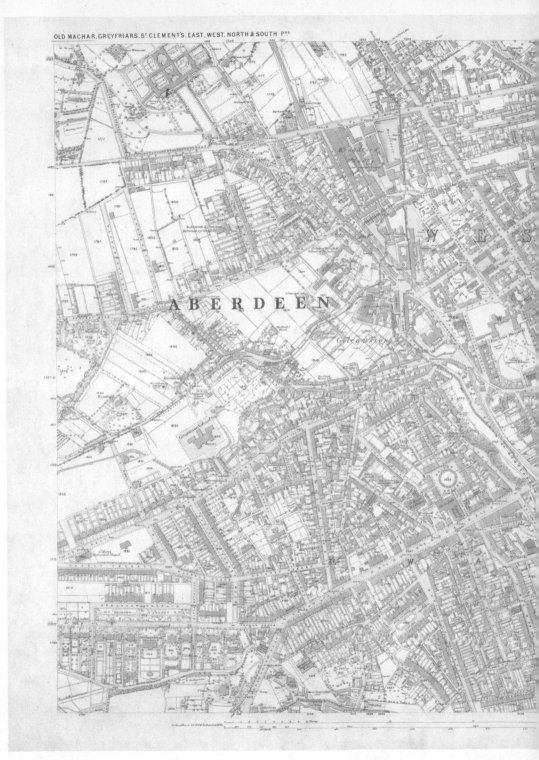

© National Library of Scotland

N O R T H

REYFRIARS

1ST   W A R D

B

E A S T

U C H

D

Gas Works

Sandford
Chemical
Works

ST. CLEMENTS

UPPER DOCK

VICTORIA DOCK

Spillwater Channel

KINCARDINESHIRE

Introduction
Aberdeen

Of all the Scottish cities, Aberdeen is the most isolated. Glasgow, Edinburgh and Dundee form a triangle that encompasses the Lowlands and within which lives the bulk of the Scottish population. Aberdeen is sixty-six miles north of Dundee and has its own hinterland and, often, its own climate. To put it kindly, Aberdeen's weather can be bracing; the snell wind is a reminder of the near presence of the North Sea, which, together with the surrounding farmland, has shaped much of the character of this city.

The origin of Aberdeen is as shrouded as an east coast haar. The Romans were certainly hereabouts, but their presence was fleeting as they marched to try to conquer a land that they, in common with later invaders, found unconquerable. There were certainly a number of small settlements that merged to form the basis of what became Aberdeen. These tiny hamlets were jammed between the sea on the east and the Stocket Forest to the west. The forest would have been alive with bears, wolves, boars and possibly outlaw men, while the rivers Don and Dee were to the north and south. Expansion would be slow and painful, but that thorough, patient, grinding advance probably helped form the character of the native Aberdonian.

This was not a peaceful coast. In 1012, there was a significant battle at Cruden Bay when the Scots defeated a raiding Danish force led by Knut, who is probably better known as King Canute, the conqueror of England. The name Cruden is said to mean 'slaughter of the Danes' and the heaviest fighting was where the golf course now sees encounters of a less bloody variety. Inland, there was bloodshed at Lumphanan, where rivals to the Scottish throne clashed and Malcolm Canmore defeated Macbeth, later immortalised by Shakespeare. Already by the twelfth century Aberdeen was a trading port, important enough to be sacked by a Norseman named Eysteinn in 1153. Whatever destruction Eysteinn caused, nine years later King Malcolm IV stayed in the town, which King David I later elevated to the status of a burgh.

Despite Norse raids and the ambitions of kings, Aberdeen was set to be the commercial capital of the northern half of the country. Isolated Aberdeen may have been, but the area was not backwards: it embraced Christianity a century or so before St Columba created the religious powerhouse that was Iona; St Mochricha, known as Machar, walked the banks of the Don; and even as the Norse were ravaging, dedicated monks wrote the *Book of Deer* in Aberdeenshire. Unfortunately, like so many of Scotland's national treasures, it was removed south, possibly when the Plantagenet English descended on the country like a plague from the Old Testament.

The medieval castle also fell victim to ravaging English armies during the Wars of Independence, until William Wallace and King Robert I and his lieutenants expelled them. The major historian for the exploits of King Robert was an Aberdonian, John Barbour. Aberdeen came through battered but unbowed to continue its existence as a market and trading town, defended from the harrying of various Highland potentates by a network of powerful castles in the Aberdeenshire hinterland.

By that time the town was split in two: Old Aberdeen beside the Don with the cathedral of St Machar as a centrepiece, and New Aberdeen by the Dee, looking towards the harbour and the sea. The two would grow separately but were interdependent. Trade flourished, with locally produced wool, hides, salmon and dried fish being exported, and flax, iron, wine, spices and timber coming in from the Low Countries and the Baltic. With craftsmen and churchmen adding to the merchants, Aberdeen was a relatively prosperous town, the third richest in Scotland behind Edinburgh and Dundee. Aberdonians put the horrors of Norse and English invasions behind them and concentrated on the sea and the trade counter; they were a hardy folk, always ready to defend themselves but, despite the occasional act of piracy by men such as the Earl of Mar, not particularly aggressive.

However, Aberdeen was a prize that promised riches for the predator. More English invasions were followed by the religious wars of the mid seventeenth century, in which Aberdeen fared badly: Covenanters and Cromwell's men both used the town as an urban punch bag. The Ulstermen and Highlanders of the Marquis of Montrose, Charles I's general in Scotland, gave the town a particularly nasty ravage, and the Aberdonians must have breathed a collective sigh of relief when that particular period of horror ground to an end. Wars and turmoil make exciting history, but they are hell on earth for the poor folk who have to live through them. The seventeenth century closed on a low note, with King William's Ill Years of famine and disease, but there was always hope in Aberdeen.

The wars might have been damaging, but Aberdeen continued to mature and grow. In the year 1495, William Elphinstone, the Bishop of Aberdeen, founded King's College, which grew to be the University of Aberdeen. It was a sign that learning and culture survived whatever the men of violence might try. A century later, George Keith, 5th Earl Marischal of Scotland, founded Marischal College, a 'civic university' or 'town college' as opposed to the earlier church creations, which required a papal bull. From that time, the city of Aberdeen had two universities, an equal number to all of England. The two universities, King's College and Marischal College, merged in 1860 and the splendid granite building for Marischal, built in 1890, is still a landmark in the city centre, although it is no longer used for educational purposes.

But it was in the eighteenth century, after the Union of 1707 had papered over the deep national and cultural divisions of Scotland and England, that Aberdeen began to properly expand. Perhaps it was because there was less fear of hostile armies coming to destroy that which had been painfully built, or maybe it was just the natural evolution of the city, but the early eighteenth century saw the city boundaries edging westwards. The opening of the granite quarries that were to give Aberdeen its alternative name of the Granite City was coming into play, and by the early nineteenth century, the streets that form the backbone of the present city were being formed. Union Street, Castle Street, King Street, the terraces of the west end, the Assembly Hall and the Music Hall all marked the progress of the city into the Victorian era.

There was progress in education as well, with the founding of Robert Gordon's Hospital for 'Maintenance, Ailment, Entertainment and Education of young Boys whose Parents are poor and indigent'. The idea of an infirmary began in 1739, and the establishment slowly expanded, not altogether without controversy at a time when the teaching of anatomy was viewed with suspicion. The ensuing riots are mentioned in a later chapter.

The nineteenth century also saw the Female Orphan Asylum and, in 1809, the Bridewell, which was a house of correction rather than a prison, an establishment that aimed to rehabilitate rather than punish. There, prisoners picked and spun oakum, with the money they earned used for buying their meals. These petty offenders were retrained to be useful members of society, whether they wanted to or not. The Bridewell was an impressive five-storeyed building with its own guardhouse and it must have awed the slum dwellers who were sent there, while the surrounding high stone wall would have served as a reminder of the situation they were in.

Aberdeen was never a fully industrial town, but it dabbled with woollen textiles and papermaking and was a notable shipbuilding centre. The clipper or Aberdeen bow was invented here, and James Hall of Aberdeen launched what has been called the first British clipper ship in *Scottish Maid* in 1839. The sea that washed the eastern face of the city provided an outlet for adventurous spirits as well as for commercial exploitation, and Aberdeen shipmasters traded with Europe and far beyond. The Aberdeen White Star clipper line was famous in the century, with *Thermopylae* recognised as arguably the fastest vessel afloat, defeating *Cutty Sark* in a number of races.

Another notable area of expertise was in the whaling industry. Aberdeen whaling masters were known for their daring, with Captain Penny being perhaps the most audacious. However, whaling was a very competitive industry and the rival masters were known to bend the law to ensure a greater profit. In Chapter 4 of this book, there is an example of the consequences. Even more successful than whaling was the fishing industry. Aberdeenshire ports shared in the herring bounty, and from its inception in the 1880s, Aberdeen became the centre of the Scottish trawling industry. Scottish deep-sea fishing centred on the northern triangle of Aberdeen, Peterhead and Fraserburgh, and all three had been whaling ports. However, although the fishing industry brought huge benefits to the area in terms of jobs and wealth, nineteenth-century fishermen were also known for their truculence. Both local and 'stranger' or outsider fishermen caused trouble for the Aberdeenshire police.

As with most towns of the period, Aberdeen's burghers and provosts usually came from the most financially successful families. At the beginning of the century, local politics was dominated by conservative merchants such as Provost Hadden. He was in place during the riot of

1802 when the military unit the Ross and Cromarty Rangers fired into a mob of his citizens. The redcoats could often be volatile, but troublesome soldiers were merely one aspect of life in the nineteenth century. Another was the advent of the railways. Building these nineteenth-century marvels of engineering created turmoil and confusion as armies of labourers descended on the local communities and demonstrated a 'navvy's randy' by drinking the pubs dry. Politics was also lively, with electoral reform easing into Chartism and then the socialism of the latter decades of the nineteenth century, but except for the occasional riot to protest about the price of bread, Aberdeen escaped the large-scale troubles that rocked cities further south. However, the citizens did share other worries.

Every community has concerns about crime. Nineteenth-century Aberdeen was no different. Compared with other cities, it had a reputation of being quiet and orderly, but that was only a relative status. The city had its bad areas and the hinterland had its share of crime, just like everywhere else. There were murders and muggings, assaults and highway robberies, and drunken brawls and riots that had the authorities begging for military help. There was a mutiny at a reform school, child murder, a mystery in which a private detective and Scotland Yard became involved, and a woman who became notorious as an international fraudster. There was also careless coach driving, child cruelty and general mayhem.

The following chapters do not pretend to be a comprehensive account of all the crime in Aberdeen and the Aberdeenshire area, nor are they in any way academic. Rather they try to show some of the variety of crime in Aberdeen and Aberdeenshire, with the major criminal events highlighted, together with some of the more interesting incidents.

1

Town Sergeants

Before uniformed police were ever thought of, Aberdeen had town sergeants to keep the peace. This post was first recorded in the Council Register of 1398, when four were elected, and records from 1616 show that an Act of Council ordered that they should be dressed in a juip (jacket) of red. The sergeants were not uniformed police in the modern sense of the word; they were not employed specifically to prevent crime. The sergeants had ceremonial as well as practical roles: they supported the Lord Provost and guarded the badges of office. They also kept order in the streets and acted as thief-catchers, while by the early nineteenth century they doubled up as sheriff officers, although that role ended by 1835.

One of the six town sergeants of the early nineteenth century was named Simon Fraser Grant, who had a long career. According to William Bannerman in *The Aberdeen Worthies*, Grant's mother came from the Highlands and it is possible that he was illegitimate. Grant worked as a kitchen servant before he became a sergeant. He was a sportsman and had a dog named Juba as well as a brace of wives and reputedly a few lovers as well, one of who presented him with a fine daughter. But it was as a sergeant that he made his living.

For example, in the last week of August 1805 there was a spate of petty vandalism in Aberdeen, with the public lamps being a particular target. At a time before electricity or gas, these lamps were fuelled by whale oil and were often seen as a major aid to curbing crime, as they lit the main thoroughfares, to the distress of footpads and pickpockets. Saturday, 24 August was a particularly bad night, with a large number of the expensive glass bowls smashed. The Commissioners of Police offered a large reward of five guineas to anybody who gave information that led to an arrest. The information was to be given to George Turriff or Simon Grant, town sergeants.

In March 1820, there was an upsurge in sheep stealing around Aberdeen and again Simon Grant was the man to whom information should be given if an informant hoped for a reward. Eight years later, in April 1828, Grant was involved in helping quell a riot in George Street on the king's birthday. On that occasion, a burning boat was hauled through the street, and when a mob came roaring to his door, John Millar defended his Loch Street house with a pistol. Grant died in the summer of 1829.

By that time Aberdeen had a functioning police force, but the town sergeants were still useful. They provided ceremonial colour to official events and helped the provost. In the winter of 1828, Aberdeen was in the middle of a mini crime wave as the number of break-ins and burglaries multiplied. The culprits were a gang of boys, known thieves who banded together and infested the streets at night. At the beginning of December 1828, two town sergeants, William Walker and Charles Dawson, learned that the boys had their headquarters in a house near the Bridge of Dee. As they were local men who had a long-standing presence in the city, the town sergeants would speak to many people and gather titbits of information, so they operated through informants and their own personal knowledge.

Dawson and Walker hurried to the house at the Bridge of Dee. In the days before search warrants they simply broke in, to find an Aladdin's Cave of stolen property. The house had a sitting tenant, who, with his wife, seemed to act as an Aberdonian Fagin to the youths. Dawson and Walker arrested both, together with three of the boys. A fourth, named Milne, was later traced and arrested as well.

In 1829, Walker was busy again, arresting Peter Dunstan, who had recently arrived in Aberdeen. His previous lodgings had been in the Watergate of Perth, but when he left there he also carried away most of his landlord's clothes with him. Walker traced him to a house in Aberdeen, relieved him of the burden of guilt and accompanied him on the Defiance stagecoach back south to Perth.

In 1834, Mr George Cockburn, one of the town sergeants, applied for the vacant position of gaoler and was chosen out of a seven-strong list. At that time he had already been in charge of the criminal prisoners in the jail for six months, during which time none had escaped. He had been a sheriff officer for fifteen years and a town sergeant for two years. With his departure, there was a vacancy in the town sergeants' department; it was not advertised until the following year. There were high expectations for the man who would replace him.

In the *Aberdeen Journal* of 6 May 1835, the advertisement was headed: 'Town Serjeant'. It said that 'all applications must be in the handwriting of the Applicants, accompanied by Certificates of sobriety and moral character. The person appointed will be required to find security for the faithful discharge of his office ... his whole time and attention must be devoted exclusively to the duties of the situation.'

Of all the early nineteenth-century town sergeants, Charles Dawson is perhaps the best remembered. He lived at Well Court in Broad Street and became legendary for his knowledge of all the local bad men. At about eleven o'clock on Thursday, 12 November 1829, a warehouseman named Robert Girvan was walking home by

Putachieside when a young man approached him and started an argument, using what Girvan later termed 'insulting language'. Girvan tried to walk on. He was near St Catherine's Brae when another man appeared; short and stocky, he stood in front of Girvan to block his passage while a third man came and landed a solid kick on Girvan's leg. Realising that he was about to be robbed, if not beaten up, Girvan backed against the wall so that nobody could get behind him. The three men surrounded him; the squat man made a grab for his watch, chain and the attached seals; and then they all ran off.

No doubt relieved to be uninjured, Girvan told the authorities, and Charles Dawson asked for a description of the attackers. Once again, local knowledge helped. Dawson thought he recognised one as William Burnett and another as a sailor and a notorious lawbreaker named William Cumming. Dawson knew the areas they lived in and soon hunted them down.

The case came before the Circuit Court on 21 April 1830, where both men were charged with assault and theft. Cumming pleaded guilty of theft but denied being 'of habit and repute a thief', and Burnett pleaded not guilty. Burnett claimed he had seen Cumming take the watch and run away. Charles Dawson knew Cumming well as a common thief, but there were a number of witnesses who said that both men had been together in Margaret Low's brothel, but as the witnesses were all prostitutes and ladies of bad reputation their words were perhaps not readily believed. Lord Moncrieff gave Cumming seven years' transportation and dismissed Burnett. Cumming was sent away on the convict ship *Burrell* in July 1830

Dawson was a busy man, as he kept his stern eye on the bad characters of the town. One family that stirred his interest were the Pirie brothers: John, Peter and Thomas Pirie, who were known thieves and housebreakers. If the criminologists' theory of a criminal class was ever true, the Piries were role models. When there were a number of burglaries in the winter of 1829, Dawson looked at the modus operandi, checked the whereabouts of the Pirie clan and put his detective skills to work.

The first break-in that Dawson could connect with the Piries occurred on the night of 14 November 1829. Burglars had hit the firm of William Mackinnon and Company, iron and brass founders of Windy Wynd. This was a lane that ran between Spring Gardens and Gallowgate, where the north bank of the Loch of Aberdeen had been. The burglars were not subtle. They forced open an iron front door to enter a short corridor that led into the premises. There was a second, wooden door with a lock that was nailed in place. The burglars forced this lock as well. That door led into a space from which doors opened onto a tin workshop and a copper workshop. The door to the tin workshop was open and the iron shutters to the copper workshop had been thrust back; there had been a fair amount of strength needed to break in.

The burglars stole a variety of objects that could be kept, pawned or sold: a number of tin dishes, a zinc-brass cover, two brass pump valves, files, brass fire irons, an oil flask, a bow saw and other objects. Dawson notified the pawnshops about everything that had been stolen.

The second break-in that Dawson linked to the Piries was on 12 December 1829, when the home of Mr Harry Grassie was burgled. Grassie lived at Holburn on the road from Union Grove to the Deeside turnpike. Once inside, the burglars had emptied a desk of promissory notes and bills, an insurance policy, nine pounds in bank notes (more than a junior domestic servant earned in a year), pocketbooks and various personal and business papers.

Dawson and the police asked for more details of the Holburn break-in. Harry Grassie was an elderly man with money, but in a move that was not uncommon at the time, he had married a young and attractive wife. His wife had fallen foul of the Excise and had been fined, but Grassie had refused to pay the fine, so she was jailed. Despite his apparent callousness, Grassie visited his wife in the jail every night between six and seven. Ironically, or perhaps with poetic justice, it was when Grassie was visiting the jail that the burglars struck, removing a pane of glass from the bedroom window to get in.

Dawson investigated the break-in with a careful eye that would have found favour with Sherlock Holmes. He found three sets of footprints on the earth underneath the bedroom window. He measured the prints: one was quite distinct, as if the heel had been lost from the boot, so that was a valuable clue. Now all Dawson had to do was search all of Aberdeen for a man with no heel on one of his boots.

Although Dawson suspected that the Piries might have been involved in the factory robbery, he had no evidence against them. However, when he examined the Piries' house in Ann Street, he took Grassie in case there was any of his property to identify. He also brought two other men in case of trouble. After Dawson had banged on the door for a good fifteen minutes, the Piries allowed him in. Dawson asked to see all the boots in the house. There were three pairs, all dirty, but that was not unusual at a time when paved streets were not universal. The boots were an exact match in size for the footprints on the earth, and one was lacking half its heel. Dawson guessed that he had found his burglars and immediately arrested them.

He searched the house and found two chisels, one of which had a piece of putty on the blade, which suggested it had been used to remove a pane of glass from a window. The colour of the putty on the blade matched that around the glass on Grassie's window. Dawson searched further; he lifted the hearthstone and found a snuffbox with Grassie's bills inside. There seemed no doubt that the Piries had burgled Grassie's house.

However, there remained the Mackinnon burglary. Although Dawson had no evidence, he strongly suspected that the Piries had been involved there as well. He remained alert and asked his informants to keep their ears open for any information. The Piries lived right next door to Mackinnon's foundry and worked in a factory in nearby

Wapping Street. As the weeks passed they must have thought they had escaped, but when Charles Dawson arrested them for the break-in at Grassie's, one of their workmates, William Ross, remembered one of the Piries using a bow saw. Ross recollected that such an item had been stolen from Mackinnon and searched the factory further. In a hidden corner of the factory he found three bags of material that had been stolen from Mackinnon. Ross took the bags to the police office.

Working closely with the police, Dawson questioned Pirie's neighbours and their servant, a woman named Moir. She lived in the flat immediately below Grassie and knew his house well. She told Dawson that John Pirie had asked her to sell a set of brass fire irons for her. When Dawson asked, she handed him the irons, which were the set that had been stolen from Mackinnon. There was more than enough evidence to charge John Pirie with the Mackinnon break-in.

The case came to trial in the April Circuit Court. The Piries pleaded not guilty and put up a spirited, if strange, defence of alibi. Although there had been a number of people who were sure that they had seen the Piries leave their work early on the Saturday afternoon, the Piries found counter witnesses who had apparently seen them hard at work. One woman, Agnes Faulkner, swore blind that she left work with John Pirie at quarter past six and that she accompanied him to the Ann Street house, where she remained until quarter past eight. Even stranger was the Piries' sister, who put herself square in the firing line when she claimed that her husband had brought home the box full of Grassie's bills and told her to hide them. She claimed that she had not known they were stolen, but she had placed them under the hearthstone, without her brother's knowledge. When the Advocate General heard that this woman was estranged from her husband, he prevented her from continuing, as she might incriminate him.

After hearing from four Glasgow criminal officers that John Pirie was a well-known thief in that city, the jury found him guilty of the Mackinnon burglary, but the case against his brothers was not proven.

All three were found guilty of the Grassie burglary. John Pirie, the eldest brother, was transported for life and his two brothers for seven years each. The Pirie brothers sailed on *Burrell* on 22 July 1830 along with another 189 convicts, including William Cumming.

The Pirie sister was not charged with perjury, although it seemed obvious she was more concerned with getting her husband in trouble than ensuring that justice was done.

But to Dawson, removing the Piries was only one incident in a busy life. For example, in December 1829 Dawson arrested James Reith, a carter, for dangerous driving. In 1830 Dawson was involved in solving the case of the poisoning of James Humphrey and in December 1830 he was again on the trail of thieves. Winter seemed to be the busiest time for the law enforcers of Aberdeen, possible because of the long, dark nights. Maberley and Company had a linen works at Loch-side and in early December thieves broke in and stole some of the weaving equipment.

Charles Dawson was told of the theft and immediately set to work. Once again he played to his strength of knowing every inch of the town and the identity of every lawbreaker and potential troublemaker. He also knew the pawnbrokers and resetters of stolen property, so after a tour he found the missing equipment and traced the thief. A weaver named Robert Gallie was arrested and jailed.

In 1831, Dawson was involved in a slightly unusual case that involved the theft and reset of whalebone. The thieves had hit two premises: Thomas and Alexander Bannerman's yard at Footdee, and the yard of the Union Whale-Fishing Company. The case hinged on the evidence of James Watt, a criminal who turned King's Evidence. He said he was on watch outside the building while John McCraw, Alexander Brebner and John Johnstone robbed the building of the valuable baleen, or whalebone. They took the bone and handed it to him as he stood beside the window. The whole party carried the bone to the links and cut it into manageable lengths before selling it to John

Walker and Lewis Sandison, dealers in whalebone, for around one shilling a pound. Walker cleaned it up and sold it for around three shillings a pound. The price of whalebone fluctuated from £200 to £375 a ton, but umbrella makers or stay makers would possibly have bought it cheaper on the black market. The thieves believed they were being short-changed, but when Watt challenged Walker for the money he thought he was due for the stolen bone, Walker whispered urgently for him to go away. Dawson was at that moment searching the premises for stolen whalebone. It was known that sailors brought home pieces of whalebone for their sweethearts and occasionally offered them to Joseph Johnston, an umbrella maker of Blackfriar Street, so there was already an established black market for the commodity in Aberdeen.

At the trial at the Circuit Court in spring 1832, Dawson gave evidence as to the bad character of all the men involved, and also confirmed that he had found stolen whalebone at Sandison's yard after acting on a tip-off from an informant. There was no doubt as to their guilt.

In 1834, Dawson was busy again. The Aberdeen area had been struck by a large number of thefts of poultry. That may sound petty, but at a time when food was never plentiful, poultry supplied both eggs and meat, and often the sale of either could mean the difference between hunger and relative plenty for a family on the brink of poverty. In April, a hen house at Fairley was robbed, and Dawson, together with a sergeant named James Horne, was sent to investigate. As so often in the nineteenth century, there were informers, and the sergeants arrested a young girl named Bisset. They searched her house and found the missing hens. Bisset was sent to jail for forty days.

Not long afterwards, a small farm at Woodside was hit, with twenty-five hens stolen. Again, the procurator fiscal sent Dawson and Horne. The sergeants saw two men named Runcie and Robb loitering near hen coops, and as they knew these two were one-time poultry thieves, they decided to follow them. Shedding their distinctive red coats, the sergeants followed – 'dogged', in the language of the time – the men to the disused quarries at Hilton. Runcie and Robb had a number of hens there, stolen from different places, so the sergeants arrested them both.

That same month, Dawson arrested a girl named Mary Bothwell, who had sneaked into the house of a ninety-year-old woman in Spa Street, grabbed a watch from the mantlepiece and run away. Bothwell melted down the case and pawned the workings, but Dawson traced her as having given the pledge for the pawn.

Dawson never knew when he might be required. On 25 February 1834, he was quietly walking home when a carpenter named Charles Reid stopped him with the information that the previous night he had been robbed of two £20 notes in a Putachieside brothel. Dawson and James Horne, who was now a sheriff officer, checked the house and found nothing, but, knowing the area, they also looked at the brothel of Jean Murray, whom they strongly suspected of being involved in murder and other, lesser crimes. Murray was in the company of a girl named Catherine Jamieson, who the sergeants also believed to be a criminal. Dawson and Horne searched the house and found one £20 note in the straw of a bed and another hidden beneath the floor. Both women were arrested: Murray, an old offender, got seven years' transportation, and Jamieson, a first offender, six months in Aberdeen Bridewell.

In November 1835, there was a horseshoe thief at large in Aberdeen. That may sound strange today, but at a time when everything was carried by horse-powered carts, horseshoes were absolutely vital. When blacksmiths, farriers and horse-hirers all complained to Charles Dawson that their stocks of horseshoes had been stolen, he began to hunt. He checked all the metal dealers until he found that Ferguson of King Street, a rag and old iron dealer, had 300 horseshoes on his property. Dawson called in the people who had been robbed, who were able to identify 200 of the shoes. One was a highly unusual ass shoe, which a man named Thomas Skene instantly recognised as his. Ferguson denied that he knew the man from whom he had bought the shoes, but said it was a man who had picked discarded shoes off the road. However, Dawson knew his Aberdeen; it would take many years to collect 300 discarded shoes in the city, but a carter named John Niven fitted the description that Ferguson gave. When Dawson confronted Ferguson with Niven, the identification was complete. Niven got sixty days.

That same year of 1835, Dawson made a number of arrests. One, Nicol Ker, otherwise known as Michael Ker, appeared at the Circuit Court in April charged with having stolen a silk handkerchief from a shop in St Nicholas Street. He pleaded not guilty, but Dawson knew him as a long-time thief and he was transported for seven years on the ship *Strathfieldsaye*. At that same court Dawson and William Walker gave evidence against Margaret Willox, another known thief, who was also given seven years' transportation. Dawson and a sergeant named George Lyall also spoke against Ann Balfour, a habitual thief who had stolen the pocketbook of a coachman called Joachim Illingworth.

Dawson was also involved in the case of Isabella Watt, Mary Sim and William Jamieson. The two women enticed a countryman into a secluded house, where Jamieson grabbed him by the throat as the women rifled through his pockets. Together with a sergeant named Grant, Dawson travelled to Edinburgh and arrested Jamieson before bringing him back for trial in Aberdeen. Watt and Jamieson were transported for life. Watt sailed to Van Diemen's Land (Tasmania) on *Hector* in June 1835, and Jamieson sailed to the same destination on *Asia* in November.

Throughout his career, Dawson relied on sheer common sense, his knowledge of Aberdeen, dogged determination and a network of informers to help keep the criminal element of the city under control. Nevertheless, the sergeants had other duties as well as suppressing crime and chasing criminals halfway across the country. They also had the unpleasant task of drowning stray dogs and the slightly less unpleasant task of donning their full red-coated uniforms on the Sabbath, escorting the magistrates to church and then taking the red coats off and touring the pubs to make sure that nobody was drinking in the hours of divine service. As if that was not enough, they had to act as heralds on ceremonial occasions, such as proclaiming King William IV in 1830.

In 1850, Charles Dawson left his position as town sergeant after he was offered the position of superintendent of the Aberdeen Railway Police, a body that had been formed two years previously. As Dawson departed his role, so did a legend, but by then the uniformed police were patrolling the streets and putting definite limits on crime in the city.

2

Resurrection Men and Anatomists

Grave robbing was a crime specific to the eighteenth and early nineteenth centuries, when anatomists needed fresh corpses to dissect for the sake of medical science. There were three cities in Scotland where bodies could be legally dissected, with Edinburgh being the most important, then Glasgow, and finally Aberdeen. However, there were still a number of cases where bodies were lifted from graves and sold to the doctors.

Early Cases

On the 29 April 1815, Lord Hermand judged a case where four medical students dug a woman's body up from a grave in Aberdeen. They were found guilty and ordered to pay a huge £100 to the infirmary, and were also jailed for fourteen days. They were not the most successful bodysnatchers, but others fared worse. In January 1830, a woman named Janet Hay died and was buried in the Old Town churchyard. To ensure it was safe from resurrection men – so named as they dug up, or 'resurrected', corpses from the grave – her grave was dug twelve feet down rather than the usual six. When the gravediggers were a few feet under the ground they came across an earlier grave with a partly rotted corpse inside. As was usual in such circumstances, the old coffin was removed, the new one lowered in place and the old one positioned on top. A stone was erected at the head of the grave, but within a few days a sharp-eyed gravedigger noticed that the stone was loose, as if the grave had been robbed. The gravediggers investigated, but rather than dig up Janet Hay, the resurrection men had only got as far as the older coffin. They had pulled this up and broken in, but when the rotted body had crumbled as they hauled it out, they dropped their booty and fled.

Resurrection Riot in Guestrow

Aberdeen's bodysnatchers were perhaps not on the same scale as the Edinburgh serial murderers and resurrection men Burke and Hare, but they succeeded in creating a public outcry and a couple of major riots. The first of these was in Guestrow.

In 1829, the UK was split over the practice of using corpses for anatomical research. There was no doubt that budding doctors and surgeons had to be taught the workings of the human body and the best method involved seeing the real thing all neatly dissected, but people did not want their deceased relatives hacked open even in private, let alone in front of witnesses. It was a time of intense suspicion, when anatomists were viewed with unfriendly eyes, graveyards had a nightly guard and anybody carrying a large box or waiting near a burial party was liable to be challenged. At the beginning of March 1829, a rumour spread that there was a surgeon giving anatomy lectures in Guestrow. The local people crowded into the street, peered through every window and tapped at every door to ascertain the identity of the occupants. Eventually they found a window that gave a view of the room in which the lectures took place and, what was worse, there was a human body lying on the dissecting table.

The lecturer must have been well aware of the impending trouble as the crowd gathered outside his anatomy theatre and howled abuse. He fastened heavy wooden shutters across his windows so nobody could see inside. However, the mob would not be thwarted. As soon as they were sure where the dissection was being carried out, they tore free the shutters and bombarded the windows with a hail of stones. They looked in what was left of the windows and saw that the corpse had already been partly dissected, with its bowels and intestines in a glutinous pile beside the body.

It appeared as if the crowd were planning a general attack on the building, but peace was restored when the town sergeants arrived and carried the half-dissected corpse to Drum's Aisle, the area between the West Church and the East Church of the Kirk of St Nicholas. The presence of the sergeants kept the crowd quiet for a while, but once they had gone the stones began to fly again. The mob poured into the anatomist's room, smashed up what they could and carried everything else into Guestrow. They threw it all in an untidy pile – surgeon's clothing, surgical equipment and even a box that had been found to contain a skull – and set fire to it. Not yet satisfied with the destruction, some enterprising men even clambered up the walls and were attempting to take off the roof of the house when a magistrate and three town sergeants arrived to restore order. The men on the roof were arrested, but it was not until the police arrived in force that the remainder of the crowd fled in all directions.

That anatomy theatre never reopened, and the shaken inhabitants of Guestrow emerged to survey the smouldering mess in the middle of their street. Aberdeen had given due warning of its thoughts about anatomists.

Riot in St Andrew Street

The second anti-dissection riot was longer lasting and even more destructive. After the wrecking of the Guestrow premises, some of the more scientifically inclined citizens had donated money towards building a more official anatomical theatre, where anatomists could lecture medical students and dead bodies could be dissected. In the winter of 1831 the building was opened in St Andrew Street, with Dr Moir as the surgeon lecturer. Although this was a perfectly legal undertaking, there were many people in Aberdeen who objected to the practice of dissection on moral or religious grounds, and many who harboured superstitious fears about their relations appearing before their Maker with parts of their body missing. The benefits to medical knowledge were rarely discussed in the crowded slums of the city.

The theatre may have been academically necessary, but it was not an architectural asset to Aberdeen. It glowered onto St Andrew Street through three false pointed windows, sightless eyes in a blank building of death. The only natural light came from the rear or from the high glass cupola on the roof. To the west and east and in the rear were patches of waste ground, so the theatre stood in splendid isolation. Its nearest neighbour was a school for girls and young women, who could, if they wished, look out their rear window and see bags of human remains thrown out for rubbish.

When the local people took a shortcut across the wasteland at the back of the theatre, they experienced a terrible smell and some claimed to have seen human bones, entrails and skulls scattered over the ground. Events suggest that they were not exaggerating. At around two o'clock in the afternoon of Monday, 19 December 1831, a group of small boys were playing in this wasteland and noticed a dog frantically digging in the ground. Being boys and therefore inquisitive, they watched as the animal unearthed pieces of a human body.

Quite possibly enjoying the horror and the attention, the boys shouted their news to everybody in the street, and about twenty people gathered around the disturbed earth. Two youths dug deeper and found more human remains. By that time quite a sizeable crowd had gathered, and when their anger grew, some barged to the anatomy theatre to voice their feelings. Two young men entered, but Moir the anatomist met them and presumably asked them to leave. Instead, the men attacked him. Moir fled, jinked past the crowd outside and ran for his life. It was a wise decision, as the blood of the mob was up. Some of the crowd chased Moir to his own house, kicked open the door and roared after him to a back room, but Moir escaped out a back window and ran into the darkening city.

Meanwhile, back in St Andrew Street, a hundred-strong crowd erupted into the theatre. They gaped in horror as they found three corpses waiting to be dissected and at once decided that thieving and destruction was the only solution. If something could be used or pawned, it was stolen, but everything else was wrecked. The cloaks used by students and surgeons, the vicious surgical instruments and just about everything portable was taken or destroyed, but then the busy town sergeants arrived to restore some peace to the place.

The sergeants ordered the bodies to be removed from the theatre and taken to the ground outside. That may not have been the most diplomatic move, as the crowd's anger increased at the sight of one of the bodies. It had already been used for lecturing purposes and the skull was sawn in two. The crowd screamed for vengeance. They knew that the only legal corpses used for dissection were executed criminals, unchristened children and orphans who had not been formally apprenticed. These bodies had presumably been unearthed from some unknown graveyard. The town sergeants quickly threw covers over the corpses and had them carried to Drum's Aisle.

By that time, the crowd was seething with anger. 'Burn the house,' somebody yelled, and others took up the cry. 'Down with the burking shop!' That was a reference to the Edinburgh murderers Burke and

Hare, who would murder their victims and sell the bodies to the anatomist Dr Knox. The killing technique of smothering without leaving a mark was named 'burking' in their honour, or at least their memory. Surging back inside the theatre, the crowd made for the fireplace, and while some tried to light a fire, others tore down lathes from the plaster to use as fuel. It was only when people brought in wood shavings and staves from tar barrels that the fire took hold, and the screaming mob danced around it until somebody yelled out, 'Come out, come out, the house is falling!'

The crowd was correct. As the people inside had been starting a fire, those outside had begun their own work of destruction. Some had dug underneath the foundations of the building and had levered out some of the stones, while others had smashed heavy planks against the walls to knock the whole place down. As the back wall fell, men and women heaped wood on the flames so the building became a huge bonfire, a funeral pyre to the hopes of the anatomist. With that wall down, the crowd swarmed to the front and began work on the wall with the three blank windows.

The Lord Provost arrived as the riot reached its peak. He was not alone; the city magistrates and a number of recently sworn-in special constables accompanied him. To his credit, the Lord Provost did not use force but spoke sensibly to the crowd, saying that 'if their feelings had been hurt, every enquiry would be made'. He also said that what they were doing was 'not a proper way to manifest their displeasure', which was a fine understatement to a howling mob out for total destruction.

Perhaps surprisingly, the crowd cheered the Lord Provost. Simultaneously, some of the 70th Regiment had been marched from the barracks to support the civil power. However, the authorities halted them at Schoolhill, so they did not get involved. Nor did the fire engine that came to extinguish the fire, as the machine carried no water and there was none nearby. Instead they watched the fine bonfire that kept them warm on a winter's evening. Despite the presence of the provost and the specials, the work of destruction continued. The front wall eventually fell so there were only the two gables of the anatomy theatre standing, with the interior a mass of flames. The crowd had swollen to an estimated but possibly exaggerated 20,000, stretching from Sim's Square to Charlotte Street, and they began to work on the gables, pushing them into the flames. It took six hours for the theatre to be demolished.

Sometime in the evening, a medical student chanced his luck and arrived to watch the spectacle. Inevitably he was recognised and chased as if he was a fox pursued by a pack of baying hounds. The student ran into a house in Schoolhill. The mob clustered outside and threatened to destroy the house unless the occupants gave him up, but when they learned he had escaped through a back window they dispersed without causing any more trouble. Another student was spotted and chased to Guestrow, but he also escaped. In that street the crowd congregated at the anatomist's house that had been wrecked two years previously, but they only made loud noises and did not attempt any further destruction.

By ten o'clock the town was as quiet as it normally was on a Monday night, except for the scent of smoke in the air and the dying flicker of flames in St Andrew Street. However, there was one last postscript.

In February 1832, Private Alexander Allen of the Scots Fusilier Guards was arrested in London. He had been seen with the mob that demolished Moir's anatomical theatre, and more than one person claimed that he had been the man who had struck the match that burned the place down. He had been described as 'a giddy wild young man' and was well educated, which was unusual for a private soldier. He had not long signed up when the riot began. The local police arrested him in Horse Guards in London and a sheriff officer from Aberdeen took the packet boat south to bring him back for trial.

In 1832, the government passed the Anatomy Act, which made it easier for anatomists to obtain bodies. From that time people who were legally in charge of dead bodies could give them to anatomists. The trade in digging up bodies ended. However, dead bodies still had the power to jolt Victorian Aberdeen.

The Nabob of Dunecht

In the nineteenth century, the nobility were treated with a mixture of adulation and awe. Their movements were followed step by step and every word they spoke was caressed by newspapers as if they were pearls of wisdom. They were the superstars of their day, titled celebrities with more power and sway than it is possible to conceive of today. They had the final word in the House of Lords, owned vast swathes of land, controlled the lives of their tenants and moved around the countryside in gilded coaches, when they were not tramping the moors slaughtering the wildlife or entertaining heads of state in their palatial mansions. The thought of insulting such a near-divine personage as a titled aristocrat was virtually unthinkable, but in 1881 that happened, and in a manner that shook the values of Victorian society to the foundations, and involved Scotland Yard, prominent politicians and a private detective.

The Earl of Balcarres was one of the most powerful men in the country. As the 26th Earl of Crawford and the 9th of Balcarres, he had an ancient seat at Dunecht House in Aberdeenshire. However, the mortuary chapel beneath Dunecht was new and was the centre of attention and scandal. The chapel was attached to the north-east of the house, but the entrance to the mausoleum was outside and to the north of the chapel, sealed by large Caithness stone slabs each weighing around half a ton. Each slab was covered in turf, and the crypt was accessible only down a flight of eight steps that descended into the calm coolness of the stone interior. There was an iron railing around the crypt, but the position of the entrance meant that nobody in the house could see it, and a gathering of bushes acted as an effective screen from casual passers-by.

In December 1880, the previous Earl, the 8th of Balcarres, had died in Florence. His body was embalmed there and brought over to Scotland to be interred in the new mortuary, and there it was left. His was the first and only body inside, as the previous deceased were interred at Haigh Hall in Lancashire, the family seat in England. The body lay apparently undisturbed for months, and then at eight in the morning of Thursday, 1 December 1881, a labourer named William Hadden was passing the vault and saw that about twelve feet of the railing had been removed, the turf had been disturbed and the slabs moved. One of the huge slabs had been raised and supported on a large baulk of wood. Hadden raised the alarm, and an investigation found that the body of the late earl had vanished: somebody had stolen the corpse.

The body had been enclosed in a succession of three coffins and all had been opened, but the thief had not touched the decorative silver mountings, which could have fetched a high price in any jewellers or pawnshop in the country. This was no simple theft after a quick profit, but something else. There was no way of discerning when the desecration had taken place, but when the police made enquiries, the staff of the house mentioned that during the summer they had experienced a strange smell. They had thought that it was only the flowers decomposing within the vault, and the entrance had been cemented shut to seal in the unpleasant aroma.

In September, there had been an ill-written message sent to the factor that suggested that the body had been stolen. The letter had had an Aberdeen postmark, but it was not taken seriously. After all, why would anybody wish to steal a dead body?

The smell and the message had been forgotten until the discovery of the grave theft. The slab was heavy so it was supposed that there were a number of men involved and that they had moved the slab to draw attention to the theft. The dowager countess, some of her family and the other members of the household had not heard anything untoward, but the night of Wednesday, 1 December had been wild and windy enough to conceal any movement of the slab. Lord Balcarres, who was the current earl, was notified, as were the police.

That same afternoon, Inspector George Cran arrived from Aberdeen and began an investigation that was to last for months. He checked the method first: the coffin was huge, oak and elaborate, with two inner lead shells. The thief had dragged it forwards on the slab it stood on. He had cut through the lower ends, unscrewed the lids of the inner and outer coffins with a nut key, removed the packing material between the inner shells and then pulled the coffin on its side to get at the body. He had left the aromatic sawdust packing and the pieces cut from the coffin on the ground, possibly to help quieten the echoes of his footsteps in the empty stone chamber of the crypt. Having done that, the thief or thieves had lifted the corpse and vanished. The police were left scratching their heads, not only as to the identity of the thief, but also the motive for the theft. Inspector George Cran was puzzled, but he knew the area and he began to work on his own theories.

As the aristocracy was involved in the case, and because of its unusual nature, it became high profile. Rather than treating it as a simple case of theft and entrusting it to the local sergeant, Major Ross, the Chief Constable of Aberdeenshire became involved, as well as Charles Duncan the procurator fiscal and Thurso-born Detective Inspector Donald Swanson of the Metropolitan Police. At that time, Swanson was probably the best-known policeman in Britain. He had been in the public eye for his actions against Fenian terrorists and he had recently arrested Percy Lefroy Mapleton, who had committed murder on the London to Brighton railway. There was also a local connection, as Swanson's brother had been the police superintendent in Aberdeen. The Home Secretary himself gave orders that no expense was to be spared in the investigation: the dead body of the Earl of

Balcarres had to be found. On that first day, around twenty constables descended on Dunecht House.

Major Ross was a frequent visitor to Dunecht as the police, aided by gamekeepers and staff, scoured the countryside around the house for any clue. The police brought in the Victorian equivalent of sniffer dogs in two Scotch terriers, which searched for any remaining scent. Three rings of men kept watch on every path and track leading to Dunecht and no strangers were admitted to the grounds or the house. However, it was like shutting the stable door many months after the horse had bolted.

The police took stucco casts of all the footprints around the tomb and compared the results with the boots and shoes of all the staff and workmen who had business on the estate. This led to one poor innocent labouring man being closely questioned before he was released without charge. All the Aberdeen police were asked to recall anything suspicious over the last few months, and one constable remembered seeing a Whitechapel cart in George Street in September, with two smartly dressed men sitting beside a large and well-wrapped parcel that might have been a corpse. That was only the first of a number of false trails.

The case created much speculation: people theorised that the man who had robbed the tomb had been skilled; that he had used some corrosive material to weaken the cement before he used a crowbar to lift the slabs; that he had not worked alone. People calculated that it had taken eight men to place the coffin in the vault; it was inconceivable that a single man could have broken in, moved the coffin, gained access and carried the body of the late earl away. But for all the theories, nobody knew the truth: the case was known as the Dunecht mystery and nothing the police did seemed to move them even one step closer to a solution.

Police inquiries continued: a workman had passed the crypt at eleven on the Wednesday night and had seen nothing suspicious, and a servant had passed at five the following morning and seen nothing, so it was assumed the crime was committed between five and eight. There had been a number of tools found near the crypt, including three crowbars, two shovels and a pick, all of which had been removed from a workman's shed in the grounds. The police had searched the locality thoroughly, including a cave that the then-present earl indicated might be a good place to hide the body, but found nothing. They checked the records of the railways and steamboat companies to see if there had been any bulky packages transported around the time of the disappearance, but again drew a blank. Their inquiries among the local people were fruitless, except to discover that most people considered the body to have been stolen in the early summer, perhaps as far back as May.

There was another, more exotic, theory that the Earl had never been interred in the vault in the first place. Before the body left Florence, ran this idea, somebody stole it to learn the skills of embalming. The scores of people who witnessed the body being deposited in Dunecht ridiculed this idea. Others scoffed at a hopeful idea that the science of clairvoyance was used to locate the entrance to the tomb. A Londoner saw a man carrying a parcel 'which looked like an Egyptian mummy'; others swore that the body was in Italy and a ransom note could be expected soon. The authorities put their view in a short statement: 'The body was there; the body is not there now and it is believed to be not far off.'

More detectives came north from Scotland Yard to aid Swanson and Major Ross; the anonymous letter received in September was scrutinised again and again; a farmer from Echt said that one early morning in June he had seen a brake being driven on the Banchory road at a fast pace with a body-shaped bundle lying inside. The police queried those people who lay on the possible route south, but found nothing. A man from Midmar thought there was a newly dug patch of ground in a plantation outside the Dunecht boundary: the police dug the place thoroughly and found only soil, roots and stones. An Aberdeen cab driver named David Neeves claimed that on 19 July on Bridge Street in Aberdeen, three rough-looking Italians asked him various questions about Dunecht. Other witnesses came forward with the information that they had seen three strange men carrying a mysterious and foul-smelling parcel through the Aberdeen streets. A man had also been seen wandering through the policies of Dunecht the day before the slab was found displaced. A servant remembered being awakened by a crash in May, but had thought nothing of it at the time. Thirty men dug up a turnip field just to the north of the house and found only soil and stones. The wells were probed with iron hooks, Craigenlow Quarry was examined and a pond was drained. There was no sign of the missing body.

The police examined the original letter again:

Sir – the remains of the late Earl of Crawford are not beneath the Chapel at Dunecht as you believe but were removed hence last spring, and the smell of decay and flowers ascending from the vault since that time will, on investigation, be found to proceed from another cause than flowers.
Nabob

'Nabob'? Who was this mysterious Nabob?

The police brought in Morgan, a bloodhound 'of great sagacity' according to the *Aberdeen Journal*, who had already assisted in solving a murder in Blackburn as well as following a pair of poachers for seventeen miles. After leaving the railway, Morgan and his keeper, a Mr Spence, travelled in a very appropriate dog cart to Dunecht. However, when a heavy frost came, even Morgan's famous nose was unable to help. Inquiries continued in a radius of around forty miles from the scene of the crime.

In late December 1881, the government offered a reward of £100 for information leading to the discovery of the body and the thief, with a free pardon to any accomplice who informed on the perpetrator. Lord Crawford's family immediately added another £500 to the total. There were a number of anonymous letters claiming to know where the body was and some asking for money for its return, but none appeared genuine.

There were further letters signed 'Nabob', which may or may not have come from the same source, but they suggested that the writer was not involved yet knew where the body was. The police tried to trace and trap the mysterious Nabob.

On 25 February 1882, two men named Thomas Kirkwood and John Philip were arrested and questioned as to the identity of the perpetrator of the theft. Kirkwood was a joiner who worked on the estate and Philip was a warehouse porter from Aberdeen. Both were in their fifties and well known locally. They denied any knowledge of the robbery, but were remanded in custody until the police made further enquiries. Philip was later questioned with the actual theft of the body, based partly on the idea that his handwriting was similar to that of the mysterious Nabob. A week later, both men were released without charge, as there was not enough evidence against them. With their release, interest faded away for a while.

After months of silence, the case surged back into public interest in July 1882 when the body was dramatically recovered. Despite the fanciful theories and the massive search by police and estate workers, the body had been buried just two feet under the surface in Dumbreck Wood, a plantation within the policies of Dunecht itself. It was still wrapped in the original grave clothes. The discovery of the body was no accident. As was so often the case with policing in the nineteenth century, an informant was involved.

All the time that interest had died away, the police and a private detective named Peter Castle had been quietly working away, asking questions, following leads and tapping into their network of informants. Castle had got in touch with a man named George Machray, who had been the gamekeeper at Dunecht Estate. He had left that job and was now a wine and spirit dealer in Aberdeen. Machray had information for Castle, but when the pair failed to meet, Machray informed the police instead. He said that a local rat-catcher and poacher named Charles Souter knew about the theft. The police immediately went to Donald's Court, Schoolhill, in Aberdeen and picked Souter up.

When he was questioned, Souter said he had accidentally come across the whereabouts of the body. Although he did not give a specific location, what he did say indicated that Dumbreck Wood was worth further investigation. At dawn next day, seventeen police, plus a number of gamekeepers and estate workers, descended on Dumbreck Wood and began to probe the ground with pointed iron stakes. At half past eleven, Michael Fraser, the head gamekeeper, and George Cooper, a stonebreaker, found the body.

Souter was forty-one years of age, a known poacher who had spent eighteen months in jail for assaulting a policeman. He had not long been released when the body was stolen. He told the police that he had been working as a rat-catcher and had been walking through the plantation when he stumbled on the body. He had been shocked and ran away, but tripped and fell. Two men with blackened faces and local accents came up to him, soon joined by two Englishmen. One of the local men held a pistol to his head and threatened that he would be 'hunted to death' if he told anybody.

The police listened but did not quite believe him, and as the law at that time allowed them to hold a suspect for eight days without charge, they held Souter in custody. Simultaneously, the police apprehended an ex-Dunecht sawmill worker. His name was James Collier and he had already come under suspicion merely because of the proximity of his house to the crypt. Collier had left the area and moved to Glasgow with his wife, but for some reason he had changed their surname to

Duncan. He also claimed to have written a book about the Dunecht mystery, which made him a very likely suspect.

Collier was hardly in the cells in Aberdeen when the police freed him without charge. That same day Souter was charged with 'feloniously abstracting and removing the body of the late Earl of Crawford from the vault in which it had been buried.' As Souter could not afford the £60 bail, he remained in prison.

On his first appearance before Sheriff Comrie Thomson, Souter said he was 42, unmarried and admitted that the person 'Nabob' was he. He said he had been poaching on the estate when he stumbled on the body and repeated nearly the same tale he had already related except with more details.

Souter was tried at the High Court in Edinburgh. The trial began on 23 October 1882 with the galleries crowded and many extremely respectable ladies pressed together so closely that they had to resort to the application of eau de cologne to keep themselves fresh. Souter was respectably dressed in a blue suit and looked pale but composed as he pleaded not guilty.

Among the many witnesses who gave evidence was an Echt farmer named William Smith Lawrie, who told the court that he had met Souter in the inn at Waterton before the discovery of the theft. Souter had asked him if he was aware of anybody disappearing from Dunecht, as he had found a dead body in the woods. George Machray, the former gamekeeper who had advised the police to look at Souter, told the court that Souter had mentioned the theft of Crawford's body as early as March. Souter had repeated the information in July, and it was he who suggested that Machray contact Peter Castle the private detective on his behalf.

Souter was found guilty and sentenced to five years' penal servitude. There was no hunt for any associates who must have helped move the heavy slabs; perhaps everybody was just pleased to put the whole case to bed and forget about it. Souter never admitted any guilt. George

Machray claimed the £500 reward and, after some legal action, was paid. The motive was never discovered. However, Aberdeen had another grave scandal to come.

The Nellfield Scandal

The Victorians seem to have had a fascination with death. It was almost a cult with them. Walking round a cemetery admiring gravestones decorated with weeping angels and chubby cherubs seemed a perfect way of spending a Sunday afternoon, while their books were laced with deathbed scenes. Of course, death was more familiar to them than it is to us. It waited in the breeding germs of congested sewers, in the filthy alleys and rotting houses of the slums, in the knives and broken bottles of predators, in the hot, humid stations of the tropical empire, in the screaming gales of shipwreck, in the poison bottles of vindictive spouses and in the blood-soaked beds of childbirth.

All these things made the Victorians very respectful of the ceremony of death. From the formality of a decent funeral to the quiet upkeep of the graveyards, they treated their dead with dignity and decorum, so there was consternation when graves at Aberdeen's Nellfield Cemetery at 27 Great Western Road were tampered with. Consternation turned into shock when William Coutts, the superintendent of the cemetery, was suspected of being involved with disturbing the graves.

It was 1899, and as the facts gradually became known, Aberdeen recoiled in horror. Nellfield was a private cemetery and William Coutts was formally charged with violating the graves. The first indication of anything wrong had come in May of that year, and there was an investigation that delved deeper and found more evidence of malpractice. A civil action was held against Coutts, but during the hearing he denied everything, which statement was soon proved wrong.

Coutts was arrested and charged with six charges of violation of sepulchres and one of having committed perjury during the civil action. At first the sheriff refused him bail, but the Lord Justice Clerk was more understanding and allowed a bail of £100. The Baker Corporation, which owned the cemetery, created the actions, saying that the actions of Coutts had damaged its reputation.

Coutts first appeared at the High Court in Aberdeen on the 26 August 1899; he pleaded not guilty. The case was delayed a little when George Cramond, a witness for the Crown, absconded and tried to catch a ship from Liverpool to the United States. The police caught him, dragged him back in handcuffs and kept him secure in Aberdeen's Craiginches Prison until the trial. That incident only increased public interest in what was already a notorious case, and when Coutts came to court a huge crowd gathered outside the building. However, the police had their orders and very few casual spectators were allowed admittance. The Baker Corporation was well represented in the audience, as were a large number of legal people, presumably professionally interested in the outcome of the case.

Lord McLaren was the judge. He said right away that there was 'no precedent in the law of Scotland for regarding as a crime the mere disturbance of bones and decomposing bodies'. Part of the case hinged on exactly what rights people had after they were buried in common ground. The legal counsel for the Crown and the defence quoted case after case to find some common ground. Eventually Coutts was charged with taking and lifting the remains from a coffin and throwing the remains into another lair – the place where coffins were interred. After a lengthy technical discussion the correct legal definition of the crime, Coutts was charged with disrupting graves. Next was the evidence, and possibly for the first time in history, the floor of a Scottish court was strewn with coffin lids, coffin ends, nameplates and other parts of various coffins. The ladies who had entered the public gallery seemed to take an especial interest in these proceedings.

Coutts was charged with moving the coffin of James Carnie from its position in Lair 517 to Lair 1519, with breaking up the coffin of Cairnie and throwing the remains of the deceased into Lair 1519, and with violating the sepulchre and raising the dead body out of the grave. He was also charged with ordering a gravedigger named William Wilson to open Lair 775 and 'violating, breaking open and destroying the coffin containing the body of Ann Caithness, and throwing the body into Lair 179'. He was further charged with having ordered other gravediggers to move from Lair 1591 the coffin of the body of Elizabeth Yule, break it open and throw the remains into Lair 20. He did the same to the body of James Rosie, Isabella Lindsay, Catherine Gordon and Ann Low.

Coutts pleaded 'not guilty, my lord' in a quiet but firm tone. Shortly after the charges were read out and Coutts saw the evidence spread out on the courtroom floor, he altered his plea to guilty of two charges of violating a sepulchre. Lord McLaren said that it was a unique case, as there was no personal gain involved. The charge was in reality a breach of trust towards these who owned lairs in the cemetery. The only people who benefitted were members of the Baker Corporation, as Coutts could increase the space for bodies and therefore the profits. Lord McLaren awarded him six months in jail.

The sentence was not universally popular; many people thought it was far too lenient. In its day, the Nellfield scandal was reported throughout the nation and echoed the fears from the past about bodysnatchers. It was a reminder of the cultural importance attached to respect for the dead.

3

Crime at Sea

The sea has its own laws and rules. Things that are acceptable on land are not always allowed at sea, and the penalties at sea can also be different. For example, from the seventeenth century until 1815, the Royal Navy Impress Service was an ogre that haunted the nightmares of merchant seamen. To be pressed into the navy meant to lose one's freedom for an unknown length of time and to be subject to strict discipline for less wages than a merchant seaman would make. Although the threat of the press gang lessened after the defeat of Napoleon Bonaparte in 1815, the government maintained the threat of sending erring merchant seamen to the navy. Fishermen and others who were caught smuggling could find themselves in warship. Such a case occurred in July 1829 when two members of the crew of *Vessa* tried to smuggle spirits into Aberdeen. They were caught and arrested, then found guilty and fined £100 each. As such a sum was unobtainable, they were ordered to serve five years in the Royal Navy instead. Other seamen broke different laws.

Fighting for a Whale

In the first half of the nineteenth century, Aberdeen was a major whaling port. One of her chief rivals was neighbouring Peterhead, and both ports sent ships north to the Greenland Sea and the Davis Strait to hunt for whales and seals. Although both these areas are vast, the actual whaling grounds could be quite limited, and ships tended to hunt within easy view of one another. Most of the time that did not cause any problems, for mutual support was welcome, particularly if the ice closed and a ship was sunk: having another vessel close by to rescue the men was a life-saver. However, there was always the possibility of having more than one ship harpooning the same whale, which caused some ownership problems.

In the summer of 1856, the Aberdeen vessel *Alibi* and the Peterhead ship *Clara* sailed to the Cumberland Straits, off Arctic Canada. On 13 October, both vessels were part of a group of whaling ships at anchor in the Bay of Niatilick on the west side of the Straits. This was a favoured spot for whaling ships, having a fairly safe anchorage and an island behind which they could shelter. The island was also called Niatilick and had the added advantage of a prominent hill. The shipmasters often climbed the hill and scanned the surrounding icy seas to search for whales. Shortly after six in the morning, Captain Sutter of *Clara* was on the hill and saw signs of a whale in the distance. He alerted an Inuit named Bullygar, who commanded an Inuit-manned whaleboat, and told him to approach cautiously so the crew of *Alibi* did not realise the whale was there.

Bullygar was an expert and came up astern of the whale, threw his harpoon and got fast to the whale without too much difficulty. The whale at once sounded – dived – but Bullygar knew all about whale hunting and kept the harpoon attached as the whale pulled the ship through the icy water. Eventually the whale lines ran out, so Bullygar attached what was known as a drog, or drogue, to the end of the line and cast it off. Drogs were inflated sealskin floats of indeterminate length, but they could be as few as two feet long and as much as five feet, with a circumference about the same. They had three functions: they slowed the whale down, they tired it out and they marked where it was.

Following the float, Bullygar steered his boat north-west, with another of *Clara*'s boats rowing beside him. About two miles from Niatilick Island, both boats landed on a small rock and watched the progress of the drogs. They had barely taken sightings when the whale surfaced, and they rowed hard towards it, but before they reached it two of *Alibi*'s boats had appeared from behind an ice floe and plunged their harpoons into the whale, and a boat from a third ship also came and thrust in the killing lance. With the whale dead, the boats united to tow it to the island of Niatilick, where the mother ships were.

Once they arrived at Niatilick, Bullygar and the other *Clara* boat tried to tow the whale to *Clara*, but the men from *Alibi* objected. The boat's crews began to argue, but mere words escalated into something more serious as the excited whaling men saw their oil-money bonus slipping away from them. Men on both sides lifted the lances, long, sharp weapons designed specifically to kill wounded whales, and tail knives, six-foot-long blades that could easily cut a man's arm off. There was a fight: a man was slashed, and things could have developed into a full-scale Arctic battle until Captain Sutter of *Clara* intervened and called a halt.

The whale was towed to *Alibi*, whose crew flensed it – stripped off the blubber – and claimed both ownership and profit. With the hunting season over and the ice closing in, all the whaling ships returned to Scotland, but the owners of *Clara* instigated legal proceedings to claim what they said was their whale. They estimated they were owed £1,200, for loss of profit and damages, with interest for 'the illegal seizure of a whale'. Captain Stewart of *Alibi* contested the claim vigorously.

It was not the first case of its kind, and it centred on the legal rights of ownership. Was the whale owned by the first ship to see and harpoon her, or by the ship whose men actually killed her? The custom in such cases was simple: if a boat had harpooned a whale and the lines broke, or became unattached from the boat, the animal was termed as a 'loose whale' and was fair game for any other vessel to claim. If this law was followed, then the whale in this case had been loose, as Bullygar had either tossed the lines overboard, or the line had run out or had broken. In either case, there was no line attaching the boat to the whale, and the drog was doing the work of the boats in tiring the whale. If that argument was correct, then Captain Stewart of *Alibi* had been legally in the right when claiming the whale.

However, the owners of *Clara* claimed that because Cumberland Straits was a new area for whaling, the old law did not apply there and that the ships should abide by the law of the native Inuit. The local law, which applied particularly to drog fishing, stated that the person who first struck the whale owned it. If that argument was proved correct, then Bullygar and *Clara* were undoubtedly the owners.

When the case came to court, Captain Sutter brought over an Inuit harpooner named Tessuin from Niatilick Island, who confirmed the Inuit law and reminded the court that the first harpoon had been made fast by a local Inuit. Captain George Brown, another whaling man, acted as interpreter.

Despite all the trouble Captain Sutter had gone to, the Court of Session found in favour Captain Stewart of *Alibi*, and Captain Sutter of *Clara* lost his case and his money.

Collision in the Harbour

Whaling ships were among the sturdiest vessels afloat; they had a double thickness of hull planking and triple thickness at the stem to ensure they could withstand the pressure of ice in the Arctic. Given their strength and size, it was not surprising that when the Aberdeen whaling ship *Princess of Wales* under Captain Woodward collided with a Sunderland schooner named *Sheepfold*, the schooner came off worst.

In the afternoon of 22 March 1818, a storm lashed the North Sea. It caught *Sheepfold* and knocked down her foretopgallant mast, so she headed to Aberdeen for repairs. She hove to off the harbour and signalled for a pilot to guide her in. After *Sheepfold* had waited for a couple of hours, a small, oar-powered pilot boat came out and led *Sheepfold* towards the harbour, moving with some difficulty because of both the boisterous weather and the damage to *Sheepfold*. At about ten in the morning, a brig named *Margarets* overtook them and both vessels tacked. After they had come about, Captain George Adams of *Sheepfold* saw the whaling ship *Princess of Wales* coming towards her with a full press of sail.

Princess was leaving the harbour before high water, for if she had delayed and had taken the ground, refloating would have been impossible on an ebbing tide. The pilot in *Princess* shouted for *Sheepfold* to go about, but there was no time. *Princess of Wales* was travelling around four knots, fairly fast for a large vessel in a confined seaway. As she turned between the piers in the harbour, *Sheepfold* was at right angles to her and *Princess*'s jib-boom became entangled with *Sheepfold*'s foremast and rigging. At that time *Sheepfold*'s sails were limp after her recent manoeuvre, so she could not move out of the way: she was dead in the water. *Princess* was in the centre of the channel: if she had moved north she would have hit rocks, while there was shallow water to the south; once committed to her course she had no choice but to continue.

The bowsprit of *Princess of Wales* thrust between the masts of the schooner and the whaling ship physically lifted and carried the schooner out of the sheltered waters of the harbour and into the bay. There was a heavy swell running, but Captain Woodward backed *Princess of Wales*' sails and after a while managed to disentangle the two vessels. However, by that time *Sheepfold* was already heavily damaged, with her decks breaking up from the force of the collision. Captain Adams ordered that the crew abandon her before she sunk beneath their feet.

He was only just in time, but rather than sinking, *Sheepfold*'s cargo of lime caught fire just as the crew pushed off in their small boat. There were great orange and yellow flames and a plume of smoke rising skywards from her as the men scrambled to safety, and a large crowd gathered to watch the spectacle. The swell pushed *Sheepfold* towards the shore, burning fiercely, until she slumped onto her beam ends and exploded in a spectacular ball of fire. She sunk in about four fathoms, with the mastheads thrusting out of the sea and a column of smoke hanging over the wreck for hours. There was an attempt to drag what remained of *Sheepfold* ashore and further away from the harbour entrance, but it failed.

In 1821, the owners of *Sheepfold* brought the owners of *Princess of Wales* to court, claiming that Captain Woodward had been to blame for the collision. The hearing took some hours, but ultimately Lord Pitmilly ruled that Captain Woodward was 'in part but not altogether' to blame. There was a small payment made for compensation, but the collision was just one of the perils of the sea.

Illegal Trawling

It may have been the Dutch who invented trawling as a technique for fishing, for the name derives from *traghelen*, an Old Dutch word meaning 'to drag'. That of course is exactly what trawlers do: they drag a bag-like net behind then and scoop up all the fish that are in the path of the net. It is simple enough in theory, but the fishing vessel needed to be powerful to tow a heavy net, and the technique was not fully perfected until the rise of steam power in the nineteenth century.

Trawling was reported in some of the Fife ports in the 1850s, but it was not popular among the more traditional fishermen, as it was thought that the vessels dragged the trawl over the seabed and destroyed herring spawn. However, it was an efficient method of catching fish and spread slowly northwards.

In 1882, a pair of English steam trawlers landed impressive catches at Aberdeen. Local businessmen bought a Dublin tug named *Toiler* and converted her; local yards launched purpose-built trawlers; and Aberdeen became Scotland's trawling capital.

However, controversy and disputes haunted the trawlers as they hauled up fish all around the coasts and far out into the seas. In August 1896, HMS *Jackal* arrested the Aberdeen trawler *Volunteer* for allegedly fishing within the three-mile limit off the Scottish coast. *Volunteer* was off Buchanness at the time but disputed *Jackal*'s claim. Captain Forrester said he had sounded the lead when they sighted *Jackal* and found they were in thirty-one fathoms of water and were around four and a half miles from land. He lost the case.

That was just one case out of many, but it illustrated how the sea impinged on Aberdeen in many ways. Crime at sea was strongly related to the city.

4

The Early Police

In common with most Scottish burghs, Aberdeen had many ups and downs. There were wars and rumours of wars, battles and plagues, good periods and bad. It was the same with the police force. It is hard to give a definite date for the origin of policing in Aberdeen, but 1179 would seem about right. Obviously there were no uniformed bobbies on the beat at that time, but King William the Lion confirmed that Aberdeen was a burgh with a provost and bailies who had the task of guarding and maintaining the 'laws and customs' of the town.

It was a good time to be in Aberdeen. The days of Norse raids were in the past and the terrible years of the Wars of Independence were well in the future. Scotland was forming as a nation with trading links to Europe, knights in armour were consolidating their position with castles and feudalism, and the church was erecting abbeys all over the country. As long as one kept on the right side of mailed authority, life was bearable.

No doubt there was crime – there is always crime – but it may be significant that it was not until 1394 that Aberdeen got its first tolbooth and courthouse. A tolbooth was an office where tolls, market dues, taxes and other finances were collected, but the building also doubled as the town jail. It acted as a reminder to lawbreakers that there was civilisation in Aberdeen and lawbreakers had better watch out. Around this time there was also the Justice Port, also known as the Thieves Gate, where the limbs of executed criminals were put on public display. The phrase 'hanged, drawn and quartered' was not meaningless in the medieval world.

The town grew, and with the larger population came more opportunity for crime. By the late 1560s there was a 'Day Patrole' as well as town sergeants to guard the good from the bad. In the seventeenth century, with the country on the brink of civil war as King Charles I and the Kirk squared up to each other, Aberdeen had unpaid constables to control crime. Perhaps because of the religious troubles of mid-century, followed by the upheavals of the disputed accession and then the Union, it was a full century later before the city magistrates appointed Charles Clapperton as the first professional constable. According to William Bannerman in his book *The Aberdeen Worthies*, Clapperton, in his blue coat with its red collar, and with his ever-present dog Help, were 'kenspeckle' (easily recognisable or well-known) characters in Aberdeen. He was a thief-taker, pure and simple, seeking out and arresting known criminals; he had no dealings with the courts. Once the thieves were lodged in the cells, they were no longer his concern.

In 1795 there was a Police Act for Aberdeen, with thirteen police commissioners appointed. In Scotland the police were not just responsible for controlling crime, but also for a whole host of regulations for the public good. The police dealt with lighting and sanitary affairs as well, so they could spend the morning inspecting midden heaps, the afternoon patrolling pawnshops and the evening checking on pickpockets in the unsavoury lodging houses of the Old Town. However, there was no permanent uniformed police presence until 1818, nearly two decades later than Glasgow and thirteen years after Edinburgh.

The establishment of the police saw Charles Baird as superintendent of a force of seven men based at the Guard House in Castlegate. There were also twenty-four watchmen, who had limited powers. These men were given the generic term of 'Charlies', which suggests a lack of respect for their person and position. With their great coats and tam-o'-shanter bonnets to supplement the long staffs that were intended to intimidate the criminal classes, they 'watched' over certain streets, carried clumsy lanterns and called out the hours to reassure the good people of Aberdeen that the streets were safe.

The police office or watch house was fairly mobile throughout the century. In 1819 it was moved to Huxter Row, but when that locality was demolished in the City Improvements of 1867, the police office moved to the Old Record Office in Castlegate and only three years later to Concert Court in Broad Street.

There were various superintendents in the early, learning years. Robert Chapman, one of the Bow Street Runners, arguably the best-known thief-catchers of the period, came up from London in 1822 to use his skills in Aberdeen. He preferred the police to use their instinct to find the criminals, rather than the old town-sergeant method of local knowledge backed by sound intelligence. Even so, the use of muscles and courage also came in handy on occasions.

The watchmen were not quite as useless as their reputation might imply. On the night of Thursday, 22 December 1824, a group of millwrights went on the spree along Broad Street, a place notorious for its drunken violence. They erupted from a public house, drunk and shouting the odds to anybody who would listen. The Broad Street watchman came across, tapping his staff on the ground, and advised them to quieten down before there was trouble. The millwrights simply knocked him to the ground and held him there, but the noise they made attracted other watchmen and a few members of the public.

The two groups began a stand-up fight in the middle of the street, but gradually the watchmen got the upper hand and arrested seven of the millwrights. They appeared at the Police Court next morning and were fined between half a guinea and one guinea each.

In the country, the early police had to contend with the extreme mobility of vagrants, tinkers and travellers, many of whom combined restlessness with criminal tendencies. One such was Charles McEwan.

Cock of the North

In common with many criminals of the nineteenth century, Charles McEwan often adopted an assumed name. Sometimes he was known as Robert McLeod, sometimes as John McIntyre, or even Charles Mackay, but very seldom did he use his real name of McEoch. Born in Armagh, to many people he was the Cock o' the North and he was a coppersmith as well as a tinker. He was a tall man, well made and muscular.

Around 1814, the twenty-six-year-old McEwan and the rest of his tinker clan took the boat from Ireland and landed in Scotland. Rather than search for work in the burgeoning industrial towns of the central belt, they headed north for the small communities and wide spaces of the Highlands and north-east. The band soon became notorious for petty and not so petty theft mixed with a casual violence that saw doors locked on their approach. The other travelling people knew McEwan well and tried to avoid him. If they were unlucky enough to fall into his company, he was quite capable of robbing them of their meagre livelihood; any resistance could lead to assault.

McEwan was a keen follower of prizefighting and was a lady's man – or rather he had an eye and a fancy for any woman who could give him what he wanted. In his ten years roaming the north of Scotland he kept company with at least three different women, and the second-last of them gave him three children. His final woman was short, well made and around thirty years old. Her name was Margaret Mooney and they had only been together for a few days when McEwan made his fatal mistake. On 8 October 1823, McEwan had speared a salmon in an Aberdeenshire river and they cooked it under the autumn stars. The drop of blood that spilled on McEwan's light corduroy trousers may have been seen as an omen, but if so he ignored it. They were walking, as always, heading south over the high hills from Aberdeenshire and enjoying the hospitality of farms and cottages on the route, as was the way of old Scotland.

Elizabeth Middleton and John Smith were shearing sheep at the farm of Kildow, and they passed a few hours with McEwan and Mooney before lodging them comfortably in a barn. The next morning, 9 October 1823, saw the tinkers trudge on to the Firmouth, a rough and lonely drove road that toiled over the Grampians from Deeside to Glenesk and the glens of Angus. They were walking side by side when a group of four whisky smugglers joined them. The smugglers were a jovial crew, with the panniers on their garrons heavy with whisky. They were not afraid of McEwan in the slightest; these men were well used to taking care of themselves against the Excise or anybody else who tried to rob them.

At a place called Lochmaven, at the apex of the pass, McEwan and Mooney sat down to rest; both were sober, despite sharing the smuggler's peat reek, but McEwan may have been a little less sober that Mooney. What happened next is pure conjecture, based on later evidence, but at some point in the late afternoon McEwan and Mooney must have argued, and he lifted a small iron anvil that he used in his tinkering trade and smashed her over the head until she was dead.

Although there were no witnesses to the actual act, there were people who used this lonely road, and their stories helped piece together something of the story. What happened after the smugglers went their separate way is pure conjecture. Later that evening, Joseph Stewart of Ballater rode past and saw Mooney lying on the heather with one hand above her head. He saw McEwan at her feet, gasped at the sight of the blood that stained McEwan's shirt and trousers, kicked in his spurs and rode on into the torrential rain without stopping or looking back.

At around two in the morning of 10 October, McEwan banged at the door of a lonely house at the south side of the Firmouth. His shirt was bloody, his trousers were sodden with rain and the deep bloodstains below his knees suggested that he had been kneeling in blood. Margaret Machardy answered the door to him and gave him lodgings for the night. Not surprisingly, she commented on the blood, but he told her little.

McEwan did not sleep well that dark morning, nor on the night of Friday, 10 October, which he passed at an inn at Balfield, about three miles north-west of Brechin. The innkeeper, Helen Young, had not wished such a bloody, battered apparition as McEwan to remain in her house all night, but she could not put him out into the dark, so allowed him to remain. Some time during the long hours of darkness he demanded whisky; he was seen furiously scrubbing at his sleeve with a wet brush and trying to wash his hat, but nobody questioned him.

On Saturday, 11 October, McEwan asked Young if she had heard about the woman killed on the Firmouth. When Young said that 'there are many lies in the country and that was one, for I would have heard of a murder', McEwan said he had seen her 'all over blood' and was sure she had been murdered.

In the meantime, Elizabeth McDonald and Margaret Cruickshanks were first to find the dead body of Mooney, at about half past seven on the Friday morning. They had been harvesting in the south and were returning home when they saw the body lying among the heather. It lay close to the road in a welter of blood and disturbed ground. When McDonald investigated, she saw that Mooney wore some rags of clothes and that there was a basket nearby with tea caddies and other items inside. The two women followed a trail of blood for about twenty metres, but it petered out in the heather and led nowhere. They hurried to the nearest cottage, some miles ahead, hammered on the door and told what they had found.

As soon as they heard the news, the scattered population gathered to see the body, but it was taken away and decently buried. Mr Garioch, a surgeon, later examined Mooney and decided that she had been killed by a blow to the head. He was shown a box of tools including a small anvil whose concave sides fitted the indents into Mooney's head. Many tinkers carried such a portable anvil. Garioch said that Mooney had been drinking spirits before she was killed. A second surgeon, Dr Murray, did not entirely agree with Garioch; he was not so sure that the anvil had been the murder weapon.

As soon as Mooney was found, the authorities began the search for McEwan. He was a kenspeckle figure in Aberdeenshire and not hard to trace with his blue coat, corduroy trousers and prominent hat. John Fyfe, a King's Messenger in Aberdeen, traced McEwan's route by the places he had stopped and the people he had passed on the road. Fyfe arrested him in Brechin and brought him to Aberdeen. The small anvil was inside the box of tools that McEwan carried with him.

McEwan denied all knowledge of the murder. He said he had come across the body in the moorland, but he had not killed Mooney. Even so, the deed seemed to affect him, and his normal false joviality altered to a sullen silence. He gave conflicting statements about his background: in his first he said he had been apprenticed to a Dublin coppersmith and had no fixed abode and had never in his life been asked for a certificate of his character. In his second he said he was a Glasgow man but had been to Dublin. In this statement he said he and Mooney lived as man and wife; he agreed that he had travelled on the Firmouth with her, but said he had left her there, hale and hearty.

During the trial in March 1824 at the High Court in Edinburgh, McEwan challenged many of the statements made by the prosecution:

he claimed he had not asked for whisky when in the houses south of the Firmouth, but only drank whey. He said that the blood on his trousers was his own, from a bleeding nose. He said he was wetting his hat to try and remove the 'cloors', or dimples, in the material. His clothes were produced in court, complete with bloodstains on the sleeve of his shirt and on his trousers. The jury had no difficulty in finding him guilty.

When Lord Gillies sentenced him to hang, McEwan said, 'Thank your Lordship, I'll die innocent. There has not been a doctor here today but has perjured himself.' As was normal in the period, McEwan was chained in his cell; he paced, clanking, back and forth as far as the chain would stretch.

He remained stubborn even as the day of his execution drew closer, and when the ministers tried to save his soul, he replied, 'I am not the better of you, or any like you.' Only when three Catholic priests came did he show any interest, but if he confessed to them, his guilt travelled no further. On the evening of Tuesday, 6 April 1824, McEwan was taken from Calton Jail to the lock-up house on the High Street of Edinburgh. At about ten past eight he was led out and he marched bravely to the gallows. He was hanged at Libberton's Wynd in Edinburgh on the 7 April 1824 and his body was given to Dr Munro to be dissected.

Murders were not common in Aberdeenshire, but when the occurred, the infant police force and their allies responded with burgeoning skill.

Policing the City

By July 1829, the streets of Aberdeen were becoming so crowded that the newspapers recommended that people pass each other on the left. That year, the Police Commission decided to augment the police presence in Castle Street 'to preserve order'. Castle Street was undoubtedly the most rowdy street in the city, with more drunk people being arrested there consistently than on any other Aberdeen street.

The Commission said 'as the headquarters for almost all the banking establishments in town there was little occasion for disorderly persons' to infest the street. There was no doubt that the Town House, the Cross and the North of Scotland Bank were all tourist magnets, but according to the *Aberdeen Journal* interested visitors were 'assailed with the discordant yells and oaths of the very worst of characters'. Not only their ears but also their eyes were assaulted as 'the passage along the pavement is obstructed by a bare-legged nymph or two stretched at full length.'

The police had the task of keeping such places safe for the respectable people of the town. In the winter of 1829, the police returned to the medieval Day Patrole. The results were impressive. The *Aberdeen Journal* of 25 November commented that 'we may anticipate beneficial effects in preserving peace and good order; as we observed them actively engaged in securing different individuals who seemed inclined to violate both.'

In 1830, Robert Chapman was replaced as superintendent of police by John Fyfe, by which time a Police Court had been established to deal with the daily dose of petty thefts, assaults and drunken behaviour that fouled Aberdeen and every urban centre in Britain. That was a landmark year, with the first handcarts used for wheeling away those Aberdonians who were too drunk to walk to the cells, and the appointment of Francis Ogston as police surgeon. Ogston would earn his five guineas annual salary over the half century he remained in the position.

The police and watchmen certainly had to earn their money as well. In the early morning of Monday, 21 June 1830, three men, Ranald McDonald, Donald McLeod and Ewan McDonald leaped on the Union Street watchman and beat him up. When other watchmen came to interfere, the three men were arrested, with Ranald MacDonald fined a guinea and the others half that.

The police had diverse duties, some of which would be easily recognisable today. For example, in early October 1830 there were two rival stagecoaches racing each other along the length of Union Street, creating alarm and sending pedestrians scurrying for safety. The police arrested both drivers, charged them with 'furious and reckless driving' and fined them a guinea.

As well as boy racers there were muggers, then known as footpads. In the early morning of Monday, 3 January 1831, a shoemaker was walking home along the Gallowgate when a woman slipped out of the shadows between the sparse street lamps and called out to him. Immediately the shoemaker stopped to talk, when a man grabbed him from behind and held him, so the woman could go through his pockets. However, they were out of luck: the shoemaker was flat broke. But his calls of 'murder' alerted the nearest watchman, who grabbed both footpads. John Watt, the male attacker, got forty days with hard labour, while the female, Jean Edward, got thirty days. Both came from Fish Donald's Close.

There were constant changes in the early years of the force. At the Police Meeting on 11 July 1831, the superintendent reported that he had had to suspend three men for neglect of duty. In February 1832, the regular Police Meeting of the council agreed that Superintendent Fyfe should employ three of the Night Patrole and four watchmen to 'apprehend all vagrants and common beggars'. During that period, the country was in political turmoil, with demands for reform and social turmoil, rife unemployment and an increase in people wandering in the hope of a better life elsewhere. Much of the time in that same meeting was spent discussing their financial restrictions, so the Day Patrole was reduced to only three men on duty in the afternoons and early evening. To counter the petty pilfering on the shore and on ships in harbour, the harbour trustees created a Shore Patrole of three men.

In March and April 1833, the Poynernook area was rocked by a spate of robberies. The wood merchants seemed to be particularly targeted and they appealed to the police committee for more men on the beat. With money in short supply there were no more men, so instead Superintendent Fyfe altered the watchmen's beats so the wood yards were better covered. One of the much-maligned Charlies saw four men break into a yard and, with great courage, arrested one of the burglars. However, the others turned on him and beat him up quite badly. With the reduction in manpower, the watchman could not summon help and the robbers got away free.

In 1834, despite their effectiveness, the Day Patrole was reduced in numbers. Only four men were retained as day patrolmen, with William Walker as sergeant. The three who were dismissed became nightwatchmen.

John Fyfe lasted as superintendent until 1835, and next year William Walker was the superintendent of the Day Patrole, with Robert Alexander as superintendent of the watchmen. Fyfe only remained in the superintendent's office for three years, after which his deteriorating health forced another change. Robert Barclay from Glasgow took his place and lasted until his death in 1854, when John Watson took command.

The Good and the Bad

The early police were not all angels. Many had a liking for the bottle, and every year saw men dismissed, or men who resigned before they were thrown out of the force. For example, the Police Meeting of January 1831 mentioned that one of the watchmen had been suspended from duty after he was found lying in his bed dead drunk the previous Saturday when he should have been on duty. Other men abused their power, such as William MacDonald, who was notoriously rough with his prisoners. In 1839 he arrested a thief named Christopher Brown, who died in MacDonald's custody. However it was a rough and ready age in some respects, and the police were still finding their place in society.

Other police proved they could be very efficient. For example, on 1 September 1845 a thief broke into a house in Courage Court, Weighhouse Square, and stole a large tartan shawl. The owner told the police, who followed the usual procedure of sending a description to the local pawnbrokers. Only an hour later, a thirteen-year-old boy named George Campbell carried a shawl into a city centre broker, who took Campbell's pledge, name and address, and then notified the police. Sergeant Watson and Constable Chesser of the Day Patrole picked up Campbell and, noticing another young lad named Alexander Allan hanging about as if expecting a share of the proceeds, arrested him as well. Both boys were already well known to the police. The whole operation, from theft to arrest, took less than two hours.

George Cran

It is unfortunate that there are no records of what life felt like for the ordinary Aberdeen policeman in the early years of the force. However, at the retirement of Superintendent George Cran in May 1883 after forty years' service, he gave some insight of his time in the County Police when he had joined in 1843. Cran remembered the last two mounted men and said there were just twenty-four men on foot for the whole county. The people 'not just the rag tag but the general public, expected the police to be more trouble than they were worth and what with the old drunken dragoons as policemen and disappointed sheriff officers it was really uphill work for the new police'.

At that time, according to Cran, Captain Anderson, a handsome ex-military officer, was general superintendent and liked to talk of his time in the military, his adventures in India and his march up the Khyber Pass. Presumably Anderson had served during the First Afghan War of 1839 to 1842. Anderson had about fifty men to police

Aberdeenshire, Banff and Kincardine, and remained in charge until the forces split in 1853. After that he remained in charge of the Aberdeen force. Cran mentioned that in his early years one of the main duties of the County Police was to rid the county of tinkers and vagrants who swarmed in great bands of twenty or thirty at a time.

Cran also mentioned the problem of juvenile crime. He said that in 1844 or '45 a squad of some fourteen young lads banded together, called themselves the Copper Company and made a trade of stealing lead from houses and copper from ships' bottoms. They also infested the suburbs very much. Cran boasted that 'after a hard run from Stockethead to Gilcomston I secured three of them'.

He continued: 'at the same time you could not turn a corner in the suburbs but some urchin from the city was found begging'. Juvenile crime troubled the police and authorities in Aberdeen throughout the nineteenth century.

A Troubled Decade

Other police also showed the mettle of the force. On Tuesday, 7 October 1845, Constable Gilchrist of the day patrole saw Janet McDonald, a twenty-year-old girl of 'notorious character', in the company of two soldiers. He watched her closely, for she had a reputation for erratic behaviour. Gilchrist could see that she was drunk, and before long she ran to the bank of the canal and simply threw herself in the water. Gilchrist had been expecting something of the sort and jumped in to save her as the soldiers watched. The police did not only control crime in Aberdeen.

The 1840s were a troubled decade, with a major economic downturn feeding social and political problems. This decade is often referred to as the Hungry Forties. The resulting lack of money led to belt-tightening in many places, including the police. On a police commissioners' meeting in January 1849, the Watching Committee recommended that the watchmen should stop calling the hours, as the thieves knew where the watchmen were by their calls. The following meeting in March 1849 suggested that the wages paid to the police were excessive and it proposed a reduction. There were forty-three night watchmen at twelve shillings a week, and the committee proposed reducing the pay of these appointed since January 1848 to eleven shillings a week. The night patrole and office clerk wages were also to be reduced, from fifteen to fourteen shillings for the patrol, and thirteen to twelve for the clerk. There were a sergeant and eleven men on the day patrole with the men at fifteen shillings plus a suit of clothing, and their wages were to be reduced to fourteen. The day sergeant was on £65 a year, the night on £49 a year, the criminal officer on shillings a week and the turnkey at fourteen shillings. It was decided to leave these wages as they were. However, the fairly generous allowance for paid sick leave was to alter from four weeks' full pay and four weeks half a year to only four full weeks.

There were other changes proposed at that meeting. Until then, an average of thirty drunk and disorderly people had been just taken into the cells each night and released in the morning. At that meeting it was proposed to treat drunkenness as a criminal offence. Some of the committee thought it was unjust to charge them, as some people who were not in the habit of being drunk might be charged as well as the regulars. Finally, watchmen were ordered not to convoy drunken people home.

Superintendent Barclay gave the following figures for crime in 1848, with the number of drunken people in the bottom row:

Crime	Male	Female	Total
Robbery	1	2	3
Housebreaking and Theft	5	1	6
Theft from Lockfast Places	2	1	3
Theft, Fraud etc	206	210	416

Reset of Theft	6	9	15
Assault	230	95	325
Breach of Peace	155	94	249
Malicious Mischief	21	22	43
Contravention of Statute	45	21	66
Drunk and Disorderly	1983	1153	3136

Country Matters

The County Police also had problems with drunks. When the Great North railway was being built, the railway navvies, or navigators, were notorious for their drunken behaviour. Rather than interfere and possibly escalate the problem, the police frequently preferred to stand back and allow them to settle their quarrels between themselves. There was even one occasion when a mass fight between Highland and English navvies stopped work completely.

The County police also had to deal with thimble riggers. These were fraudsters who enticed naive people into a gambling game that invited them to choose under which of three thimbles an acorn sat, and then shuffled the thimbles. The game was rigged, and the farm servants would be virtually robbed of wages that they had sweated blood to earn in all the weather possible. In 1855, one thimble-rigging group had a semi-permanent encampment about a mile south of Huntly. Their practice was to waylay the farm labourers as they walked to the market, before they had the opportunity to spend their wages. When the farm workers realised what was happening, they told the police. The constable took the labourers to the local landowner, 'Laird' Stewart, who was less than sympathetic. Stewart said that the labourers were partly to blame and said they should have given the thimble riggers 'a good thrashing'.

When they left the Laird, the workers got into a coach and returned to the spot where they had been robbed. The thimble riggers were gone, but the workers asked in which direction and followed them to Colpy, a few miles north of Insch. The coach halted, and the labourers jumped out and attacked the thimble riggers with fire and fury. There was no contest between the burly farm servants and the conmen; the farm workers quickly recovered the money they had lost and threw the thimble riggers into a handy ditch.

Ellon was another town with problems. It was normally quiet during the week, but woke up on Saturday nights when the farm servants descended on the shops, particularly the shoemakers and tailors. The congregation of so many workers attracted half the pickpockets of the north-east and the police were hard pressed to keep the town under control. It was worse on market days, when Aikey Fair was a hive of pickpockets and conmen.

Superintendent Cran mentioned the less diplomatic side of policing that was common in his early years: 'In the beginning of my time the spengie switch [cane] by day and the oaken staff by night were the two principal supports of the police force. Indeed if a policeman was not pretty swift and could not use these instruments very freely he could not hold his own at all.'

So according to Cran, force was a prerequisite for effective policing in the rough early days of the Aberdeenshire police. Having brains and a logical mind also helped.

Detectives

Aberdeen was a bit later than some other towns in the appointment of detectives, or 'criminal officers' as they were then known. In a Police Board meeting in July 1856, the Watching and Lighting Committee recommended an experimental addition of two plain-clothes officers to 'increase the efficiency of the day force'. Some of the committee had opposed the idea, but when they learned that in the year ending 1 July 1855 there had been 1,244 cases of undetected crime in Aberdeen they changed their mind. Bailie McHardy disapproved, as did Mr Rose, who spoke against 'the spy system – it was neither wished for nor required by the town'. However, that same year plain-clothes detectives were set loose in the city. They knew the general public had little time for such an addition to the force, but also that they were usually dedicated and efficient.

In a meeting of the police commissioners in June 1857, Super-intendent Watson explained the work and success of the criminal officer they had appointed. At first his audience was critical, but when he explained that the plain-clothes detective had been crucial in a number of arrests, and that thefts had decreased and detections increased, the Committee agreed to retain the services of a criminal officer. Detectives were in Aberdeen to stay.

Annual Reports

In 1859, Colonel Kinloch, the Inspector of the Constabulary of Scotland, gave his report on every police force, including Aberdeen. He said that there were sixty-five police officers in Aberdeenshire, which was one constable to every 2,150 people. In the city of Aberdeen itself, with a population of 71,973 in 1851, there were seventy-seven police, giving a proportion of one officer to every 934 people. The city was fairly well covered.

The Aberdeenshire force was divided into six divisions: Aberdeen, Peterhead, Old Meldrum, Huntly, Alford and Aboyne, with the headquarters at Aberdeen having 'good accommodation' but lacking cells for the prisoners. Kinloch said that the chief constable earned a very decent £275 a year, plus the keep of his house. There were two superintendents, with one acting as deputy chief and earning £80 a year and the other £75. From there, the wages descended to £65 a year for an inspector and between twenty-one and twenty-three shillings a week (about £55 and £60 a year) for a sergeant. There were fifty-one constables, divided into three classes, with the highest class earning nineteen shillings a week (nearly £50 a year), then seventeen shillings for the second class (nearly £45 a year) and sixteen shillings for the third class (nearly £42 a year). The sergeants' and constables' pay was enhanced by a two shilling and twopence monthly boot allowance. Despite the earlier reluctance to use detectives, the inspector at headquarters acted as the principal detective officer.

Two years later in his Annual Report of the Inspector of Constabulary for 1861, Colonel Kinloch said that crime had declined throughout the country and the police were more efficient: 'it was not so much owing to the increased numbers of the police as to the superior intelligence, education and character of those who now enter the service, from the social position of a constable being in some degree raised above what it was even a few years ago.' However, he thought that better accommodation should be provided as well as a pension. 'Of the nineteen burghs reported efficient last year above 5,000 inhabitants, I now have the satisfaction of adding Aberdeen and Inverness,' he wrote. Aberdeen was gradually improving the quality of its police force.

Although the police were gaining the upper hand and the complete chaos of the early decades of the century had eased, there was still plenty of crime to combat.

5
Riots in Aberdeen

Every city and most towns were afflicted with riots and civil disturbances in the nineteenth century. The trouble could be for political reasons, or a riot for bread, or because the police were thought to be too heavy-handed. If the trouble became too bad for the civil authorities to handle, they could call on the army, but that option was not available if it was the army that was rioting.

'Like a Parcel of Wild Beasts'

In his poem 'Tommy', Rudyard Kipling says that soldiers 'aren't thin red 'eroes, nor we aren't no blackguards too' and 'sometimes our conduck isn't all your fancy paints'. The nineteenth century was often coloured by riots in which the military played their part, and Aberdeen shared the experience.

In March 27 1802, the French Revolutionary Wars between Great Britain and France ended. Europe had been at war since 1789 and both sides were sick of slaughter. There had been invasions and plundering and bloody battles, while the British Army had lost the early campaigns in Europe but redeemed some honour in Egypt. Now both sides drew back, took a breath and prepared for the next round in a war both surely realised was not yet finished.

As regiments were either disbanded or brought back to barracks in Britain, tensions were bound to rise. The presence of thousands of fit young men, trained to fight but underemployed and possibly frustrated, was a natural flashpoint for trouble. In those days it was traditional that the King's birthday should be celebrated with riot and disorder and, it was on that day on 4 June 1803 that trouble erupted in Aberdeen. It started fairly innocently. John Garioch was an Aberdeen merchant who happened to be staying in Gordon's inn and coffee house on Castle Street. He heard a noise outside and saw a number of boys throwing dirt and wet straw at each other, and then at any unfortunate person who happened to be passing by. The boys were also throwing dirt at the soldiers of the Ross and Cromarty Rangers, who occupied the barracks at the east end of the street. The Rangers had recently returned from Ireland, where they had been too late to be involved in the ugly fighting of Wolfe Tone's rising, but they had witnessed the brutal aftermath, so may have been suffering from taut nerves.

The guardhouse was opposite the hotel. Garioch went upstairs to the highest room in the inn, from where he could get a better view of the disturbance in the street. He realised there were men as well as boys throwing dirt at the soldiers. Many of the officers and most of the great and the good of Aberdeen were in the Town House celebrating the birthday of the king.

At about eight in the evening of 4 June, Garioch saw Lieutenant Colonel George McKenzie marching towards the barracks, while a young ensign named George Lanigan was also present, making ineffectual thrusts with his sword at the mud throwers, who seemed not to take him seriously. Another Aberdeen merchant, ex-provost John Dingwall, thought McKenzie was drunk; he saw the colonel fall down, so that two officers had to support him as he walked. Dingwall said the boys were laughing at the colonel but did not pelt him with mud.

Garioch continued to watch and at about half past eight, Captain James MacDonogh appeared in the street. Sometimes he was shouting at the boys and once he joined the celebrating crowd, raised his hat and shouted 'huzzah' along with them. The boys seemed to take special delight in attacking MacDonogh, and on one occasion a boy grabbed a handful of mixed dirt and horse dung and threw it in his face. Not surprisingly, MacDonogh lost his temper, drew his sword and chased after the dung throwers, who ran away at great speed. After that incident, at around five to nine, MacDonogh decided that enough was enough and called out the guard.

However, a town sergeant was not pleased with this escalation in events and he hurried over to MacDonogh and asked him to recall the guards. A few moments later, Garioch saw MacDonogh hurrying towards the Town House, flanked by marching soldiers. Ten minutes later the barrack gates opened and about thirty men marched out to augment the guard.

The crowd had gathered again, and Lanigan was still flapping his sword around futilely, although he and a private soldier did grab a young boy and drag him into the guardhouse. At about quarter past nine Garioch saw Lanigan pulling a soldier by his coat as others filed out past the guardroom. The Rangers seemed incensed, with some having fixed bayonets to chase away the mud throwers; one or two even fired live ammunition. As they did so, Captain MacDonogh raced into the barracks and returned leading out the whole regiment. They marched to the guardhouse and formed in a double line across the street, muskets on their shoulders, with MacDonogh in front. By this time Garioch was naturally alarmed and when he saw Captain Anderson he asked him to try to stop any trouble. Garioch then left the hotel and met Sergeant McPherson of the Aberdeen Volunteers, the Territorial Army of its day. He asked McPherson to go and find Provost Hadden, tell him what was happening and try to get the city magistrates to come and take command of the Ross and Cromarty Rangers from Captain MacDonogh. It was now half past nine.

For some reason, Garioch did not try to find the provost himself. Instead he returned to the hotel and watched events from the window. There were other officers in front of the soldiers now, and he heard MacDonogh give the order to prime and load the muskets.

Dingwall also head the order: 'with powder and ball, prime and load'. He was not sure if the order was given in earnest or merely to intimidate the gathering crowd.

The Rangers obeyed and now there was a line of trained redcoats with loaded muskets barring the entire width of Castle Street. They began to walk down the street, some firing their muskets; two civilians fell, one near the inn, and a young boy named John Ross near the plain stones, but at the time Garioch suspected he was faking, as the army were not firing in that direction. In fact, Ross had been shot under the eye and died. Garioch saw a group of four soldiers run up to a man who stood with his arms crossed; they battered him to the ground with clubbed muskets, then bayoneted him as he lay helpless and bleeding. MacDonogh was with his men, cheering and raising his hat in the air, and then he led them in a column into a lane that was near the barracks.

After witnessing the bloodshed, Garioch ran from the hotel to try to find a magistrate. He ran to the Town House and saw the provost and some of the magistrates.

'Good God, gentlemen,' Garioch said, 'what are you doing here and why don't you come out?' He told them what he had seen and offered to lead them to the trouble, but the magistrates were less than willing.

'Perhaps we will be shot too,' one said, timidly.

Garioch suggested that they march in a body, accompanied by the uniformed town sergeants so that there could be no mistake of their rank and position. The provost and magistrates agreed and walked to the soldiers, but by that time the firing had stopped. There were some men throwing stones at the guardhouse in retaliation but there was no major response. Most of the Rangers had gone to the East End of Aberdeen, but the provost and one of the town sergeants found a group in a lane near the hotel; he had to push through a barrier of bayonets, and some of the Rangers pointed their bayonets at him.

Hadden ordered them back to barracks. 'I am the provost of Aberdeen' he said, and showed them his chain of office.

Sergeant Mackay of the Rangers was not impressed: 'You are no officer,' he said, 'and I don't care for a magistrate.' Having come to quell the trouble, however, Provost Hadden was not inclined to back off. He grabbed Mackay and hustled him back to barracks. Most of the other soldiers formed around the provost as a bodyguard.

Garioch was incensed at the behaviour of the Rangers in general and Captain MacDonogh in particular and said that 'hanging was too little for him'.

Other witnesses to the event remembered the details a little differently. Most of the great and the good had been celebrating the King's birthday in the Town House. Charles Adamson, who had been an officer in the army for twenty-two years, had been in the Town House with the rest of them when the trouble started but hurried along to the New Inn later. A waiter informed him that the Rangers had shot somebody dead. Adamson investigated and advised MacDonogh to take his men back to barracks.

'You have no business,' somebody in the crowd shouted, 'he is as great a scoundrel as any of them.'

Even so, MacDonogh was about to do so when somebody in the crowd threw a brick that cracked him on the head. MacDonogh drew his sword and chased the brick thrower as the remainder of the crowd, about twelve strong, persuaded Adamson to return to the safety of the inn. Shortly after, the soldiers formed a line and marched down the street, firing at will.

A third merchant, John Collinson, lived in Castle Street and saw the boys throwing mud at the soldiers and then witnessed the soldiers form up. He left his house and tried to persuade the boys, who numbered around two to three hundred in his recollection, to behave themselves, and warned them that the soldiers might open fire on them. He also joined some other men in asking MacDonogh to take the soldiers back to barracks as the boys had done nothing to provoke such a response. Collinson said that instead MacDonogh ordered the soldiers to form into divisions and shouted: 'On the right, counter march.' MacDonogh led them past the boys and into a lane near the barracks, but once they were gone the boys gave a 'derisive huzza'. However that was not a good idea. Collinson heard one of the soldiers order the men to 'halt, front, charge', and according to Collinson the Rangers 'came running back like a parcel of wild beasts'. Most of the crowd scattered and ran, except one man, who stood still beside the railings. One soldier approached him and patted him, but another group attacked him with musket butts. Afterwards the soldiers formed a line and began to fire. Collinson thought two men were shot and another bayoneted in the back.

William Skene was another ex-military man who saw some of the events. He described a great crowd running, with the soldiers chasing them with bayonets and musketry. William Copeland was the town clerk and he spoke to MacDonogh shortly after the mud-throwing incident. MacDonogh said he had been insulted, but Skene said that such things happened on the King's birthday, and anyway it was only a parcel of boys. He offered to act as escort to the captain and ordered two of the town sergeants to follow and arrest anybody who insulted MacDonogh. Shortly after that, Copeland had to run from a body of soldiers with fixed bayonets. George Turriff, one of the sergeants who was with MacDonogh, said he saw nobody attack the captain.

Other witnesses thought Sergeant Mackay of the Rangers was one of the prime instigators of the firing and were certain that many people were injured. They thought Mackay was in a great rage and said that 'none in Aberdeen should make me go back to barracks unless I choose'. Mackay used his halberd as a weapon when he arrested a printer named David Chalmers, who had said the Rangers were behaving 'very ill'.

By the end of the incident, MacDonogh had been arrested and brought to the Town House.

The case came to trial in Edinburgh on 6 January 1803. Lieutenant Colonel George McKenzie, Captain James MacDonogh, Ensign George Lanigan and Sergeants Mackay and Sutherland were all accused of murder. Lanigan failed to appear and the others pleaded not guilty.

As would be expected, the story the Rangers proffered was very different to that related by the civilians. They said that the crowd had insulted their Highland antecedents and called them 'Highland buggers'. They said that the sentinel in the sentry box outside the guardroom had been driven from his post by showers of filth and stones. They said that a volley of stones had bruised and bloodied Colonel McKenzie.

When the point came up that MacDonogh had ordered the men to load, they pointed out he had said 'with cartridge, prime and load' and had deliberately missed out the word 'ball' so the muskets would only fire blanks and not bullets, and even then the Rangers fired high, into the air, just in case of accidents. The soldiers said there were hundreds in the crowd, men as well as boys, and mentioned an incident when a butcher lifted a knife to threaten a corporal. The soldiers, as well as some of the civilian witnesses, swore that there were stones as well as mud being thrown at them. They said that MacDonogh had been severely hurt by a stone and another six or seven soldiers had been variously injured.

Although there were four civilians reported as killed, the trial was for the murder of John Ross, who had been shot in the face. After a long trial, McKenzie and MacDonogh were found not guilty while the case against the two sergeants, Sutherland and Mackay, was not proven.

That riot ushered in the century, but other riots racked Aberdeen.

Meal Riot

Poverty linked to inequality could encourage crime, and when poverty was enhanced by near starvation and hungry people saw shipments of grain leaving port, it was not surprising that they should react with violence. That was the situation in January 1847 in much of Scotland, including Aberdeen.

The Irish potato famine is well known, but the northern parts of Scotland experienced a similar situation. The potato was as important across great swathes of the Highlands as it was in Ireland, and starvation seemed a near certainty for much of the population. In Aberdeen, there were shiploads of grain leaving port at a time when bread prices were high and people were in real destitution.

At eleven in the morning of Friday, 24 January 1847, the townspeople of Aberdeen mustered on the links as speakers told them of the situation in the town and in the country as a whole. Not all who gathered were locals, as around 200 railway navigators crossed from the other side of the Dee to join in. Another crowd rallied in front of the Town House and yelled their discontent and frustration. The provost and the magistrates were in the council room inside the building, but when the provost addressed the crowd and asked them to dispel, they retaliated with a deputation reminding them of the extreme poverty of many of the people. The provost and magistrates promised to help all they could, and shortly after they met the merchants and asked them to stop sending grain out of the city, so bread prices could stabilise.

There was still agitation in Aberdeen, however, and at three that afternoon a number of special constables were sworn in to ensure that any disturbances could be controlled. In the streets, groups of desperate people attacked carts that were laden with grain for the ships in harbour. Superintendent Barclay arrested a man who was actually in the act of rolling a sack of grain from the back of a cart. The evening witnessed crowds gathering again, boys, youths and adults all intent on protesting, or perhaps doing something more active.

When the crowd started to stone windows in Castle Street and Marischal Street, shopkeepers hurried to put up their shutters. The stones continued to fly, with a fair number directed at the watching police. However, the police had been expecting trouble and at about seven at night the entire Aberdeen police force, day and night combined, lifted their batons and charged a hundreds-strong crowd that had been throwing stones at them. There were a desperate few moments as the blue-uniformed police struggled with starving men and women, and then the crowd withdrew, leaving some of their number as prisoners of the police. There were other, minor skirmishes, but although the town was tense, the trouble subsided that night.

Compared with other places, Aberdeen had got off lightly; the police had coped well. However, there was plenty other crime for them to worry about.

6

The Kittybrewster Axe Murder

Peter McRobbie farmed at Sunnybank, near the village of Cotton, which was then about a mile from Aberdeen. On the evening of Monday, 4 October 1852, he had been threshing bere in a barn beside the cottage of one of his tenants, Barbara Ross, commonly known as the Widow Ross. Mrs Ross lived in a house that sat on its own, near to the old road, about forty metres west of the Inverurie turnpike and just north of the Kittybrewster toll bar.

When McRobbie left the barn he noticed that there was a light moving in Mrs Ross's house, as if somebody was carrying a lantern from room to room, and he stopped to get the key of the barn so he could secure it for the night. He stepped inside the house and through the lobby into the kitchen.

'Are you all bedded?'

Rather than Mrs Ross, it was a man who replied: 'No!' The man was at the fireplace and came to the door; he carried a lamp but blew it out as he approached McRobbie. 'What do you want?' the man asked.

'I want the key to the barn,' McRobbie told him. He tried to make out who the man was by the light of the kitchen fire, but the room was too dim.

'Who wants it?' the man asked.

'Peter McRobbie wants it,' McRobbie said, and the shadowy man handed it over straight away.

As the man turned away, McRobbie glanced into the kitchen and saw what he believed were two pairs of legs sprawled beside the fireplace, and he thought he heard a man snoring, as if he was sleeping off too much drink. McRobbie did not enter any of the four rooms in the house, and left when the shadowy man handed him the key.

As soon as McRobbie walked away from the house, he saw that 'a light sprang on' and that the man spread some sort of covering on the windows, as if to conceal what was happening inside. By that time, McRobbie was suspicious. He walked to the house of a neighbouring farmer, William Grant, which was between the cottage and his home, and asked if Barbara Ross was 'in the habit of keeping bad company'. When Grant answered in the negative, McRobbie asked if she kept lodgers, but Grant answered no to that as well. McRobbie pondered for a moment and asked if Grant would accompany him back to Ross's house, and they returned, walking through a rising wind.

It was shortly after nine when they got back to the cottage, and again McRobbie saw a light moving in the kitchen window. McRobbie knocked at the door and found it was closed and locked, but when Grant lifted his heavy stick and knocked hard a second time, the man opened. This time he held a candle and McRobbie recognised him as George Christie, a man who had been employed to help with the threshing. No sooner had the door opened than the wind blew the candle out, and when Christie retired to relight it at the kitchen fire, McRobbie heard moaning inside the house.

When Grant asked who was moaning, Christie explained that Mrs Ross's young grandchild, John Greig Louden, was ill with a 'sair belly'.

'Is Mrs Ross not in?' McRobbie asked.

'No,' said Christie.

Grant asked if he could have a lantern so they could examine the interior of the barn and the work that had been carried out there. However, Christie said there was not a lantern in the house. Christie brought his candle and accompanied them to the barn. They remained inside for about four minutes while McRobbie inspected the threshed grain. McRobbie had intended to lure the man away from the cottage so he could ensure Mrs Ross was safe; but in case there was an innocent explanation, he was trying not to interfere too much or offend Mrs Ross. The plan did not work, for as soon as McRobbie and Grant were in the barn, Christie split his candle in half and returned to Mrs Ross's cottage, with the wind blowing out the flame as he walked. Grant and McRobbie stood in the shadow of the barn and watched; a light appeared in the window of the cottage and then Christie adjusted the covering on the window. About five minutes later Christie left the cottage, locked the door and walked into the night. He was 'soughing' – whistling softly – as he walked. He carried a bundle under his arm, greeted them in passing, said it may rain later and walked in the direction of New Aberdeen.

Without any hesitation, McRobbie and Grant knocked at Mrs Ross's door, but there was no answer. They tried to enter, but the door was locked and their attempts to force an entry failed. The two men asked another neighbour, James Foote, if Mrs Ross kept male company but were told 'no'. Two of Foote's sons accompanied them to Mrs Ross's house and one, Skene Foote, banged on the door and windows and demanded 'I must get in!'

There was no reply, but he was sure he heard a low moaning from inside. The other brother, John Foote, knelt at the door and put his ear to the keyhole. He confirmed that there was somebody moaning inside.

Grant took hold of John Foote. 'Run for Richardson at the Printfield,' he ordered, 'and get him here as fast as you can.'

Richardson was the local policeman. While Grant and Skene Foot stayed at the cottage, McRobbie returned home for a while. After about twenty minutes, Constable Richardson and John Foote arrived at the cottage. Richardson rapped on the door three times, stated that he was a policeman and demanded entry. There was only silence from within. He then said that unless there was a reply he would break in the door. When nobody replied, Richardson stepped back and rushed forward, smashing his way in with his shoulder. There was a candle handy on a shelf in the lobby, so they lit it and tried the kitchen door: it was locked against them. Grant found a hoe and they forced it open. They stepped inside, with the candle pooling flickering light into the dimness of the room.

Although they had been prepared for tragedy, they still stopped in shock at the scene. Mrs Ross lay near to the fire in the kitchen, with the footstool at her feet; it was this stool that McRobbie had initially mistaken for a second pair of legs. Young John was also lying on the ground in front of the chest of drawers, and McRobbie thought that he looked dead as well. Both the bodies were covered in blood, with Mrs Grant's injuries concentrated around her throat and her head. Young John's head had been split open like an apple, with his tiny skull cleft to his nose. There was also a deep cut in his chest. His body was still warm, but there was blood pooling and congealing all around him. One of the drawers was smashed and there was a large axe lying between the two bodies, with dark blood on the blade. There were also bloody fingerprints smeared over the lid of the chest that sat in a corner of the room. Incongruously, there were some freshly baked oatcakes on a table in the midst of this scene of carnage.

As Grant and Constable Richardson were taking in all this horror, McRobbie entered the house. McRobbie told Richardson about Christie, but added that he did not know where the suspected murderer lived. Richardson brought in Constable James Cran and Mr Simpson the procurator fiscal. They consulted with Constable Nicol of the night patrole, who knew that James Humphrey, a gardener and contractor, had employed Christie to thresh the barley. Humphrey would know Christie's address.

Humphrey took Constables Richardson and Cran to Denburnside, New Aberdeen. It was about one o'clock on the Tuesday morning when they arrived, and they found Christie fully dressed and drinking with his partner, a woman named Marshall, in his house. Constable Richardson laid a hand on Christie's shoulder and said, 'I suspect you are the man I am in search of.'

'No,' Christie said simply, and promptly denied any knowledge of the double murder. He said he had not been at Sunnybank that night. The constables examined him and found blood on his shoes and trousers and spattered on his wrists and on the cuff of his shirt. He also had a woman's purse and gold ring in his pockets, and there were various items of clothing in the house that he could not account for. The police arrested him: the time between the murder and the arrest was less than four hours. They took him to the watch house, where he was stripped so that Dr Ogston and Dr Jamieson could examine him. When the police questioned Christie, he said, 'This should have been done long ago.'

They dug deeper into the life of George Christie. He was around fifty-one and originally came from Skene, in Aberdeenshire. After a youth as an agricultural labourer, Christie joined the Bengal Artillery and served in India for twenty-seven years, making it up to sergeant before he was reduced back to the ranks. He was discharged in June 1850 with a 'bad' character and a pension of a shilling a day. Returning to his old haunts, Christie turned to theft, and got sixty days in jail, after which the East India Company stopped his pension. He had to earn his living as a casual labourer, either at the farms or in the quarries.

After his arrest, Christie sunk into silence and refused to confirm his guilt. He was tried at the High Court in Edinburgh in December that year. He was charged with murdering Barbara Ross by hacking her with an axe on her head and face and other parts of her body. He was also charged with stealing a purse, rings and a number of items of clothing. Further to that was a charge of murdering young John with an axe. He pleaded not guilty.

A number of witnesses spoke at the trial. One was James Sangster, who had worked with Christie and remembered him mentioning that Mrs Ross must make good money by selling her cows. George Ross, a son of Barbara Ross, identified the ring and purse as belonging to his mother. He told the court that she kept her money and valuables in the top drawer of her chest of drawers: the same drawer that had been smashed open. Mary Brownlie, a pawnbroker in Aberdeen, said that Christie had come to her on the Monday night with some items of clothing; Joseph Ross, another son of the murdered woman, identified them as belonging to his mother.

When Christie was questioned, he admitted that he had been at Mrs Ross's cottage but 'declined to answer' whether or not he had struck either of the victims with an axe, or to explain from where he had obtained Mrs Ross's possessions.

It took the jury only seven minutes to find Christie guilty of murder despite the defence's attempts to lay the blame on a second, unknown man, who may have come into the house unseen, murdered Mrs Ross and young John, and slipped away into the night. Lords Cowan and Anderson sentenced Christie to be transported under a 'secure guard' to the prison of Aberdeen, to be 'detained and fed on bread and water' until 13 January. Then he was to be hanged and his remains buried within the prison.

Christie seemed to accept the sentence without much emotion. He certainly did not show any deep remorse for the murders he had committed. When he was in prison he confessed his crimes to Mr Baxter, the chaplain. He told Baxter that on the afternoon of the murders he had gone to Humphrey to pick up his wages; however, there was no money for him, so he walked over to the barn beside Mrs

Ross's house to collect some small bits and pieces he had left there. He had left a flagon in Mrs Ross's house, and when he saw her in the byre, he asked for it back. She refused and he followed her into her house, where she told him that he owed her money for some milk and she would keep the flagon as payment. That was enough for Christie: he was already under financial stress, and lifted the axe. He killed Mrs Ross, and when John ran between them, he killed him as well. After that he smashed the place up, robbed it and left.

William Calcroft, the famous English executioner, performed the deed in front of a crowd of around 8,000 people. It was not uncommon for the spectators to voice sympathy for the condemned man or woman, but on this occasion the crowd were all on the side of the executioner. The attendant police and special constables were hardly needed; there was no disturbance among the crowd. After hanging for an hour, George Christie was cut down and buried inside the prison.

7
Theft and Robbery

Three crimes were ever-present in nineteenth-century towns: assaults, drunkenness and petty theft. To take one year in Aberdeen as a sample: in 1888, the police recorded fifty-four thefts from the person. Of that number, prostitutes committed at least ten, but only one occurred when the victim was sober. Men or boys were known to have committed twenty, eleven of which were when the victim was drunk. Women who were not prostitutes committed another three at least, and twenty-one of the victims were unable to say who stole from them, but eleven admitted they had been drunk at the time. The police were hard-pressed, but sometimes the general public could be more than useful.

Quick Capture

On the afternoon of Friday, 9 April 1852, the coach from Banchory to Aberdeen pulled up at Kirkton of Durris on its scheduled stop. Alexander Leys, the coach guard, accompanied Donald Finlay, an Aberdeen ostler, and some of the passengers to the local public house. Finlay hurried to the counter and ordered a glass of whisky to refresh him for the remainder of the journey. He paid at once, and the shop assistant put the money in the till. Finlay then asked her for a piece of cheese. When the girl walked through to the back shop for the cheese, Finlay leaned across the counter, opened the till and purloined a £5 note. The girl noticed the loss and suspected Finlay, but a quick search failed to find the money, so he reboarded the coach and continued to Aberdeen.

Leys was sure of Finlay's guilt, however, and as soon as they arrived in Aberdeen he grabbed hold of the ostler and manhandled him to the constable in Union Street. Finlay tried to struggle, but Leys, like many coach guards, was a burly man and used to dealing with unruly passengers. Finlay was escorted to the police office and stripped naked, with all his clothes thoroughly searched. At first the police thought that Leys was mistaken, but just when they were about to apologise and release Finlay, a policeman found the crumpled £5 stuck deep in the toe of his boot. Finlay spent some time in jail.

Career Thief

Sometimes people just gave way to temptation and committed a single crime, but there were also those who made a career of crime. Many of these hopeful criminals were not particularly good at what they did and spent more of their life in prison than outside, and rarely gained anything by their actions. Mary Mackay was one such unfortunate career criminal.

Her first serious conviction was on 13 August 1862, when she appeared before the Sheriff Court. She was convicted of petty theft and sentenced to sixty days in prison. On 30 May 1863 she was before the Sheriff Court again and this time was locked away for twelve months. She came out in 1864 and either lived an honest life or was not caught for a while, but on 20 September 1865 she was in the Circuit Court and was sentenced to a hefty seven years' penal servitude.

She survived that but did not reform, and on 10 September 1878 she was given another eight years' penal servitude for stealing money from a gentleman. The man had the misfortune, or bad judgement, to accompany Mackay into a close off the Netherkirkgate. He should not have been too surprised to have his pocket picked there, but the nineteenth century seemed to produce a breed of very naive men to supply the thieves with their daily bread.

Mackay was released on a ticket of leave when she still had two years of that sentence to survive, but on 22 May 1884 she was in trouble once more. Mackay had inveigled her way into the friendship of Mrs Walker of Flourmill Lane and her stepdaughter, Williamina Walker. Mackay came into the house at around four in the afternoon, when Williamina was in bed. Mackay had been drinking and was looking for a pair of boots. Williamina told her to come back when she was sober and Mackay left the bedroom.

About half past eight that evening, Williamina noticed that she was missing a pair of earrings that had been on the dressing table. She asked if Mackay had seen them, but got an instant denial. Williamina told the police, who did their usual search of the pawnshops, and the earrings were found. Mackay had pawned them. The police arrested her and she was lodged once more in Aberdeen Prison.

The procurator fiscal would have been well within his rights to send her to the High Court, which may well have sent her back to complete her unexpired sentence, while adding another period of years for the latest theft. Instead he took the more lenient step of sending her to the Sheriff Court. Sheriff Brown heard the case on 7 June 1884. Mackay stated that Mrs Walker had invited her to her house, and she and Williamina had begun talking in the bedroom. Williamina, apparently, asked if Mackay would 'stand one' – meaning buy her a drink – and thereafter the conversation turned to the earrings. Mackay said that Williamina had allowed her to borrow them for the day. However, there was no doubt that the earrings were pawned for two shillings and five pence. Sheriff Brown sent Mackay back to jail for another sixty days.

Pocket Picking

Pocket picking is an ancient skill, but perhaps reached its apogee in the nineteenth century. It was an age when crowds frequently gathered at major events and offered tempting targets for the professional 'dip'. Sporting events were always good places for such thieves to practise their craft. When there was a regatta held at the Inches in Aberdeen in September 1852, pickpockets flocked to the town from all over the country. However, the police and town sergeants were also on watch.

It was Town Sergeant Mellis who recognised a thief carrying a purse away from a victim and immediately pounced. The man claimed he was an innocent Dundee fish dealer named James Grant, but Bailie Sim gave him thirty days to cool off.

Ship-breaking and a Rash of Theft

Ships in harbour were often tempting targets for a thief. They were often unguarded, the dockside was frequently quiet, and seamen were not known for their security consciousness and could leave their possessions lying in the forecastle or cabins. Of them all, the whaling ships were amongst the largest in Aberdeen. They held a fairly large crew and the master earned a substantial wage, making the ships doubly attractive for a thief. The ships sailed out early in the year and returned in the autumn when the ice closed in, so they were often laid up over the long, dark nights of winter. In October 1821, a whaling ship in harbour was broken into. The robbers may have had seagoing experience because they went straight to the captain's cabin and stole everything they could before vanishing into the night.

That same month there were robberies in James Street, North

Street and in various shops in the Green during church service. At a period when church attendance was so high as to be almost universal, burglars simply waited until all the respectable and the godly were worshipping and their houses were empty and then struck. It was a simple system that seemed to work. That was a busy time for thefts, so the *Aberdeen Journal* reported that 'the town seems to swarm with vagrants and loose characters. We would strongly impress upon all persons keeping lodging houses the necessity of giving notice at the Town House of the arrival of all unknown characters who may come to them requesting accommodation.'

Although most thefts were petty, some of the criminals made a decent living. In March 1824, a householder in Union Street heard noises in his house at night-time. He rose from his bed and came downstairs, but the thieves had heard him and fled. They had entered by the back and were after only the silver plate in the drawing room, using a crowbar to force the iron door that protected it. They got nothing, but escaped in a gig. Among the respectable, only the wealthy could afford a coach; it seems that Aberdeen thieves had their own hierarchy.

Some people lived by stealing.

Habit and Repute a Theft

Hugh Thompson did not always use his own name. Sometimes he called himself William Cameron, while his working companion, James Watt, was also known as James Duncan. The line of work they were involved in made it necessary to alter their names from time to time, for both were thieves and if they had been convicted using the same name too often, the result would invariably be transportation. But even with that horrendous possibility hanging over their heads, they continued with their chosen profession.

They had been working in Edinburgh, but decided on a change of location so moved north to Aberdeen. On Sunday, 12 May 1843, they watched as the Munro family filed out of their Union Street house to go to church, ensured the house was empty, and then broke in. Mr Munro was a surveyor of taxes, so the thieves guessed he was relatively well paid. They were right: their visit netted fifty-six silver spoons, from tiny tea spoons to heavy ladles; eighteen silver forks; twelve silver toddy ladles; twelve silver spoons; and a selection of other items, including a silver watch, a snuffbox, a gold watch, four gold rings and a lady's gold chain.

Delighted with their good fortune, they looked for their next victim. Charles Playfair also lived in Union Street and as a gunsmith he was equally respected and equally as well off. His door was locked, of course, but professionals such as Thompson and Watt had a great many lock picks and false keys to surmount that obstacle, and once inside they helped themselves to silver toddy ladles and dessert spoons, a gold brooch, a gold ring and other valuables. Their trip to Aberdeen was proving a success.

On 23 May, they visited Aberdeen Race Course at the Links, but did not waste their time gambling on the horses. Instead, they cast around for what they could gain without any risk to themselves. Miss Christian Kennedy had left her carriage unattended near to the winning post, so that was an invitation to any of the light-fingered profession. Thompson and Watt found a silver snuffbox, a silk bag and two handkerchiefs in the carriage, which they took for themselves.

Three days later, on Sunday, 26 May 1843, they again used their selection of keys to enter Mrs Hutcheson's house in King Street and lightened it of five pounds in notes and thirteen shillings in silver, following that with a visit to Mr Connon the grocer's house in the same street. That was where things started to go horribly wrong. As Connon was a respectable man and had a respectable house, it should have been empty during the hours the family was at church, so it was just bad luck that Connon's servant was present. She had decided to visit a friend at two in the afternoon that day, but was unsure when she was to be back. As the whole family would be out at church and the house locked, she asked Mrs Connon for the key in case she returned before them.

Unfortunately the servant had forgotten her money for the church collection so hurried back to the house for it. Her timing could not have been worse, for she arrived just as Thompson and Watt were busily looting the place. She put her key in the lock and found the door already open, so entered slowly. She was in the kitchen when Thompson and Watt came out of Connon's bedroom. They either saw her then, or had already heard her, for both made a dash for the stairs that led down to the outside door. 'Stop, thief!' the servant called out, and again, 'Stop, thief!' She chased them down the stairs, shouting at the top of her voice, but of course they did not stop.

Thompson was first out and ran into the street, but Watt was slower. He slammed shut the door and held it as the servant tried to open it to chase him. There was an impasse for a few moments as Watt held the door and the servant continued to scream out 'Stop, thief!', and then Watt let go and ran for his life.

However, he had delayed a fraction too long. During the time he had been holding the door, the servant's shouts had attracted attention, and now the sight of a running man with a woman chasing him, yelling her head off in the quiet of an Aberdeen Sunday afternoon, was enough to waken the devil himself. As Watt ran down Frederick Street, he bundled a bunch of keys into a silk handkerchief and threw them over a stone wall into a wood yard. He also dropped the lock picks that had gained him access to the various houses, but he offered no resistance when a hefty coachman by the name of Alexander grappled him and brought him to the ground. In the meantime, Thompson escaped.

There was no thought of going back to help his friend; there was no honour between these thieves. Thompson divested himself of his lock picks and ran for freedom. Without looking back he caught the coach for Stonehaven, leaving Watt alone. The police soon collected the false keys, which were perfect fits for the burgled houses, and the lock picks that both men had discarded.

The next day, Monday, 27 May, Superintendent Barclay rode to Stonehaven. He saw Thompson board the mail coach for Pettycur, and followed and arrested him. When the interior of the coach was cleaned later at Aberdeen, the cleaner found several of the small articles stolen from the houses of Munro and Playfair pushed between the side of the coach and the cushion.

The case came to the Aberdeen Circuit Court in April, and three Edinburgh detectives stated that Thompson had been known as a thief 'by habit and repute' in Edinburgh for the last five years. One of these detectives was James McLevy, who was arguably the best-known criminal officer in Scotland at the time. When the jury heard the evidence they had no doubt that both men were guilty and Lord Medwyn sentenced Watt to ten years' and Thompson to fourteen years' transportation.

Both convicts were transported on the ship *Mount Stuart Elphinstone* in February 1845, landing in Van Diemen's Land

Methods of Burglary

Although most thefts in Aberdeenshire were opportunist, with the thief slipping through an open window or forcing a door, there was a cadre of professional thieves that used more sophisticated methods to break into premises. For example, on the snowy night of Saturday, 29 November 1868, a burglar broke into the office of the Town and County Bank in Alford, and then into the neighbouring agent's house. The thief must have been a professional, for he took his time. Before he even tried the bank he cut the glass of a carpenter's shop window and stole a forming iron, which he carried with him. He ensured he would not be disturbed by fastening the bank's doorknobs together with ropes and securing them with crossbars so neither could open.

Assured of no interference, he climbed the eight-foot-high railings that protected the bank, dropped to the far side and used the iron to tap out two panes of glass in the window. That gave him access to the internal wooden shutters, which were fastened on the inside. He broke the lower ring, inserted his fingers between the two shutters and forced off the keeper bar, so he could push them open and enter the office of the bank. However, all his efforts were pointless. He raked through the drawers and the till, but they had been emptied and the contents put in the safe. He tried, but failed, to break into the safe. In his frustration, he wrecked the room and then burgled the house next door. All he got away with was an old sword and a bottle of whisky. The police followed his footsteps in the snow, but did not find who he was.

Other thieves used different methods. James Robertson was a forty-year-old labourer who had a sideline in housebreaking. In November or December of 1880, he broke into the smithy at Rosehill, Oldmachar, by going on to the roof, removing some tiles and cutting through the lathe and plaster beneath. He stole ninety-one yards of lead pipe, and as he had seven previous convictions, he was given eight years' penal servitude.

An Inept Burglar

Thirty-six-year-old James Hill was a respectable engineer who lived in Urquhart Road, Aberdeen. However, he also had an alternative occupation: he was a burglar, but not a very successful one. On the night of Tuesday, 8 May 1897 he proved his ineptitude for his second occupation when he broke into John Esslemont's grocery shop in King Street.

He started the burglary with a degree of skill and forethought, but it then degenerated into a piece of spontaneous stupidity that had a painful ending. He had been drinking that evening, which may have been to give himself some courage for his nocturnal activities, or the reason for them. Either way, he was not quite sober when he entered the common close beside the shop. He had mounted the staircase within the tenement stair, which brought him to a level equal to the roof of the shop. He pushed the window right open and climbed onto the roof of the shop. There was a skylight in the roof and Hill carefully cut out a three-foot by two-foot pane of glass. It was a windy night, which would carry away any noise that Hill made, but he must have been prepared and experienced to successfully remove a pane of glass without breaking it or making a noise.

There were a number of methods a Victorian burglar could use to remove a window, from scraping away the putty to cutting a hole in the glass, but once that was done, Hill realised he faced a twenty-foot drop to get to the shop floor and he had not brought a rope with him Nevertheless, he was an adaptable man and quickly thought of an alternative. Taking off his boots, he laid them beside the skylight and stripped off his long johns so for a moment he stood exposed to the swirling wind. Then he pulled his trousers back on, tied the long johns to the frame of the window and used them to swing himself down.

Or that was the general idea, but woollen underwear were not designed to take the full weight of a grown man and either they ripped or Hill's knot slipped. Either way, Hill fell to the ground. That was where John Esslemont found him when he opened the shop the next morning, semi-conscious and in pain with a broken leg. Esslemont called the police and Inspector Forbes soon worked out what had happened. Forbes ordered Hill to the infirmary, as well as putting him under arrest.

However, the roads of Aberdeenshire could also be dangerous.

Highway Robbery

On Monday, 21 June 1830, William Reid, the carter between Aberdeen and Huntly, was passing Inverurie when a man walked up and began talking to him. Pleased to have the company, Reid was enjoying the crack until they neared Kintore, when his travelling companion lagged behind, pulled out a pistol and shot Reid in the back. Reid felt the ball enter his back, but had enough energy left to turn around before he fell down.

It is possible that the attacker thought Reid was not seriously hurt, or that he had missed completely, for rather than remain to finish the job or rob the carrier, he took to his heels and ran away. Reid was unable to walk properly so he used the shaft of his cart as a prop as he carried on to the nearest farmhouse. The farmer's wife sent for a doctor, but Reid was gravely hurt and later died. The attacker was never found.

Robbing the Farmer

William Imlach and John Young were enterprising young men of Aberdeenshire. It was December 1847, poverty stalked the land, and unemployment and disquiet was abroad from the smallest hamlet to the largest city all across Europe. However, Imlach and Young had decided that they knew how to defeat the recession and make money for themselves at the same time. It was easy: all they had to do was wait for others to spend time and energy in making money, and then rob them.

Accordingly, on 9 December they waited on the turnpike road between Huntly and Rhynie, just south of the Manse of Huntly. When they saw a farm cart approaching they jumped on and robbed the owner, a farmer named James Petrie, of eight pounds and two shillings. They tried the same trick on 27 December, when their victim was a man named George Durno. He had been riding on the turnpike road to Inch when, near the toll bar at Greenhill, Imlach and Young approached him, hauled him from his horse and grabbed him by the throat. Unhorsed and faced by two desperate men, the shocked Durno had little chance to resist, and Imlach and Young got away with his pocketbook containing £13, which was a substantial sum back then.

Caught and brought to court, the highway robbers were transported for fourteen years each. Imlach sailed on *Oriental Queen* in October 1852 but there seems to be no record of Young being transported. As Lord Moncrieff and Lord Cockburn both happily pointed out, if they had been caught a few years previously they would have been hanged.

However, housebreaking was much more common than highway robbery.

Housebreaking

In September 1887 there was a series of robberies and attempted robberies in Aberdeen. One of the robbers was a thirty-nine-year-old labourer named Alexander Gibb. He lived in Seamount Place, but on Tuesday, 27 September he had been caught housebreaking in Golden Square.

The beat constable was an observant man. He had passed along Golden Square about half past five in the afternoon and had noticed something moving in the window of number 10, the home of ex-baillie Duffus. The constable knew the family were away in the country, so paid particular attention to the house. The Duffus family had attempted to prevent prying eyes by placing grey paper on the inside of their windows, but that paper could also act as a shield for anybody who broke into the house. The constable knew that there was no reason for the paper to move in an empty house, so he investigated further. A pane of glass had been completely removed from the window, and the burglar had put his arm through, unfastened the window and crawled inside. It was the draught through the empty windowpane that had stirred the paper.

There were a number of people in the square, so the constable elicited the help of a couple of passers-by. He told them he suspected that there was a burglar in the house, but he could not guard the front and back doors at the same time. He asked the gentlemen if they would guard the back door while he waited at the front. In the nineteenth century, people seemed more than willing to help the police and the men hurried around the back entrance, which was in a lane off North Silver Street. From there they could see Gibb at work, ransacking the house. Eventually Gibb noticed them watching, and he dashed through to the front of the house to escape.

Unfortunately for Gibb, the policeman was waiting there for him, so he quickly turned around, retreated into the depths of the house and looked for somewhere to hide. The constable saw him disappear, entered the house and began a search. He found a basket of stolen property at the back door, ready to be taken away, but there was no sign of Gibb until the constable looked under the bed. Gibb was cowering there and was arrested there and then.

The policeman questioned the neighbours as well. Some of them had seen Gibb leaving Duffus's house by the back door on previous occasions, so he was systematically stripping the house of all its valuables while the family were away on holiday. Indeed, Gibb was such a regular visitor that the neighbours believed he was a workman that Duffus had hired.

Gibb appeared at the Sheriff Court on Monday, 24 October and pleaded guilty to breaking into the house on three separate occasions. He was not a first offender, with a string of mainly minor offences stretching back to 1869. He was sent to prison for six months. He was no sooner released than he was arrested again. In May 1888, there was a break-in at St George's in the West Parish Church in John Street and the police picked him up on suspicion; that time he was released.

Robbing the Manse

Not long before the burglary at Golden Square there was an attempted break-in at Mannofield Manse at Great Western Road in Aberdeen's affluent West End. The Reverend William Forbes was at home at the time, and at one in the morning he heard his front doorbell ring. He rose from his bed, donned his dressing gown and walked to answer the door. He moved slowly, as he was recovering from a long illness, but before he reached the door he heard footsteps around the back of the house and then somebody shoving and pushing at the back door.

Forbes realised that the front door had only been a trick by the burglars. They had rung the bell to see if anybody was inside, and as he had taken so long, they assumed the house was empty and safe to burgle. Rather than face what could be a number of determined and dangerous men, Forbes thought it better to merely make it obvious that the house was occupied, so he walked around each room, lighting the gas lamps.

That was enough to scare away the would-be robbers. Forbes heard the sound of feet running around the side of his house, and then he heard the hooves and grinding wheels of a horse and cab on the road in front. He smiled, expecting instant panic from the burglars. Instead, the cab halted in front of the manse and the two men who had been attempting to break in calmly got on board. It drove away, leaving Forbes safe but concerned.

Jewel Robbery

Jewellery shops were always targets for crime. They held an accumulation of valuable and easily transportable merchandise and were not always adequately protected. Andrew Malcolm was the proprietor of a jeweller's shop at 13 Union Place. The shop was on the ground floor of what was known as the Arcade Buildings, with a single large window looking onto the foot of Chapel Street. There were no shutters on this window, but Malcolm had a blind pulled down behind the glass.

The burglar had no pretence at finesse: shortly after one o'clock in the morning of Wednesday, 28 September 1887, he just walked up to the eight-foot-wide plate-glass window and threw a stone through it. Then he thrust his hand through the hole, shoved the blind to one side, grabbed whatever he could and ran away. Presumably he had already worked out exactly what he wanted to steal, for the window was broken exactly where the watches were on display. He must also have known the routine of Constable Grant, the beat policeman, who passed the shop every thirty minutes.

Constable George Grant found the window broken when he passed at twenty-five to two and blew his whistle to get assistance. With the broken window a tempting target for any further thievery, he could not leave, and it was a frustrating twenty-minute wait before a fellow constable appeared; that gave the burglar plenty of time to make his escape.

The second policeman woke up Malcolm in his home at Thistle Street and they inspected the shop to see what had been stolen. The only stock missing was in the window. The burglar had stolen six gold and nine silver watches, together with ten gold, eight stone and three diamond rings and nine gold Albert watch chains: a good collection for a few seconds' work. The total value was around £100; two years' wages for a working man.

At that time, the police were worried that there was a professional gang of burglars on the prowl in Aberdeen, as there had been a spate of robberies during the previous week. There had been burglaries at Ruthrieston and Cults the week before, and at Golden Square and Mannofield Manse since then. As usual, the police alerted the pawnbrokers in Aberdeen and sent details of the stolen jewellery to the other Scottish forces. It was often easier for the police to wait and see who was selling stolen goods and trace them backwards from there to the point of origin. On 7 October, the first of the stolen items turned up as a travelling hawker named Thomas Townsley swapped one of the watches at Stonehaven. The police were quickly notified, and when on 11 October a member of the same hawker family tried to sell more of the stolen items at Auchinblae, the police pounced.

They searched the caravan and horses of two hawkers, Thomas and Hugh Townsley, but found nothing. The police released them, but the suspicion remained. The investigations continued, with the police asking questions in the places they knew to be haunts of resetters. George Deans, a barman in a pub in West North Street, told them he had seen the Townsleys selling a silver watch chain to a carter named Thomas Dickson. The police spoke to Dickson, who told them that the Townsleys had spoken of other jewellery. That was information enough, and Detective James Dey traced the hawkers to Fettercairn and arrested them on 16 October.

When Dey was bringing back the Townsleys to Aberdeen, Thomas Townsley said they had bought the goods from two men in Market Street. He did not know who these men were. However, he also offered to show Dey where he had hidden some of the jewellery. Dey agreed and recovered some of the stolen property from a hole in a wall at Water of Cowie.

On 9 November, Thomas and Hugh Townsley appeared before Sheriff Dove Wilson in the Aberdeen Criminal Court and were charged with resetting stolen property. Both pleaded not guilty. One of the witnesses called against them was their nephew, John Townsley. He was also a travelling hawker, who worked with his father from a caravan. He told the court that on 11 October, when the police searched the accused men, they had some of the stolen goods hidden in the padding of the saddle while a watch was hidden in a nearby field. That watch was subsequently destroyed. The defence argued that both men had co-operated with the police after their arrest. Sheriff Wilson sent Hugh to jail for sixty days, as he had been previously convicted of theft, and Thomas for six weeks, which seems surprisingly lenient.

In the meantime, the hunt for the actual thieves continued. In the first week in October, a man named William Washington was arrested in Edinburgh as he tried to sell some of the watches. Detective Wyness travelled down to bring him back up to Aberdeen. A few days later the Stirling Police arrested an Aberdeen leather cutter named James Jamieson on suspicion of the burglary. He had walked from Dundee and was on his way to Glasgow with a number of gold and silver watches in his pockets. Detective Innes brought him back to Aberdeen to be questioned. On 9 December, two men, William Washington, an ex-soldier, and Jamieson, were found guilty of the robbery at the Sheriff Court in Aberdeen but sent to the High Court to be sentenced. Jamieson, who had a record, was sentenced to five years' penal servitude and Washington to fifteen months in jail.

Stealing Fifty Watches

On Thursday, 2 September 1880, at about eight at night, John Lavie, shop assistant, closed the shop at 46 Upperkirkgate in Aberdeen and went home. The shop was one of two owned by ex-bailie Benjamin Duffus of Janefield Cottage in Cults. Lavie made all the usual security checks on the door and the windows, for he was well aware how much of a temptation the watchmaker and jewellery shop could be. The shop was on the ground floor of a tenement building with two windows facing the street; there was a close entry named Burn Court at one side, which led to the back of the shop in George Street. The shop had two windows that faced onto the close. One of the windows was very securely protected with iron bars spaced about ten centimetres apart. The second, the west window, was not quite so well protected, with bars further apart; however, because the shop was situated on a slight hill, the west window was about two metres above the ground so more difficult to enter. Both Duffus and Lavie thought the height and the bars were sufficient protection.

At nine in the morning of Friday, 3 September, Lavie returned to open the shop. The west window was open, the interior of the shop was in a shambles and the place had been burgled. Lavie immediately informed Duffus, who came at once from his Market Street shop to investigate and take a stock check. Duffus thought that around fifty watches had been stolen, along with marble clocks, lockets, gold Albert watch chains and other pieces of jewellery. Altogether 256 articles were missing: it was a major calamity.

There was no sign of a break-in except for the open west window, and Duffus decided that nobody could have squeezed between the protecting bars. There were no broken windows and the lock had not been forced. The only clue Duffus found was a small jewellery case lying outside the open window. He surmised that the burglar had used a skeleton key to enter by the front door and passed the stolen goods out to an accomplice who waited in the Burn Court. The use of a skeleton key argued for a professional rather than just a casual thief. The burglar had also gone to the window where the best of the stock was held, so it appeared he had studied the shop in advance.

As soon as the police were notified, they began work. Superintendent Wyness notified police forces in other Scottish cities and towns and ordered his men to scour Aberdeen for known thieves and burglars. The detective force began their usual search of the local pawnshops. The police also asked Duffus to take a thorough stock check to see what exactly had been stolen. Duffus found that his original estimate had been wrong: only fifty-one silver and ten gold watches were missing, with twenty gold and thirty-six silver Albert chains and other pieces of jewellery. The police also checked the shop thoroughly and discounted Duffus's elaborate theory. They believed that the burglar had lifted the sash of the back window and squeezed in between the security bars, despite the lack of space.

Only a day later, two men came into the pawnbroker's shop of William Fyfe in Perth. They handed over a gold Albert watch chain that one Neil McPherson claimed to have bought in Edinburgh. Fyfe took the pledge but soon realised he was handling stolen property. McPherson had given his address as 6 Skinnergate, which was a bakery, not a house. Fyfe kept Macpherson occupied in the shop and sent his assistant to notify the police. Inspector Duncan Cunningham arrested McPherson, but his colleague ran for freedom and was never caught. When he was brought to the Perth Police Station, McPherson said he lived at Heave-away Close in Edinburgh's High Street.

Detective Baird of the Perthshire force escorted the supposed burglar to Aberdeen. He was a twenty-two-year-old Dundonian, a bootsprigger who had already served sixty days in Dundee jail for the attempted robbery of a jeweller's shop. He was not the cleverest of thieves, for he had given his own name when he pledged chains in two different pawnshops in Perth, while his associate had used the name McPherson when he handed in a chain to a pawnbroker in Dundee.

Dr Ogston, the police surgeon, measured McPherson's head and found it was one-sixteenth of an inch smaller than the six-inch-wide gaps between the bars on the west window of the shop, so he could have manoeuvred himself inside. Ogston also found some scratches on McPherson's chest, which he thought were caused by scraping against the bars on the window, which were also marked.

The case came to the High Court in Edinburgh on 31 January 1881. Witnesses proved that McPherson had been in Aberdeen that day, staying at the Crown Inn, Shore Brae. He came into the inn at around ten at night but was gone before six the next morning, ostensibly to catch a train. John Salmond, a George Street confectioner, opened his shop at half past three in the morning. At that time he saw a man carrying a heavy green and red carpet bag. The man passed under a gas lamp but crossed the road when he noticed Salmond.

Two criminal officers gave their evidence. William Baird, criminal officer of Aberdeen, said that there was a frame nearby that McPherson could have used to climb up to get access to the window. David Ross, criminal officer from Dundee, searched McPherson's home and found a green and red carpet bag. He said he had known McPherson as a common thief for years and that he had been in Dundee Prison some of that time. McPherson was found guilty and was given five years' penal servitude.

The Old Machar Robbery

It was a mild night, as befitted the 17 May in the year 1878, and two men were hard at work. There was Robert McCombie, aged thirty-four, and forty-one-year-old James Wilson, both experts in their profession. They were at Arbour Cottage at Hammerfield West, Old Machar. They crouched beside the washing-house window with their sharp knives and darkened paper. First they cut through the putty around the windowpane and then they attached a lump of putty to the glass and gently pulled it free. They were so well practised in the art of burglary that there was no sound to alert the inhabitants of the house. One of the men cautiously pushed his hand through the space where the glass had been and unfastened the snib. He lowered the upper sash and both men snaked in, slowly and carefully.

Once inside, they rifled through the drawers but did not find very much: certainly not much for the risks they had gone through, for robbery could mean penal servitude. They had a quiet conversation and decided to go for broke. They would find the proprietor of the house and persuade him to hand over all the money there was in the house.

John Strachan had been an accountant most of his life. He was not married and lived at Arbour Cottage with his sister Isabel. About nine that night they had checked the doors and shutters of the house and had gone to bed. Strachan was soon asleep, but at about one in the morning Isabel came into his room with the alarming news that there was somebody else in the house. Strachan had hardly looked up when two men came hammering up the stairs and burst into his bedroom.

'Your money or your life,' Wilson said. He was obviously not a man given to original thought. McCombie lit the gas as Isabel cowered in the corner. Strachan recognised McCombie immediately; he had been employed as a labourer on a building site next to the house. He also thought he recognised Wilson, although he could not put a name to the face.

Strachan replied that he had no money to give them, whereupon both men grabbed hold of him. Wilson spoke to McCombie: 'Either strangle him or use your revolver on him.'

As they spoke, they dragged Strachan out of the bed, grabbed him by the throat and threw him to the ground. Strachan struggled up, so they threw him down again two or three times, which convinced him that he had better comply. He lay still on the floor for a few minutes as they went through the house and found sixteen shillings in silver. When they returned, they demanded a pound and then they would leave the house. Strachan fetched a pound note from a drawer in the wardrobe and handed it over.

'That's no use.' Wilson was the spokesman again. 'There must be more!'

Strachan asked the pair to go to the door, which they did, and he returned to the drawer where he kept his pocketbook. He gave them another pound note, but they demanded yet more. They grabbed a bag that held about £3 of silver, snatched a silver snuffbox and took hold of the pocketbook. They saw it was empty and threw it away, but they found about two shillings in copper and a needle case. All the time they threatened to shoot Strachan and pointed what he thought was a pistol at his head.

After half an hour, the burglars left the room and clambered out through the window through which they had entered. Isabel was inclined to go downstairs after the two men, but Strachan said she had best not. It was about two hours before Strachan mustered the courage to venture downstairs and found the gas lit but the house empty of burglars.

The Strachans called the police and gave descriptions of the two intruders to Constable James Diack. Inquiries began: Constable Sim had been on duty in Holburn Street, about a quarter of a mile from Strachan's cottage, and he saw two men pass him. As it was late at night, he thought they might have been poachers and he noted their appearance. One was definitely Wilson. Less than a week later, Diack arrested McCombie while his colleague Constable Middleton grabbed Wilson.

The case came to the Circuit Court in September. Strachan claimed he had never been frightened but 'it was nonsense to try and resist two men', which amused the audience, who always enjoyed the free entertainment of court trials. Both Strachan and Isabel immediately recognised McCombie and Wilson as the two men who had robbed them. The judge, Lord Deas, rushed the case through and did not allow any certificates of character to be read for the defence, while the defending solicitor did not offer any alibi, so the jury did not even have to retire to consider their guilty verdict. Lord Deas said 'there could not be a more daring case' but was interrupted when Wilson asked to be allowed to speak. He denied having a gun and said he had never been in the house. Lord Deas said it was no use after the verdict of the jury and gave each man twelve years' penal servitude.

It was not only men who were given to burglary. Women were also prone to breaking and entering.

The Harpooner's Wife

At the Circuit Court of Aberdeen in October 1821, Grizel Samuel, the wife of the harpooner Alexander Willox of Peterhead, was charged with three acts of housebreaking and theft in and around Peterhead. She denied the thefts but confessed she had reset the stolen goods and was sentenced to a year with hard labour in Bridewell.

The preceding text has given a few examples of the types of theft common to the streets of Aberdeen. The following table shows the number of thefts and arrests for theft in Aberdeen in some given years.

Year	Theft by Shop- or Housebreaking	Simple Theft	Thieves Arrested
1863	3	456	234
1868	16	390	
1869	4	324	
1876	Not known	337	
1877	7	351	
1878	22*	409	147
1879	11	448	190
1882	23	498	261
1883	11	527	342
1884	10	500	268
1885	13	461	
1886	31	563	257
1887	16	559	284
1888	50	691	275
1889	27	794	330
1890	20	787	
1893	22	986	471
1894	21	894	394
1895	19	818	381

1896	23	822	431
1897	41	948	435
1898	80	1048	
1899	43	988	581

* most by cutting glass

The figures show that housebreaking and shopbreaking was not a major threat to Aberdeen, but increased as the century progressed. Simple or opportunistic theft was much more common, while the Aberdeen police had a good arrest record for the number of thefts. Housebreaking and robbery may have been a concern for the people of Aberdeen, but there were worse crimes.

8
Murder Most Foul

Of all the crimes, murder is always the one that creates most interest. While even the cleverest robbery will be forgotten in time, murder, especially a brutal murder, has the ability to cause a thrill of horror years or even decades later. Aberdeen and the north-east had its share of murders. Some were in the city, but the countryside, often viewed as a haven of peace, was never quite as restive as the police would have liked.

Travelling could be hazardous in the nineteenth century. There were highwaymen on the lookout for coaches and footpads waiting for unwary walkers. The roads around Aberdeen were no safer than anywhere else.

Murder at the Den of Culter

Along with many people around Peterculter, Ann Harvey worked at the Culter Paper Mills. She claimed to be seventeen but looked older, and was a middle-sized young woman who lived with her friend Janet Esson in Burnside of Culter, about three miles west of Aberdeen on the Deeside road. On 6 May 1854, Harvey was walking along the turnpike on her way westward from Aberdeen, carrying a basket and with her head partly covered with a shawl. Harvey should have been happy; she had told Esson that her sweetheart Francis Forbes was in Aberdeen and she might be returning with him. She had told a carter called Alexander Mathieson the same thing when she met him on her way to Aberdeen and he had given her a lift. As they passed a place called Middleton, she pointed to it and told Mathieson that her sweetheart lived there and would be with her on the journey back.

Margaret Davidson was friendly with Harvey and knew about Francis Forbes. She also knew the two had recently had 'a small strife' but it was nothing serious. Harvey had been smiling when she told Davidson that Forbes had been 'devilish saucy' to her. Harvey appeared happy, but she had her own fears. She had allowed Forbes, 'Francie' as she called him, to be 'too intimate' with her, and now she was afraid she might be pregnant. That was worrying, but she also expected to marry him before too long, so it was not as desperate as it could have been.

However, at the Den of Culter a man stabbed Harvey in the neck, cut her throat from ear to ear and slashed her across the face. Harvey died nearly instantaneously. Once he had killed her, the attacker lifted Harvey's body and threw it over a drystane dyke that separated the turnpike from a small plantation of trees. There were no witnesses to the attack.

James Tosh worked as a servant at the house of Mr Campbell at West Cults. He and Alexander Stewart were out on the morning of Sunday, 7 May 1854. They walked towards Aberdeen and at the Den of Cults they saw a crumpled plaid lying beside the dyke. When they got closer they saw there was blood on the material and a pool of blood in a shallow ditch directly below the dyke. Tosh noticed that the wall was also splashed with blood; he looked over the top and saw Harvey. She lay on her back with her gown thrown up to cover her face and one leg exposed. Her hands were cut and battered as if she had thrown them up to try and protect her face and throat, while there were a number of other cuts and gashes on her body. Not sure what to do when confronted with such a terrible find, Tosh and Stewart ran to fetch Andrew Ellis, the grieve. As was normal, a host of other servants also rushed to see what was happening.

Ellis sent another servant, William Bothwell, to find a policeman, and Constable Alexander Aiken arrived forty-five minutes later, followed by the sheriff and a couple of doctors. Tosh remained when the doctors examined Harvey's body. Her bonnet was still in place and one of the parcels in her basket was addressed to a Mr Cruickshank of Castlegate in Aberdeen. There was also one shilling and eight pence in the pockets. Constable Aiken noticed that the ground around the dyke was churned up and bloody, as if there had been quite a struggle and Harvey had fought back. Aiken found some letters in Harvey's pockets: one was a valentine. The police took the body to the workshop of George Barclay, a nearby farmer.

Knowing that Harvey had intended meeting Francis Forbes, Constable Aiken hunted him down to his brother's house at Middleton, on the Aberdeen road. When Aiken came to the door, Forbes greeted him with a loud 'holloa' and later said, 'You need not come ben, it was not me that did it.' All the same, Aiken arrested him that same morning, in front of a house full of people. When Aiken took Forbes to identify the body, Forbes agreed that it was Harvey and turned away at once; he seemed visibly upset. Constable Aiken examined Forbes and found he had one finger cut and swollen, and blood around one nostril. He also had some blood on his clothes, but Aiken thought that could have come from his nose rather than from the wounds on Harvey.

Forbes was well known in the locality. His friend James Emslie had seen him at about half past seven on the morning of the murder. He had been wearing a wide-awake (broad-brimmed) hat and a dark-grey coat and was walking towards Aberdeen. Pensioner James Kinnaird also knew both Forbes and Harvey; he saw them walking together in

Market Street at about quarter past nine. Mary McDougall, whose husband Peter ran stables at the Steps of Gilcamston at the end of John Street, saw them walking together at around eleven o'clock on the Saturday night. Harvey had been shopping and had some articles in her basket. Richard Cameron, who then lived in Albion Street in Aberdeen, knew Forbes well; he saw Forbes and a woman walking past him. Later that day Cameron was out snaring rabbits and he saw them both walk past, about a hundred metres from the murder scene.

After Forbes was arrested, Superintendent Anderson searched his house. He found a smock coat and a pair of trousers marked with blood but no weapon of any sort. Forbes did not deny that he had been with Harvey on 26 April. He said he had left her about one o'clock and then he went home. He also said that he had an agreement with Harvey that they would get married. His sister-in-law said that Forbes lived with her and her husband, but she said he had not been with Harvey on the day of the murder. She was backed up by a number of other people who lived in the same house, including her husband.

With two directly opposing bodies of evidence, the jury had a hard task ahead of them, but they played it safe and found the case not proven. Rather than random attacks by strangers, most murders were by family members, or by people that the victim knew well.

Murder by Abortion

Sometimes the finest intentions can go bad, and somebody trying to help the best way that they can only makes things worse. When that person also breaks the law, the result can be tragedy for all concerned. Such a situation came to light at the High Court on 3 July 1888.

There were a number of victims, but the attention of the court centred on the accused, Charles Rae, a fifty-two-year-old post runner – postman – from Maryculter, a few miles south-west of Aberdeen. He was a stocky man with a long beard that was more black than grey, and he pleaded not guilty to the charges of murder and procuring abortion for two young women, Jeannie Greig and Christina Reaper. Both abortions had been performed earlier that year, and one of the women, Christina Reaper, had died. The court had to decide if her death was a result of the abortion, and if so, whether Rae was guilty of murdering her.

Christina Reaper had made a deposition on 29 May 1888, just before she had died in hospital, and this statement was used against Rae by the prosecution. Reaper had known she was dying, and the deposition was made in the presence of Charles Wilson, the deputy procurator fiscal. As always on these occasions, the court ensured that the witness had been duly sworn in and had given her oath so what were nearly her final words could be legal in a court of law.

The first witness in Rae's trial was 23-year-old Jeannie Greig. She was the granddaughter of Francis Shepherd, the farmer at Millbank, Maryculter. She said that she and Reaper had both become pregnant around the same time, in late 1887. The father of Greig's child was a man named William Bruce, who had worked at the farm during the summer, while the father of Reaper's child was another farm worker named George Robbie. The two women discussed their condition and decided to do something about it. As neither of them was married and neither wished to have a baby, they thought the best thing to do was to terminate the pregnancies: procure an abortion. At that time, abortions were illegal, so the women knew they could not ask a doctor. They had to find somebody else who understood the procedure. In that area of Aberdeenshire it was Charles Rae, the postman, who was reputed to be the man to ask on such occasions.

As a postman, Rae came to, or walked past, the farm most days. Greig approached him and said that Reaper was pregnant and asked if he could help. Rae said that he could perform an operation; according to Greig, 'he did not ask if I was hoaxing him'. This instant acceptance of the situation suggests that Rae was experienced in this situation, which begs the question of how many other illegal operations he had carried out on desperate young women. Greig and Rae arranged that he would come to the farmhouse to do what he had to do.

Greig was unsure exactly when Rae came to the farmhouse but thought it was at the end of February or the beginning of March. It was a dark winter night and the farmhouse was sufficiently isolated for nobody to see him come. He entered by the front door, with Greig waiting for him at the specified time. The only other people in the main house were Greig's grandparents, both elderly and both already in bed. Mr and Mrs Shepherd, son- and daughter-in-law of the old couple, lived in the flat above. They entered and left their home by an outside staircase and a side door, so they were out of the way.

By that time Rae knew that he had two women to work on: according to Greig, he took them into a spare bedroom one at a time. Greig was first to visit Rae. Unfortunately his mysterious operation failed, although it was not until the next morning that she realised she still carried the baby. She left the room and sent in Reaper. The procedure seems to have been simple, for Greig said that a few moments later Reaper came out and said the operation had been successful.

With the procedure complete, Rae asked Reaper for sixpence with which to buy a bottle of laudanum. He came back the next morning and told Greig to take nine drops to stop the bleeding after the operation. He returned that same night and operated again on Greig, this time telling her that he had been successful. On the Saturday of that week, Reaper told Greig that she had miscarried. Strangely, Rae asked Greig for the body of the child. Greig had her own miscarriage on the next morning, but rather than hand over the body of her child to Rae, she buried it in the dunghill, telling Rae she had burned it. Interestingly, Rae did not ask for payment for his actions; all he asked for was the foetus.

Greig said that she had not had much pain during the operation or the miscarriage and was able to work quite normally, but Reaper had 'suffered a good deal'. She had taken to her bed. Jane Shepherd, the daughter-in-law of Francis Shepherd, saw that Reaper was unwell and found out she had miscarried Robbie's child. Robbie also found out, came to see her and they arranged for Reaper to leave to live with her sister. Constable Nicol arrived to ask awkward questions, but Greig denied that she had any knowledge of Reaper's condition.

About a month later, Greig had toothache and had to visit the doctor; she took carbolic acid for the pain and 'nearly poisoned myself'. The story of the abortions was also aired.

Dr Rannie gave evidence at the court case. He said that when he was called to Millbank Farm on 20 March, Mrs Shepherd told him she thought Reaper had miscarried a baby. Reaper had a bad pain in her right side and on her thigh and admitted that she had had a miscarriage the previous week. Rannie only saw her one more time, on 22 March. On 26 May, he was back to see Greig, who confessed her abortion to him.

Dr William Stephen also gave evidence at the trial. He said that on 30 March he saw Reaper at her new home in Millden, Belhelvie. He treated her for rheumatism, a swollen hip and an abscess at the top of her left thigh. He recommended that she go to Aberdeen Infirmary. Dr Stephen told the court that blood poisoning could have caused the abscess and sometimes followed a miscarriage. When asked by the judge, Lord Shand, Stephen said that the unskilful or rough use of instruments during an abortion could cause blood poisoning.

Dr Garden of Aberdeen Infirmary stated that Reaper had had an abscess on her left thigh, as well as a fever, wasting, perspiration and 'a peculiar smell on her person'. She developed a further abscess on her opposite thigh, and when she told him about her miscarriage he examined her internally. He discovered 'evidence of mischief round about the womb'. Reaper grew worse over the next month, with a 'dusky colour of skin' and other symptoms. In his opinion, 'the use of instruments' had created the 'diseased condition' around Reaper's womb, which had caused the blood poisoning. However, Reaper did not mention that Rae had used any instruments. She told her brother Alexander Reaper that Rae had given her some 'black stuff' to drink. Christina Reaper died on 13 June.

Dr Hay carried out a post-mortem examination of Reaper; he also believed that blood poisoning had caused her death. Rae was arrested on suspicion of murder and illegal abortion. When Charles George, the chief constable of what was then Kincardineshire, searched his house, he found three 'knitting wires' in Rae's bedroom.

There was not much said in defence of Rae. He refused to answer any questions, but Duncan Shepherd, the farmer, said that if the operation had been carried out in the room the women claimed, the light would have been visible. He was trying to defend Rae by denying the act had taken place.

Lord Shand summed up by saying, 'If for an unlawful purpose a dangerous instrument was used, and in consequence of its use death was caused, that was murder.' The jury had to decide if an instrument was used, and if so, if it was unlawful and if it had caused death. The jury took only ten minutes to find Rae guilty of procuring a miscarriage, but found the murder charge not proven. Lord Shand awarded him seven years' penal servitude.

Child Murder

One of the most prevalent serious crimes of the nineteenth century was also one of the saddest: the murder of a child by his or her mother. There could have been many reasons for the murder, from postnatal depression to shame at having conceived an illegitimate baby, or simply an inability to cope with another mouth to feed.

On 11 June 1833, Christian King became cook to Mrs Dewar, a minister's wife of Albyn Place, Aberdeen. It was about 13 July that

Mrs Dewar first noticed that King was looking a little bit pregnant, and asked if her suspicions were correct. King said, 'I would be behaving very ill if I had come to you in such a state.'

Mrs Dewar let that pass, but she still suspected that King was with child and watched her closely. Two days later, Mrs Dewar asked again and got exactly the same response. King swore blind that she was 'not in the family way'. However, other people also harboured suspicions about her. One was another servant named Charlotte Grant, but when she asked about it, King told her she was not and that her size was natural to her.

About two weeks later, King fell sick with a sore stomach, but recovered. On the first Saturday in August, Mrs Dewar and most of the household went for a day trip to the beach, leaving King in charge of the house. Mrs Dewar returned shortly after four and found King in the outhouse; she noticed that King made a few trips to the outhouse and King told her she had a bowel complaint. Mrs Dewar sent her to bed, but instead King found it more comfortable to just sit on a chair. Mr Dewar set for Dr Keith to check on her. Charlotte Grant had been watching King's frequent trips to the outhouse as well, and thought the cook had been in there for about ten minutes. Grant saw blood on the floor beneath the chair that King had sat on.

The doctor accompanied King to the outhouse. After quite a length of time, Dr Keith returned with a small baby boy in his arms. Blood was flowing from a cut on the baby's temple and blood was flowing from it and dripping onto the floor. The temple also had an ugly purple bruise. Williamina Campbell, another servant, checked the outhouse and saw no blood there, but she did see a broken clothes pole about five feet long in the garden; there was blood on the end of the pole. Campbell was a long-time friend of King and had recommended her for the position of cook.

When Dr Keith first examined King he thought she had recently given birth, but King said she 'had never been pregnant in her life'.

Keith said that the outhouse floor was 'swimming with blood' and there was also blood on the seat. There were two holes in the seat, one small and one large. The clothes pole was inside the outhouse, thrust inside the smaller of the two holes. Dr Keith pulled it out and saw blood on the pole, and heard a child scream from the soil beneath. Keith went outside the outhouse and opened a small door that allowed access to empty the contents. He found a newborn baby amidst the mess; he stepped inside and pulled it out.

The child was alive and crying hard, but when Keith examined him there was a deep, bleeding wound on the left-hand side of his forehead and another beneath his left eye. The entire left side of his body was also bruised and battered. Keith asked King if he could examine her properly and she agreed, afterwards admitting that she had given birth about two hours previously. Dr Keith called for a wet nurse and a Mrs Goodall looked after the baby for a while. The baby survived that night, but grew sick the next day and died in the evening of Monday, 5 August 1833. When the boy was fully examined after death, it was found that the wound in his head had caused significant injuries, including brain damage. In other words, the blow to the head had killed him.

When Christian King appeared before Lord Mackenzie and the Circuit Court in September 1833, she was obviously upset. She kept her head bowed so her face could not be seen by the audience or the jury and spoke so softly that she was not heard. Her counsel, Mr Neaves, said that she had pleaded 'not guilty'.

Dr Keith spoke at King's trial. He said he had been in Aberdeen for about ten years after practising in India and was a member of the London College of Surgeons; he was a man of long medical experience. He thought that the boy had been thrust down the hole in the outhouse shortly after birth and then killed with a blow to the head from the clothes pole. Dr Campbell gave a second opinion to the Court. He had been a doctor for fifteen years, was also a Member of the London College of Surgeons and had worked as a surgeon on East Indiamen. He had examined the baby and agreed with Dr Keith entirely.

Neaves gave the best defence he could. He agreed that King had concealed her pregnancy and that she had thrust the baby into the soil, but he said that was merely to keep it safe until she could retrieve it later. The jury preferred to believe the prosecution and found her guilty: she was sentenced to death but later reprieved and instead sentenced to transportation for life. She sailed to New South Wales in December 1833.

Other women were equally capable of murder.

Killing the Husband

'Oh it's a sair thing to wash for the gibbet; but I hope I will be washed in the blood of my Redeemer.' Those were the words of Catherine Davidson on Thursday, 7 October 1830, the day before she was hanged for murder.

On 23 July 1784, the very young Catherine Davidson had been part of the crowd that gathered to watch the execution of a woman named Jean Craig for stealing linen and clothes. After Craig had dangled on the end of the rope for the required length of time, the executioner had cut her down and removed the rope from around her neck. As was usual, he had thrown the rope into the crowd for a souvenir. Davidson had flinched as the knot smashed against her breast, and the memory had always remained with her. Now it was her turn to be the object of a gaping crowd's attention.

Davidson was born in Keith Hall but moved to Aberdeen when she was very young. She met and married James Humphrey, a dashing light cavalryman in the Windsor Foresters, but like many women she had been taken in by the supposed glamour of the uniform and had not considered the ordinary man beneath.

Humphrey transferred to the Aberdeenshire Militia and Davidson spent ten years of her young life following the drum: that was probably the happiest time she ever knew. She seems to have given birth but lost the child, which was not uncommon at that time, and there were no more children to come. They were destined to be childless.

When the Napoleonic Wars ended, Humphrey was discharged in Aberdeen and became a butcher. Davidson opened a public house and began to suspect that the quiet, inoffensive man she had married was having affairs with other women. She became unhappy in her marriage. From a naive girl in love with a romanticised figure, Davidson turned into a bitter, bad-tempered woman with a vicious tongue and, as was not uncommon in the period, a fondness for the drink that she sold. She made Humphrey's life a nightmare with her nagging and was never averse to telling the world how much she disliked him.

After some years of this, Humphrey also caressed the bottle and the two had some fine stand-up fights. The marriage that had once been so successful deteriorated into a grim affair of two people who disliked each other but were bound by ties they could not legally break. More than once Davidson said, half in jest and whole in earnest, that she would kill her husband, and once she had hinted she would poison him. The pair kept a single servant named Janet Petrie and she often watched them fight, particularly when they had both been drinking. Petrie had seen Davidson hold a knife and a razor at Humphrey's throat and had heard her utter death threats.

At the beginning of March, Davidson sent Petrie to Anderson the druggist to buy a phial of vitriol, which was sulphuric acid. Davidson said it was to burn away a wart on her wrist. Petrie bought it; such purchases were normal at the time.

Life, then, was not good in the Humphrey household, and it was about to get worse. On 16 April 1830, the two had a major confrontation that ended in mutual violence. Humphrey had been displeased when Davidson brought home a woman named Mrs

Walton who was suspected of poisoning her husband. Humphrey said she had a bad character and wanted to throw her out into the street. Davidson replied that she could bring anybody she liked into her house, and their argument developed into an exchange of abuse and then slaps.

The house had four apartments on two levels. There were two rooms on the ground floor, the kitchen and a room in which guests were entertained over a bottle or three, and two small rooms upstairs. Humphrey left the drinking room and stomped into the kitchen in a foul temper. When Davidson followed him, he chased her out with a torrent of bad language. Petrie and Davidson both went into the drinking room and belatedly put Mrs Walton out of the house.

There must have been a minor reconciliation because a man named John Roy came into the house and shared a dram of whisky and a bottle of ale with Humphrey, while Davidson cooked them both beefsteaks. When Roy left the house, Davidson sent Petrie upstairs to bed, which was highly unusual, as servants were habitually last in bed and first out. The other upstairs room was Davidson's private domain, while Humphrey and Davidson usually slept together in the kitchen. Before Petrie had changed into her night things, Humphrey called her downstairs and asked her to clear away the plate that had held the beefsteak.

Petrie asked if Davidson was going to bed, but she replied that she would wait and see if her husband settled first, adding, 'Lord God, if anybody would give him poison and keep my hand clear of it!'

Like many couples, when Humphrey and Davidson argued they did not share a bed at night. Humphrey slept in the kitchen, usually lying on his back with his mouth open, and Davidson shared Petrie's bed upstairs. That night Petrie left them to their sulking and returned to bed, but no sooner had she fallen asleep than Davidson came into her room wearing nothing but her stockings. Davidson told her that Humphrey had taken ill and was making strange noises. Despite her news, Davidson did not seem concerned; she smiled to Petrie as she spoke.

Petrie got up and dashed downstairs, no doubt wishing that she could find a position where she could get a decent night's sleep.

Humphrey was yelling in pain. 'I'm burned' he said. 'I'm gone, I'm roasted!'

Davidson knelt over her husband, suddenly all concern. 'My dear,' she said, 'you have taken bad drink.'

'Oh, woman, woman,' Humphrey replied between his moans, 'whatever I have gotten, it was in my own house.'

Petrie knew she could not help so left the house and sought out a neighbour named Mrs Knowles, who was useful at such times. She also tried to find a Mr Anderson, who had some medical knowledge, but he refused to help at such an ungodly hour of night. Finally Petrie thought to find Dr Jamieson. When she got back to the house, she saw Davidson holding her husband. Humphrey was still in pain. 'Oh, woman, woman,' Humphrey said, 'you have tried to do this often and you have done it now.'

By this time it was mid morning and the house was like a fair with people coming and going. Humphrey told a neighbour it was 'bad work' and added, 'May God Almighty forgive them who have done this to me.' One visitor was Simon Grant, the town sergeant. When he arrived, Humphrey was lying in bed and in a lot of pain. When Grant asked him who had given him the poison, Humphrey replied that he did not know who had given him it, he had been sleeping at the time. In reply to Charles Dawson, another town sergeant, Humphrey said that somebody had poured something down his throat.

Humphrey lingered all Saturday, with Davidson pretending grief as the couple denied any rift. However, the police thought otherwise. The nearly empty phial of vitriol was a clue, as was a suspicious glass on the table. When a visiting child tried to drink from the glass and cried in pain, people could hardly doubt what the contents were.

The town sergeants asked their questions. Petrie remembered the phial of vitriol she had bought for her mistress. When she had last seen it, the phial had been nearly full. Now it was nearly empty. It seemed possible that during the night Davidson had taken advantage of Humphrey's vulnerability to take the phial of vitriol and pour the contents into a glass and then into his open mouth. There was no doubt that the vitriol had been used.

Davidson could hardly have been surprised when she was arrested, and she appeared at the Circuit Court in September 1830. There were a number of witnesses who testified to the bad feeling that existed between husband and wife.

John Roy said he had often heard Davidson wish her husband dead. He added, 'When in drink they always quarrelled.' A Mrs Riddel said she had seen Humphrey hold a razor to his throat and put Davidson's hand on it, saying, 'Do it now, for you will do it sometime,' and claimed 'his wife would hang with her face down Marischal Street for him yet'. The Aberdeen gallows faced that direction. A James Cowie had heard Davidson say that 'arsenic is the best thing for that scoundrel'. The doctors were in no doubt that sulphuric acid had killed Humphrey.

When Davidson was found guilty she appeared composed, but later broke down in tears. She admitted her guilt the next day, but denied any intention to kill him.

'I am the person that murdered my husband, by administering vitriol, which occasioned his death; it was nothing but jealousy which caused me to commit the crime; I had it in my heart two years ago for to murder him, but I always thought to get some other person to do it, in order that my hands might not be stained with his blood. My sentence is just; I deserve to die for what I have done. The temptation of the devil has been strong in me when I committed such a crime. I hope my fate will prove a warning to every person, particularly women, not to follow my example, and deep from jealously and revenge.'

According to contemporary newspapers, Davidson found religion in the period between conviction and execution. On the Thursday night before her hanging, Davidson hardly slept, which was perhaps not surprising with the noise of carpenters and joiners erecting the scaffold a few yards from her cell window. At half past two on the Friday, the Lord Provost and magistrates came in stately procession to the Old Court House to watch the show, with Davidson escorted to the gallows shortly afterwards. She was fifty-one years old and dressed in black.

Nearly fainting and not looking up, Davidson was taken directly to the drop. 'Oh my God,' she said as she dropped her handkerchief, which was the signal for the execution to pull the lever that opened the trapdoor beneath her. The watching crowd stretched from Castle Street to St Catherine's Wynd in Union Street, but if there was no misbehaviour, neither was there sympathy for the condemned woman. Davidson died at five minutes to three and her body was delivered to Dr Pirie at Marischal College to be dissected.

Two days later there was a break-in at the Upper Kirkgate during the hours for church attendance, and a purse full of silver was stolen. However efficacious the sight of a hanging was intended to be, crime went merrily on.

Poisoning a Family

Aberdeen was not cursed with a great many murders in the course of the century, but when they occurred, they could be quite spectacular. There were a number of celebrated cases of poisoning in nineteenth-century Scotland and many others that history has neglected. The affair at Burnside near Aberdeen in 1821 is one of the latter, even though there were multiple victims, one died and the others were left with permanent affects.

Four members of the Mitchell family lived at the farm of Burnside: James, William, Helen (known as 'Nelly') and Mary, all siblings. The brothers lived in one house at the farm and the sisters at another. There was a third sister, Jane, who was married to George Thom, who lived at Harthill on the Skene road in the nearby parish of Newhills, which was then about four miles out of Aberdeen. Jane and Thom had been married in 1820, although her brothers and sisters were not totally happy with her choice of man. When they were courting, Thom had come to the farm fairly regularly, sometimes staying the night, and even though the Mitchells did not particularly like him, they tolerated him for the sake of their sister.

Once she was married, Jane was a rare visitor to Burnside farm, and Thom even rarer, so it was a bit of a surprise when both arrived on the night of Saturday, 18 August 1821. However, they were family, so the Mitchells made them welcome, shared their evening meal of porridge and invited them to stay the night. The sisters retired to their own house and the men remained in the farmhouse. The brothers asked Thom if he would stay to breakfast, but he declined, saying he was having breakfast at the Mains of Cluny, a nearby farm. However, Thom asked if he could sleep in the box bed in the kitchen that night, which was something he had never done before. When the brothers turned him down, Thom did not insist. Instead he shared a room with William, while James slept in the kitchen, as was normal.

Early on Sunday morning, James heard somebody moving about in the kitchen; a few moments later he heard the sisters come in from milking the cows, and Thom talking to them. Helen asked Thom if he wanted to stay to breakfast, but he said no. She saw him shake some crumbs of bread from his pocket onto the table and saw a white powder among the crumbs. She dismissed the incident as unimportant and waved goodbye as Thom left the house for Mains of Cluny. He arrived there at the back of eight, but neither Ann Donald, the wife of William Gillanders the farmer, or Barbara Gillanders, the daughter of the house, had expected him. He breakfasted there and went to look for William Gillanders.

When James rose from his bed in Burnside, Thom had already gone, without having breakfast. The breakfast porridge was put on the table, but when James tried it he found it not to his liking. He thought it sickeningly sweet, and ate a little, but not much. Helen mentioned the strange taste, but the others had no complaints. Of them all, William enjoyed the heartiest breakfast.

James was getting ready to go to the church at Tough when he felt a bit sick. He contemplated whether he should go to the church or not, but as it was Sacrament Sunday he thought it best to go. He regretted that decision when he was in church and felt worse with each passing minute. He attended Holy Sacrament, but afterwards had to leave the church. Half blind and staggering, he met William in the kirkyard, who said he was also sick but was going to church anyway. James limped home, vomited yellow-red fluid on the way, and felt as if his stomach and belly were burning hot.

When James nearly fell into the farmhouse the sisters asked what tho matter was. Helen and Mary were also sick, but William was the worst of them all. He became nearly blind and the whites of his eyes turned red, his chest swelled up, his breathing was laboured and he shared the same burning sensation as James, but worse. After three days he lost the use of his left arm, while his feet also ballooned up to twice their normal size. Despite his condition, William rode the mile to Whitehouse to pay his rent, and visited Dr Murray at Smiddyhill in the nearby parish of Alford. The doctor gave him a plaster to put on his breast in the hope it would ease the swelling and visited them on the Saturday, nearly a week after the visit of Thom and the beginning of all their troubles.

Things seemed to have improved after the doctor gave them all medicine, and on the Sunday William rose from his bed and went for a drink. He returned to bed, stretched and groaned out loud. After that he lay still, covered in a cold sweat. James was concerned and tried to revive him, but failed. There was no response. William was near death; he lay still, barely breathing. James brought in the sisters and they were all present in a classic nineteenth-century deathbed scene when William gave a last breath and passed away.

Helen and Mary had also been sick. From the Sunday of Thom's visit until the following Tuesday, they had intermittently vomited a white liquid. On the Monday, Helen was at her worst, with a burning pain in the region of her heart and no sensation in her feet. She was very thirsty and had sore eyes. The feelings continued all week, but with a slow improvement from the Tuesday onwards, so she was nearly herself when her brother died. Mary had the same loss of feeling in her arm and the same vomiting, but she also had a terrible pain in her head. She lost the feeling in her lower legs and was not fully recovered before William's death.

Thom and Jane were not invited to William's funeral, but they arrived at Burnside anyway. Helen spoke to Jane and said she thought they had been poisoned. Thom suggested that it could have been water from the burn that had poisoned them, with all the toads and paddocks there, but Helen said that was unlikely, as there were no toads or paddocks, and anyway the porridge had been made with milk, not water.

James sent them away, saying they had 'done ill enough already'. The couple left; they seemed surprised to be rebuffed, but did not ask what James meant by his words.

John Fyfe, a King's Messenger from Aberdeen who later became superintendent, was ordered to arrest Thom for the murder of William Mitchell and the poisoning of the other members of the household. When he arrived in the late evening, Thom was in bed and claimed to have been sick for days. Fyfe saw two doctors, Fraser and Henderson, in a carriage outside Thom's door and called them into the house. They examined him and said he had 'an inward complaint', but still they thought him well enough to travel and bundled him into a carriage and taken to Aberdeen Bridewell.

When the case came before the Aberdeen Circuit Court in October 1821, James Barron, an Aberdeen druggist, thought he recognised Thom as a man to whom he had refused to sell rat poison, while Peter Farquharson of Whitehouse said he knew Thom well. Farquharson said he had met Thom about seven miles from Aberdeen on the Sunday of the poisoning. Thom said then that he had been sick and claimed it had been something he had eaten at the Mains of Cluny.

Dr Murray had performed the post-mortem on William Mitchell's body. At the trial he said that William had died 'by means of some deleterious matter received into the stomach'. He thought it might be 'sugar of lead' and considered it unlikely that a stomach complaint would attack a whole family at the same time.

When all the evidence was heard, the jury decided by a large majority that George Thom was guilty of murder. The judge ordered him executed in Aberdeen on the 16 November and gave his body to Dr Skene and Dr Ewing for dissection.

'Gentlemen,' said Thom as he heard the verdict, 'I am as innocent as any of you sitting here.'

Killing in a Cornfield

Crofting may be seen as a desirable lifestyle by many city people who hope to escape the rat race. These people may view marginal farming as an idyll, living close to nature while working in the great outdoors. The reality of nineteenth-century crofting was somewhat different: a daily struggle with often poor soil and an unforgiving climate, with hard labour from morning until night and no guarantee of even a full stomach let alone anything else. When the human equation is added, life could be dangerous as well as hard, as Margaret and James Thow discovered in September 1834.

The couple worked a croft at Moss-side of Arnhall, by Fettercairn.

They had been married for some time, but, as was not uncommon in times of stress and hardship, the marriage had come under some strain. James Thow had been known to raise his hand to Margaret, and she strongly suspected that he had been having an affair with Ann Wallace, a neighbouring crofter. Wallace was married with three children, but her husband had left her for another woman.

On 17 September, the three of them had been harvesting, with Ann Wallace and James Thow binding the oats, and the Thows' son John watched and helped all he could. They had stopped in the evening. Margaret Thow went into her cottage for a few moments and when she came out again her husband and Wallace were holding hands. She said nothing, but on her appearance they all began to walk home together, and Margaret and he began to sing a song, the last word of which ended in the word 'whore'.

Wallace reacted at once. 'You damned wretch,' she said, 'will you call me a whore?'

James Thow turned back to her. 'Will you say I called you a whore?' he asked.

Wallace was obviously incensed. 'Yes, you called me a whore and I'll take your wife as a witness that you did.'

Margaret Thow joined in then. 'He said whore, but mentioned no name.'

'If you call me a whore, I'll cleave you with a stone,' Wallace threatened.

James Thow was still calm. Walking to Wallace, he gently took hold of her hands and tried to defuse the situation, but Wallace was not to be placated. She was holding a hook – a small sickle – in each hand and, shaking her hands free, she thumped Thow with the curved steel. According to Thow's eleven-year-old son John, Wallace was foaming at the mouth and she called Thow a 'damned bitch' and said she would 'send him to hell'. Thow lost some of his calm and replied that she 'would need to let him see the road'.

Perhaps not too unhappy that her husband was fighting with the woman she suspected of being his lover, Margaret Thow stepped between them and took away the hooks. 'Try yourselves,' she said, meaning 'fight it out between yourselves'. She threw the two hooks away: 'Ye'll nae hurt ither now.' Without a qualm, Margaret walked away as James Thow and Wallace continued to argue.

Wallace's heavy boots were reinforced with iron on the toes and heels; she launched a series of mighty kicks at James Thow, catching him in the groin and the lower belly. Thow would have gasped or yelled, but as Wallace closed in and began to punch him, he grasped her by the arms and threw her to the ground. He left her there and tried to walk away once more, although he was now in considerable pain.

Wallace got up, lifted a large stone and threw it at Thow, who ducked his head so it missed him. He grappled with her again and put her back on the ground. 'You are mad,' he said, 'I will tie you and send you to bedlam.' As she lay there, Wallace kicked up, once more catching him in the belly with her iron-shod boots. Even although he must have been in considerable pain, James Thow kept his temper. When Wallace stood up, he patted her on the shoulder and advised her to go home. She swore foully at him and punched him on the side of his head. His hat flew off and landed in a ditch. 'You're a damned ugly wretch,' Wallace screamed at him.

Thow left her then and limped home. He watered the horse, entered the house and asked if his supper was ready yet. Margaret Thow fed him bread and milk; she must have seen he was in pain and asked if he was hurt. Thow confessed that he had 'sair guts' and was 'hurt in the bottom of the belly'.

As the evening wore on, Thow's pain increased and he began to moan. He found it easier to sit than to lie down. Shortly after five the next morning, Margaret Thow went to Dr Stewart, who came along in the middle of the afternoon and gave Margaret a bottle of medicine.

He came again in the evening and, along with Dr Pretwell, remained beside James Thow all night. Dr Stewart was familiar with Thow; he had attended him the previous year when Thow had been accidentally injured in exactly the same place.

'She has broken my inwards with her feet,' James said, and sometime after seven at night, he died.

As Wallace was working in the fields next day, one of her neighbours shouted across to her: 'It was you that killed the man.'

'Devil care though he had lain on the spot,' Wallace replied. 'I did not spare him with feet nor hands.' She added, 'I garr'd my feet ring in his belly [kicked him in the groin] and flung stones when I could get them' and, for good measure, she said: 'I know where to strike him.'

The police arrested Wallace and she appeared at the Spring Circuit Court in 1835. Although the doctors agreed that Wallace's kicks had killed Thow, she was found guilty of culpable homicide rather than murder, and Lord Mackenzie jailed her for a mere six months in Stonehaven jail.

Other killings were even more brutal.

The Killing in George Street

Ann Wilson was about thirty years old, short, slender and pale. She lived at 111 George Street, Aberdeen. The house was entered through Beattie's Court, and had a room, a kitchen and a closet. It was on the ground floor of a two-storey building, just opposite a row of cellars, and sheltered by a flight of outside stairs that led to the upper floor.

On 10 December 1898, Wilson climbed onto a box to look out of the window, slipped and fell awkwardly. Later that day she was killed. She was beaten to death by fists, boots and a poker so she lay on the bed in a mess of blood.

Wilson shared the house with her partner James Robertson, who worked as a drainage labourer, and with Isabella Dundas, the estranged wife of John Dundas, a Dundee marine engineer. Isabella Dundas was no angel, having spent two periods in jail. Although Robertson was Wilson's partner, the two were not on speaking terms. Both were habitual drinkers, but Robertson had withheld any money from her so she could not buy any drink. Wilson was a new mother; her second child had been born a few weeks before and she had not fully recovered. The three had been lodgers at Crooked Lane before taking the very short step across the lane to George Street. Young James, the son of Robertson, was also in the house; he was seven years old and considered Wilson to be his mother; there were two other children, an infant under two and the five-week-old baby that Wilson had borne to Robertson. But now Wilson was dead.

Suspicion fell on James Robertson senior and gradually the events of the day were pieced together. On Saturday, 10 December, he had been working all morning, but at about two in the afternoon he returned to the George Street house for his dinner. As usual, Robertson had been drinking, and rather than eat, he lay down on the bed in the kitchen, where he remained for some time. After an hour or so he asked Wilson to fetch the vest (waistcoat) that he had pawned, but she said she did not have time. Robertson swore at her; he was bitterly angry not to have his vest. Dundas calmed things down and said that she would get it when she was out. A few moments later, Robertson left the house.

Wilson must have gone outside as well, for when Robertson returned at about six, Dundas asked him where his wife was. He replied that he did not know but that 'if I get haud of the bugger I'll tramp the guts of her in, although I should be hanged for it'.

At that point a neighbour came to the door and told Dundas, 'Margaret Wilson wants you.'

'Where is she?' Dundas asked.

'Outside,' the neighbour told her.

Dundas heard Wilson's voice call 'Bella' and thought she was either in one of the cellars outside the house or in the outside water closet. In reality, she was hiding from Robertson in a small space between the cellars and the water closet. When she emerged, Dundas gave her two shillings and Wilson walked to the pawnshop and retrieved the vest, bringing it back home. Robertson dressed and at about seven in the evening he went out. Dundas also left, but returned at about half past eleven at night. She walked into the house and stopped in horror: Wilson was lying across the fireplace on her back, bloody and battered, and Robertson was standing over her. The light was burning low, but Dundas's view was clear enough.

'What's been ado here?' Dundas asked. 'This is dreadful!'

Robertson looked up briefly, and then landed two sharp kicks, one on Wilson's legs and a second in her ribs. Dundas rushed forwards, lifted Wilson from the ground and sat her on a chair. But Robertson was not finished yet. As soon as Wilson was in the chair, Robertson shouted: 'You dirty pig! Where's my supper?'

He thumped her across the head, just behind her ear, and knocked her back down again. Wilson fell on the fender, and this time when Dundas lifted her up she noticed all the blood. Wilson was bleeding from her nose and mouth as well as her ear, but there was far more blood seeping from beneath her petticoat. Rather than leave her in the room with Robertson, Dundas helped her to the bed closet and placed her on a chair. Wilson said nothing and Dundas wondered if she was unconscious. However, Robertson followed them, grabbed Wilson by the hair of her head, dragged her back through the kitchen and threw her out to the lobby. He slammed the door shut behind him.

Dundas left the bed closet and pleaded with Robertson to bring Wilson back inside the house. When he refused, Dundas threatened to call the police.

'If you do,' Robertson said, 'I will do the same to you as I have done to her.' Leaving Dundas, Robertson brought his son out of bed, but he either had a change of heart or Dundas's words had struck home, for he told her that Wilson was nearly naked and would freeze to death out in the lobby.

'Come ben,' Dundas said, 'and help me in with her.' Surprisingly, Robertson agreed and they carried Wilson back to the bed closet. She had been in the lobby for about quarter of an hour and still seemed to be unconscious.

Robertson barely glanced at her. 'You can put her on the bed or do what you like. She is inside now.'

Dundas gave Wilson a drop of whisky, which seemed to revive her a little.

'Bella,' Wilson said. 'Get me to bed; wash me; bring water, hot.'

Dundas removed Wilson's blood-sodden skirt and both her petticoats; she wore a tight bodice beneath, but Dundas had to fight to get it off before she washed her. Wilson was bleeding heavily from her private parts. All her clothes were ragged, torn and bloodstained; her body was battered and bruised. There were bruises and cuts on her legs and back, and a deep gash under her eye. Her private regions were in 'a fearful mess of blood' according to Dundas. As Dundas lifted her onto the closet bed, Wilson's moaning turned to deep sobs that lasted until four in the morning.

Mrs Helen Robertson knew something ugly had happened. She lived at 11A Crooked Lane, a house that was back to back with Wilson's at 111 George Street and she had been getting water from a well that was between both houses and only a few yards from Wilson's back window. While she was out there, she heard Robertson beating Wilson and a volley of 'very bad language which I would hardly like to repeat'. She looked through the window and saw Robertson 'tearing her by the hair of the head and skelping her at the same time and telling her to rise up and make his supper'. He used both his fist and his open hand and 'he was striking her as fast as he could make his hand go ... the blows were all on the face.'

Helen Robertson 'rapped at the window' to try and get Roberson to stop, but the assault continued with Wilson partly on the floor and partly lying against her bed, moaning 'oh me, oh me' in a voice that grew weaker as Robertson continued to hit her.

The son, James Robertson, at all of six years old, was also aware what had happened. He had been in a closet bed and heard Robertson and Wilson arguing over the waistcoat. He saw Robertson kicking Wilson on the leg as she lay on the kitchen floor.

After she had attended to Wilson, Dundas stepped into the kitchen to look after the baby. About half an hour later, Robertson went to bed. Dundas sat in front of the fire with the baby until about six in the morning, when she checked on Wilson. She did not try to wash away the blood that was on the kitchen floor; it was also on the floor of the bedroom and the lobby.

'Are you asleep?' she asked, but there was no answer. Dundas left, but returned about nine o'clock. Wilson looked cold and pale, so Dundas put a hand on her head. Wilson was rigid.

Dundas returned to the kitchen, where Robertson was in bed. 'Jim,' she said, 'she is dead. She is cold and stiff.'

Robertson looked up from his bed. 'Oh me, me,' he said. 'What am I to do? I have murdered her.'

'You will have to report the death,' Dundas said.

'I'm frightened,' Robertson replied, frankly. He noticed the blood on the floor and ordered Dundas to clean it up in case the neighbours saw it.

Dundas tried to wash away the bloodstains. She failed; it had soaked through the carpet onto the floorboards below, and in the lobby the blood had flowed three or four feet from the door. When she had finished, Robertson stood with his back to the door.

'Now, you'll have to say this,' he told her, 'else I'll do the same to you.

Say that she went out at twelve o'clock and did not return until six in the morning; the folk will think that someone outside has done it to her.'

Robertson left and called at the house of another neighbour, Mrs Charles, who spoke to Dundas through the window but did not enter the house. A few moments later a police constable arrived. Dundas told him exactly what Robertson had ordered her to say, adding that Wilson had come in covered in blood, but the policeman asked about the bloodstains on the floor. Dundas said it could have been flooding. Robertson said virtually exactly the same thing to the constable.

The chief constable arrived shortly afterwards, with a number of policemen, and both Robertson and Dundas were taken to the police office. Robertson was arrested and charged with murder.

Dr Thomas Milne examined the body. He saw all the wounds, including five fractured ribs, but decided that death had been caused by wounds on the vulva and a haemorrhage of the vagina that may have been inflicted by a kick from the rear, or from a fall, but they might also have been caused by getting up and being active too early after giving birth to her baby. Dr McKerron, assistant professor of midwifery at Aberdeen University, agreed that both external and internal wounds could have been caused by either a kick or from her earlier fall but more likely the latter. He added that in his opinion there had not been enough blood to cause death from haemorrhage of the vagina unless it had been bleeding for some days previously.

The Advocate General tried to sum up the conflicting facts. He said that the jury had to decide how the injuries on Wilson were caused and if Robertson had caused them, and if so was it murder or culpable homicide. The police had found marks on Wilson's hips that matched the studs in Robertson's boots, so he had certainly kicked her in the area where the fatal bleeding had occurred.

The jury found Robertson guilty of culpable homicide and Lord McLaren sentenced him to penal servitude for life.

The passage of time puts a patina of romance over events, but murder is always sordid and often cruel. That was as true for Aberdeen and the north-east as it was for anywhere else. However, the police were efficient and the consequences for those caught could be extreme.

9

The Consequences of Detection

Although there is frequently a perception that punishment in nineteenth-century Scotland was savage and unrelenting, much of the justice system was aimed at rehabilitation rather than retribution. There were graduated penalties, from admonishments to fines to small periods in prison, and then, if the offender reappeared, from the Police Court to the Sheriff Court, which could inflict longer sentences in prison. Finally there was the Circuit Court and the High Court in Edinburgh. The Circuit Court toured the country, while the High Court only sat in the capital. Only these courts could award the death penalty. In between the two extremes of execution and admonishments, there were various other penalties, such as banishment or its cousin, transportation, or the extremely unpleasant penal servitude that replaced it.

The mainstay of nineteenth-century justice was the prison, either for a short, sharp shock or long, weary years of confinement, but despite a conception that nineteenth-century jails would be packed with petty offenders, the number of inmates was often surprisingly low. In 1809 there were only eight felons in Aberdeen jail, with seven petty offenders.

Aberdeen's first known prison was founded by a charter of King Robert III in 1394, the same year that Aberdeen's tolbooth and court house were opened in the Castlegate. The Laigh Tolbooth was the council chamber, while the High Tolbooth was also the prison. Nothing of this building exists, but there are vestigial traces of the Old Tolbooth of 1616. A house of correction was built in 1636 for people such as 'incorrigible harlottis', of which Aberdeen seemed to have a great many. When the Bridewell was opened for business in 1809, men of the 75th Foot escorted a solemn procession of the magistrates, town sergeants and the great and the good to bless this august building with their presence. Ten years later the architecture of justice was enhanced with a new court house just to the rear of the Tolbooth, and the East Jail along Lodge Walk, a street that was named after the Freemason Lodge. Justice in Aberdeen was ready for business.

The Sheriff court house and the Laigh Tolbooth were much altered in 1820. The High Tolbooth, also known as the East Jail, also housed the Aberdeen City Police for a while. After 1829, the East Jail was the burial place of many of those hanged in Aberdeen, but their graves were disturbed in October 1893 when the jail was demolished. Before 1829, the bodies of the deceased could be handed over for dissection, or simply dumped at sea.

Among the convicts who were buried here was Catherine Davidson, who was executed for poisoning her husband, and James Burnett from Fyvie, who murdered his wife in 1849. That same year, twenty-two-year-old James Robb of Auchterless killed an elderly lady and was duly hanged and buried here. Adding to the grisly company was George Christie, who murdered two people at Kittybrewster in 1852, and lastly John Booth, who despatched his mother-in-law.

Although the prison was a place of punishment, the authorities were not totally inhumane; they constantly strove to make the prison more effective in its purpose in turning the inmates away from crime. For example, in September 1836 the proposed new regulations included having a separate cell for every prisoner and painted glass or shutters on the windows so they could not corrupt each other or spend time watching what was happening outside. There was a sensible proposal to recruit a female turnkey, who should be the wife of the head turnkey, and an idea that prisoners who were not yet convicted should be encouraged to work while they were in prison, and could keep half their earnings. If inmates were allowed to keep all their earnings it was believed that people might commit crimes to get free board and lodging in the jail while still making money. It was also recommended that visitors be restricted to once a month for convicted prisoners and that a 'competent person' be appointed to teach the prisoners.

Total of People Imprisoned: 1841–51

Year	Male	Female	Total
1841	474	405	879
1842	471	288	759
1843	520	222	742
1844	468	245	713
1845	484	267	751
1846	421	262	683
1847	465	335	800
1848	461	316	777
1849	609	402	1011
1850	617	326	943
1851	539	261	800

Source: Table of Crime, *Aberdeen Journal*, 28 January 1852

The table above shows that the number of people imprisoned rose sharply in 1849, a year when the Hungry Forties were releasing their grip and there was more employment in the city. The figures may indicate that destitution was less of an encouragement to commit crime than excess money, which could be spent on drink.

Sometimes prisoners tried to escape; occasionally they were successful. John Watson Laurie was one of the most famous convicts of the nineteenth century. He had been jailed for the murder of Edwin Rose, a young Englishman, on the Isle of Arran. He was sent to Peterhead, where he behaved like a model prisoner so became a 'prisoner of the first class' with certain privileges and freedoms. He worked in the carpenter's shop in Peterhead and was with a group of men erecting scaffolding to build new warden's houses near the main road to Aberdeen. The prisoners were retained within a barrier, which was mainly a high stone wall but partly a wooden fence.

About half past seven in the morning of 2 August 1893, there was a sea haar rolling in from the North Sea. The haar restricted visibility to around a hundred yards, and Laurie took his chance. He clambered over the fence and ran onto the public road to Aberdeen. His timing was bad, for he ran straight into one of the civil guards, a man named Graham. The guards carried carbines, so Graham loaded and aimed, but his weapon misfired. Luckily for Laurie it was a single-shot carbine, so Graham had to extract the cartridge and reload, by which time Laurie had vanished into the mist. Graham gave the alarm and called out the guard and the wardens.

As long as the mist lingered, Laurie had a chance, but the rising sun dissipated it and he was soon exposed and out in the open. He ran to cross the Blackhills Road and bolted for freedom, just as the wardens blew their alarm whistles. When the local people heard the whistles and saw a man in his convict clothes trying to run for freedom, they withdrew inside their houses and locked the doors and windows. Laurie saw a warden race to the Blackhills Road on a bicycle, so he tried to hide in a small wood, but the wardens were right on his tail and he was caught in a matter of minutes.

Laurie faced a bleak future as he was marched back with his wrists handcuffed behind his back. As well as losing all his privileges he would be placed in irons, with an iron belt around his waist and bands around his ankles, all heavily chained together. He was to remain in prison for decades, although there is still some doubt as to his guilt.

Even if the authorities tried to help the convicted get back on the path of lawfulness, some Aberdonians were less sympathetic to those who committed even petty offences. In the 1840s at least, one source of amusement on a Sunday morning was to stand outside the police office and mock the unfortunates who had been arrested the previous night.

The Bridewell continued to be used until 1842, when it changed its name to the West Prison; in 1864 it closed for good, and it was demolished four years later. In 1878, the East Jail was thought unsuitable, with small and dark cells, so a new jail was constructed at Craiginches, being opened in 1891. This three-storey granite building had sixty-one cells for male prisoners, twenty-one for females, and a padded cell for those of unsound mind.

Despite all the efforts of the authorities to help the criminal classes by providing decent accommodation and a chance of a respectable life, some objected to being sent to jail and tried their best to avoid such an educational experience.

Heroic Coach Driver

In August 1849, the jail at Dumfries was being renovated and the authorities sent the prisoners elsewhere. As the supply of local jail accommodation was limited, some were transported to Aberdeen, at the opposite end of the country. Six men were placed on top of the mail coach, with a police superintendent and three constables to guard them. Perhaps naturally, the prisoners were not keen on the long and draughty journey. On the evening of Thursday, 16 August 1849, they reached Bervie, about ten miles south of Stonehaven, when they became truculent. Despite the guard, the prisoners had managed to manufacture and hide a variety of weapons. One man had a pointed razor tied to a pole, three had hefty two-pound weights and fourteen-inch-long bludgeons, and the fifth had a hatchet. They also had files to use to break free of the handcuffs that confined them.

On the journey through the summer countryside they tried to rock the coach from side to side in an attempt to either overturn it so they could dash for freedom or to force Alexander Leys, the driver, to lose control. This had failed, so at Bervie they jumped off the top: a unified mass of desperate men, all linked by steel handcuffs. The police followed, but they were outnumbered and were getting the worst of the struggle until Leys joined in. He was a broad-shouldered man well used to handling a team of horses or unruly passengers, and he set to with a will.

One punch removed the teeth of the nearest convict and Leys knocked another senseless to the ground. With two of their number out of action, the convicts began to waver. The police saw their advantage and gained the upper hand. They removed the weapons from the convicts, bundled them back on top of the coach and the journey started again, but with a few changes. Now the superintendent sat on top of the coach, facing the prisoners and with a pistol held in each hand. One of the inside passengers also said that if any of the prisoners should manage to jump off the roof, the superintendent would shoot them before they got ten paces. The convicts responded with a volley of mocking oaths, but they did not again attempt to escape. Grateful for the help, the police superintendent handed Leys a hefty reward.

Sometimes, the trouble began after the prisoners reached the jail.

Escapee

In late August 1849, a prisoner named McCallum escaped from the West Prison in Aberdeen. McCallum had been sentenced to ten years' transportation for housebreaking and was something of an expert in prison breaks, having escaped from Dumfries in the past.

When he clambered out of Aberdeen West he immediately returned to crime, stealing a suit of clothes from a house at Cloghill, presumably to help him blend in with his surroundings. However, his freedom did not last. He had travelled as far as the farm of Culsh, north-west of Ballater, when he was caught breaking into a chest. Mr Douglas, the farmer who caught him, took him to the local constable, who, helped by a sheriff officer, took McCallum back to Aberdeen. The authorities ensured there were no more escape attempts by riveting leg irons on him.

Transportation

Of the 166,000 men, women and children who were transported from Great Britain and Ireland to Australia, around 8,000 came from Scotland. Some were professional criminals with a string of previous convictions, others were destitute unfortunates forced into prostitution or theft through desperate poverty or terrible stress. Scottish convicts in Australia had the reputation of being the best educated, which was a reflection of the state of Scottish education on the wider public at the time, but they were also reputed to be the most hardened and desperate. This latter was equally revealing, as the Scottish authorities were less inclined to inflict transportation for a first offence than their Irish, English or Welsh counterparts were.

The process of transportation created a number of sentimental broadside ballads, most dealing with the sadness of exile, either for seven years or the term of their natural lives. As one, the anonymous narrator of the poem 'Convict Maid', put it:

In innocence I once did live,
In all the joys that peace could give
But sin my youthfull heart betrayed
And now I am a convict maid.

However, life was not quite so simple, and Scottish judges were often more careful whom they sent to Australia, when they had a choice. Sometimes transportation was seen as a merciful punishment.

Killed by the Devil

At the Circuit Court in April 1844, nineteen-year-old William Ritchie was transported for fifteen years for culpable homicide. On 9 October 1843, he had been making or repairing a shoe with an iron last – or a 'devil', as it was known – when he fell out with his father. The two exchanged angry words and the father lifted a stick and thumped Ritchie with it. Without thinking, Ritchie struck back. He smashed his father across the head with the iron devil and the older man fell backwards, killed immediately by the single blow. There was no doubt it had been an accident and all the neighbours agreed that William Ritchie was a quiet and well-behaved lad, but the blow had been struck and his father was dead. If it had been a premeditated act, Ritchie would be liable to execution or at least transportation for life, but culpable homicide was a lesser crime and Lord Moncrieff only sentenced him to fifteen years' transportation, adding that Ritchie's own guilty conscience would be a worse punishment. Lord Cockburn added that fifteen years' transportation was a much less severe punishment than twenty years, for not only was the term of exile shorter, but a man transported for life was subject to 'severer treatment in penal settlements'. Cockburn said that 'although your father had struck you a blow, it was not only his right, it was his duty to do so, and perhaps it had been well for you had he chastised you more frequently in your younger years'. Cockburn's statement affords an interesting example of authority's views of parental skills.

Even so, Cockburn augmented his speech with the comforting words 'in the country you will be transported to, you will be treated as a slave and although your sufferings will be severe ... by behaving yourself well you will mitigate the severity of your punishment and you may indulge the hope of even returning to your own country after a few years of exile.' Ritchie sailed to Van Diemen's Land in the convict ship *Hyderabad* in October 1844.

After sending the young man to work as a slave for the best years of his life, Cockburn did not think the case worth even a mention in his book *Circuit Journeys*.

In that same court, Mary Robb was transported for seven years for a career of theft that had seen her rob six houses over three months: she was hardly an innocent wee girl who had been forced into a single theft. She sailed on *Tasmania* in September. Nor was William Ross a blameless angel with a lily-white conscience. He was a hard man who refused to leave his cell and come to the trial, so he was subdued and dragged before the bench by four sturdy men. He had already been sentenced to seven years' transportation for theft, but had been allowed his freedom. This time Lord Moncrieff was less inclined to mercy; he said that Ross 'had made very bad use of his liberty' and sentenced him to fourteen years' transportation. If His Lordship expected pleas for mercy he was disappointed, as Ross said, 'I can stand on my head for fourteen years.' He accompanied Ritchie on *Hyderabad* in September that year. At the same sitting, John McQueen got seven years from Cockburn for stealing three silk handkerchiefs.

Life for transportees could be hell on earth if they were sent to places such as Van Diemen's Land or ended up on Norfolk Island, but the convict could also behave, be released early on a 'ticket of leave' and settle into a new life in a country of vast spaces and some opportunities for those willing to work.

Penal servitude replaced transportation. There were two Penal Servitude Acts – 1853 and 1857 – but in essence the acts ultimately replaced the near slavery of transportation with an equal length of time in prisons at home, though in conditions nearly as intolerable as those in Australia. The 1853 Act had the Progressive Stage System, where the prisoner started as a virtual slave working on the treadmill or crank for up to eight hours a day and sleeping on a bare plank, and working through four stages and many years to a more comfortable but still monastic lifestyle. The sentences of both transportation and penal servitude could be shortened by the 'ticket of leave' system, where the convict was released on licence, but would be recalled to complete his sentence on the first hint of trouble.

Transportation or penal servitude for life was one step below execution in the pantheon of punishments. Hangings were rare in Aberdeen, but they happened. There was an execution for murder in 1801, one for robbery in 1810, one for sheep stealing and one for theft in 1818, George Thom for murder in 1821, two more for murder in 1822, three for stouthrief (robbery in the home) in 1823, one for stouthrief in 1824, one for murder in 1826, Malcolm Gillespie the Exciseman for forgery in 1827, Catherine Davidson for murder in 1830, two for murder in 1849, George Christie for murder in 1853, and one for murder in 1857. That was a total of eighteen hangings in nearly sixty years, and ten of those were for murder. It was grim enough as a total, but compared to the 270 who were hanged in Scotland in the same period, including fifty-four in Edinburgh and fifty-eight in Glasgow, Aberdeen was not so bloody.

Last Word

In November 1898, Colonel McHardy, chairman of the Prison Commissions of Scotland, spoke about crime and prison in Edinburgh's Free Assembly Hall. After he stated that there were two types of crime

– the serious, such as murder, robbery and theft, and the trifling, such as breach of the peace and drunkenness, he mentioned the effects of prison on people. McHardy said that some felt degraded by the experience and intensely disliked the lack of conversation, but still could be fairly comfortable inside jail. Others even seemed to like the life. McHardy said that at the end of their sentences most prisoners were determined to lead a better life and the Prisoners Aid Society was there to help.

McHardy believed that a lot of crime was caused when people had nothing to spend their wages on but drink. He pointed out that the prisons were at their fullest when there was plenty work and so more money, while in his frequent prison visits he had never met anybody imprisoned for stealing bread for starving children. In a typical Victorian swipe at drink, McHardy said that heredity and physical development were not major factors, while intemperance was. Men turned to drink when their home life was uncomfortable and the State should have more power to remove vulnerable children from drunken parents.

It would be interesting to match these statements with somebody in a similar position today.

10
Railway Randies and Related Crime

Railways were a great boon to the Victorians. They connected communities in a way never before visualised; they allowed the less wealthy to travel on holiday; they moved goods around at unheard-of speed and they created employment for thousands of people. However, they also created different centres for crime. In April 1854, the Caledonian Railway put up posters warning passengers that there were sets of professional gamblers and pickpockets on the line and asking passengers not to join in but to tell the guard if anybody asked them to play cards.

There were other, more widespread troubles. The embankments scarred the landscape and could split up communities, while the railway navvies who built the viaducts and hacked through the hills and moors had possibly the worst reputation for drunken violence of any group of men in Britain.

Most people are familiar with the term 'navvies' and know that it can be applied at times to just about any manual worker who uses a pick and shovel. However, that is to misname a group of workers who have little in common with the original navigators except the fact that they all used manual labour. The name navvy is short for 'navigator' and they were the men who built the canal-navigation network that improved communications across Britain in the eighteenth and early nineteenth centuries. They had a reputation for hard drinking and the occasional riot, and when the canal age slid into the railway age, both the name and the reputation crossed seamlessly to the railway navvies.

An experienced navvy could dig twelve cubic yards of earth a day, every day, whatever the weather, and travelled from one engineering work to another. He was a migrant worker who lived apart from the communities around which he was employed, stayed in rowdy camps and settled his disputes by battles with fist or shovel. As the railways snaked across the landscape, huge numbers of these thirsty, rough-mannered servants of the spade, unwilling to bow to man, God nor devil, descended on quiet towns like plagues of raucous Huns, spreading fear and mayhem. They were often divided into three national groups: Irish, English and Scots. In Aberdeenshire, it seemed to be the Highland Scots who caused most trouble.

1847 and 1848 were bad years on the Scottish railways: in June 1847, there was a major riot in Fife when the Highland and Irish navvies came to blows. The trouble began after a Saturday payday when the Highlanders attacked the Irish, but escalated the following week when between 500 and 1,000 Irishmen, armed with rails, pokers and shovels, marched through Kirkcaldy to confront about 200 Highlanders, some of whom carried knives. Seeing themselves heavily outnumbered, the Highlanders prudently retreated. At that time there were over 8,000 labourers employed on the railways, about 5,000 of who were from Ireland or the Highlands.

There were two types of railway navvies: the local labourer who was hired for one particular job, and the professional railway navigator, the hard-working, hard-drinking and hard-fighting man who dressed distinctively and followed the railway lines as they snaked across the countryside. As the contemporary popular song ran:

I am a navvy bold, that's tramped the country round, sir
To get a job of work, where any can be found, sir

This latter type of worker created the popular image of the nineteenth-century railway navigator. The name came from the original labourers who dug the canals, the 'navigations' that opened up the country before railways were ever conceived. When the railway age began, camps of labourers sprang up, with hordes of often-itinerant men pushing the railway lines through countryside that was not used to strangers. The ubiquitous railway navvy ate two pounds of beef and drank a gallon of beer a day; he dressed in moleskin trousers, canvas shirt, square-tailed coat and studded boots, with a felt hat on his head and a bright kerchief around his neck. He earned good money and spent it in 'randies', drinking binges that often ended in riots.

On Wednesday, 5 January 1848, it was the turn of Stonehaven to experience a navvies' randy. This section of the East Coast line was around five miles long, from the Slug Road, which was a pass between Stonehaven and Banchory to Auchengowans farm to the south. The main contractor was a man named Forbes, who had up to 1,000 men working for him, the majority of whom were Highlanders. It was not easy work, with six embankments, one viaduct and twelve bridges to create, but these were navvies, the toughest manual workers in Europe. By that date the Highlanders had often abandoned their traditional clothing in favour of the more 'flash' gear of the Irish navigator, so they wore tight moleskin trousers and brightly coloured waistcoats or 'fancy vests' as they visited the town. However, they were still recognisable as Highlanders, which may have been the original cause of the trouble. Many of the navvies lived in the town. They lodged at five or six shillings a week and supplied their own food.

The summer of 1847 was a time of crop failure, trade depression and high prices. The Highland navvies did not understand that it was a Europe-wide problem and thought that the Stonehaven merchants had combined against them. The belief rankled and the navvies began to turn against the people of Stonehaven. As the trade depression deepened, Mr Forbes, the main railway contractor who employed some hundreds of navvies, had to lay some off and cut the wages of others.

The navigators were paid on Tuesday, 4 January 1848, and next day some approached William Bowman, the Stonehaven bellman, or town crier, and paid him sixpence to call for a meeting of the navvies in the square. He was warned that if he did not do it properly, others would do it for him. However, before Bowman could do his work, a navigator named Munro stopped him, saying that it was wrong to call the meeting. All the same, around 200 to 300 navvies gathered in the square, some armed with pikes, staffs or knives. But as it was a local holiday, Old Christmas Day, the town was otherwise quiet. The navigators shouted their grievances about the suspected conspiracy to raise the prices against them and make them lose their jobs, but as they spoke in Gaelic, the townspeople could not understand what they were saying.

As the men in the square shouted the odds, other navigators marched to Dunnottar Woods and cut themselves sticks. At around three in the afternoon, the whole crowd began a movement to the Old Town. They paraded through the streets, drinking the local pubs dry before threatening and terrifying the law-abiding townsfolk.

By half past five the roaring mob paraded through the town throwing rocks at every window where there was a light. They beat up a man named James Murray at the bottom of Ann Street. They smashed all the windows in the Commercial Inn but failed to break through the door. They moved to the Mill Inn and tried to attack John Melvin, who lodged there. Melvin was the timekeeper to Mr Forbes the chief contractor, who had recently paid some of them off. The navvies smashed the windows but could not force an entry. Instead, they beat up Melvin's son. They charged to the house of Knox the saddler and stoned the windows, but Knox and his sons prevented them entering the property. Then they stormed through the town beating up everybody who did not speak Gaelic. The town rang to cries of 'murder' until about nine at night, when the navvies dispersed and the people of Stonehaven wondered at the Highland storm that had wrecked their peace.

There were many witnesses, all with their own tale to tell. At about three in the afternoon, Alexander Weir, the Kincardineshire Police superintendent saw a group of navvies gather around Wadsworth's Inn. Weir ordered all five of the local police to get ready for trouble. Around four, the mob charged at the house of a man named Smart. Constables Reid and McRob tried to hold them back, but a Highlander named William McDonald tried to crown Constable Reid with a bottle. After that, the navigators ran back the hundred metres to Wadsworth's Inn. Some pushed their way inside while others milled around the Market Place, shouting and yelling and generally causing trouble.

A teenager named William Walker watched as a mob of navvies marched down Allardyce Street towards the bridge. He recognised the leader as Donald Davidson, while John McKinnon and Donald McKenzie were also in the front, carrying sticks and looking for trouble. They crossed the bridge to the Old Town, came to William Thomson's house and smashed the windows. As they were doing so, two local men, a slater named James Walker and his friend John Carnegie, walked towards them. They were going to watch game shooting and Carnegie carried a gun. Walker and the navvies were not friendly, possibly because he had helped to pacify earlier trouble against them. Walker told Carnegie that they had better get back in case there was trouble, but when they turned away the navvies ran after them.

'Hold the fellow with the gun,' a navvy shouted, and another leaped on the back of Walker. He tried to run, but McKinnon hauled him back from the door of the house and cracked him over the head with his stick; Donald Davidson and Donald McKenzie then began kicking and punching the defenceless man. James Walker thought that Davidson tried to hold the others back, but William Walker thought the opposite.

Local woman Mrs William Thompson said that Davidson attacked her husband and tore his coat, as well as hitting her three times with a stick. Mary Webster also saw Davidson leading the rioters and yelling at them to follow him to the cross and then to the shore. When a group of navvies met a man named William Gordon from Blackhills, Donald Davidson asked him if he could speak Gaelic. Gordon said 'no' and the navvies smashed him over the head with a stick, opening his scalp and blackening his eye. He was then knocked to the ground and the crowd surged past him and around a man named Charles Grahame. Somebody thumped Grahame on the head with a stick and somebody else smacked him on the arm; he ran to hide in the nearest house.

They also smashed the shop windows of Knox the saddler and then hurled stones through the windows of his house. The Commercial Inn was next, so its windows had to go, and Mrs Elrick the proprietor cowered inside as the stones came hurling through. The house of a Mr Stephen who owned a factory was also wrecked, and then they looked for people to attack as well as buildings. As it was the middle of winter, the town was dark; nobody lit the street lamps and the inhabitants cowered behind the windows, put up shutters where they could and doused their lamps in case they attracted unwanted attention: Stonehaven was under siege.

John Carnegie saw most of the troubles, but missed the worst of the lot. After escaping from the initial assault with Walker, he had stopped in Allardyce Street to talk to a young man called James Murray, but Murray had got a little behind him. A navvy cracked Carnegie on the cheekbone and he staggered around when something smashed against his arm. He heard Murray shout: 'Run, Carnegie!' and 'Ah! Ye Highland butchers.' He did not see what happened next, but Christian Thain did. She saw Donald Davidson lift his stick and knock Murray down with 'a very sore blow'. Murray tried to get up, but Munro shoved him down again.

'Good God, Donald Davidson,' Christian Thain said, 'I'll tell Jamie Reid the night.'

Davidson and Munro ran away and Thain lifted Murray up. Murray complained about his sore head and allowed Thain to help him to the house of Robert Milne.

Elizabeth Cowie came to help them. 'I've been killed by the navvies,' Murray said. He lost consciousness, and Mary Milne, Robert's wife, sent for the doctor, who at first thought he was in a drunken stupor. Carnegie came in then and Murray died between 11 p.m. and midnight on Wednesday, 5 January. When Dr Thompson examined him, he thought that he had died from the blow on the head.

Christian Thain also recognised both Davidson and Munro as being two of the main perpetrators of the trouble. She saw the attack on William Gordon; she saw the mob smashing the windows in Knox's house; she saw a navvy hit Carnegie with a walking stick; she saw the murder of Murray, and told Constable James Reith that Davidson had struck the fatal blow.

On Thursday, 6 January 1848, the Justices of the Peace held a special meeting and sent to Aberdeen for the army. Captain Leith Hay brought in twenty men of the 93rd. The police had been vastly outnumbered on the night of the riot, but they counter-attacked the next morning and arrested Davidson and ten other navvies. Five men were summoned to appear before the court in April: Donald Davidson, William McDonald, John McKinnon, Donald McKenzie and Colin Munro. McKenzie chose not to attend and was duly outlawed. At the trial, the navvies all pleaded not guilty; they denied there had been a breach of the peace and said there was only a 'slight disturbance'. They claimed they had only held a demonstration to show the town of Stonehaven 'how powerful the Highlanders were'. Davidson denied any participation in Murray's killing, and said he had been home at the time, although he had taken part in other events that night.

The Advocate-Depute told the jury that he was not asking for a verdict of murder, as there was insufficient evidence, but he wanted a verdict on the charges of mobbing and rioting plus malicious and wanton mischief. The jury found the accused guilty of all charges, plus culpable homicide. Lord Cockburn sentenced Munro to one year in jail, McKinnon and McDonald to eighteen months, and Davidson to seven years' transportation. In June 1850, Davidson sailed on *Nile* for Van Diemen's Land.

In 1849, after a break, work restarted on the line, and it was not long before the navvies began to make their presence felt. In May 1849 they had a minor dispute with each other at Drumlithie, but ended up throwing stones at the windows of every house in the neighbourhood instead. Navvies were capable of causing trouble in other ways as well, with poaching fairly common. For example, on 28 December 1846, a railway labourer named William Robertson appeared at the Justice of Peace court in Stonehaven for trespassing and poaching and was fined, with the alternative of twenty days in prison.

Navigators were also suspected of the occasional casual murder without the excuse of a riot.

Death of a Blacksmith

Margaret Fraser was a very young girl, the daughter of Peter Fraser, who lived in the parish of Lumphanan. She left her house at around half past eight in the morning of Sunday, 30 January 1859, but within a few minutes she ran back to tell her parents that there was a dead man in a field beside Lumphanan village. Her father informed the local police, who called out Dr Walker from the nearby town of Kincardine O'Neill.

The dead man was Fenton Petrie, who had lived at Collieston and worked on the Deeside Extension Railway at Wester Beltie. He was around forty years old and married with three children. He was a skilled, hard-working, muscular man, but his skull had been fractured like an eggshell.

Dr Ogston inspected the body and the police began their investigation. Petrie had been the railway blacksmith, working on all the metalwork required for this section of the line, including sharpening the tools of the navvies. He had drawn his month's wages the previous Saturday and settled his bills; he paid his twenty-eight shillings for board and lodgings, sent £2 and two shillings to his wife at Bishopsmill, near Elgin, and jingled the remainder, around twelve shillings and sixpence, in his pocket. He spent some on a scarf and a handkerchief in a Collieston shop and entered George Cromar's unlicensed drinking house in Lumphanan, where the railway employees gathered. Petrie shared a few drinks with his colleagues before leaving at around six in the evening.

Wherever Petrie had intended going, he did not get far. His body was discovered at the foot of an embankment only a few yards from Cromar's shop. His jacket and waistcoat were found a few yards from the body, as if he had either taken them off to fight, or the killer had stripped them from his dead body to search for his wages. However, as he still had two shillings and sixpence in his pocket, the search had not been thorough. There were a number of bloody marks on Petrie's head, so it was unlikely he had stumbled in the dark of a winter's night and cracked himself on the rocky ground. The doctors were of the opinion that somebody had cleaved in Petrie's skull with an axe.

Inspector Cran and Sergeant Richardson, with a number of constables, began to ask questions of the local people and the railway navvies. Although the residents of the village told all they knew, Cran did not learn very much, and the railway workers gave nothing at all away. Cran questioned them all, especially those who had blood on their clothes, but many had injuries sustained at work, and others were poachers, so the blood could easily have come from any of the animals they had killed. Cran suspected that one of them had murdered Petrie, either as the result of an argument or to get his wages, but the more he asked, the less he learned. The navigators had a way of clamming up when outsiders interfered with what they thought was their business, and that murder was never solved.

Even when the construction was complete, the railway could bring other crime to the land.

Assault on the Train

Nearly as soon as they began to stretch across the countryside, railways became sources of contention. There were disputes over the steam trains terrifying farm animals, disputes as the railway navigators unleashed their own brand of fear on isolated rural communities and disputes about travelling in the carriages. Some carriages were infested by travelling sharps who invited innocent passengers to a game of cards and then fleeced them of all their money. However, probably the most feared possibility was of a sexual nature.

At a time when women were arguably less likely to travel alone than they are now, there was a fear that unaccompanied women in railway compartments might be liable to unwelcome attention from men. In the early decades of train travel, it was not unknown for women to carry long hatpins in readiness to repel the expected assault from men whenever the train entered a tunnel. Even late in the nineteenth century there were some occasions when such events actually transpired.

On 23 November 1886, Elspet Wilson, a sixteen-year-old domestic servant of Harvieston, Kinneff, had been at the feeing market (where farm workers hired themselves out to farmers for the next term, or period of employment) at Brechin to find a situation for the following year. She caught the evening train home, stepped into a compartment and sat beside a woman, a girl and two men. However, most of the passengers left at the next stop, so that when they left Laurieston station she was alone with a seventeen-year-old farm servant named James Bruce, from Pitcarry, in Arbuthnott.

According to Wilson, as soon as they were alone, Bruce immediately assaulted her. He thrust a hand up her skirt and knocked her onto the floor of the carriage.

'If you don't leave me alone,' Wilson said, 'you will suffer!'

Bruce ignored her threat and pushed her against the seat, grabbed her by the throat and covered her mouth. Wilson was not a girl to tamely submit, however, and she struggled free. Bruce knocked her down again, but she fought back and dashed to the window, which she slid open. She thrust out her head and screamed for help.

Alexander Stephen, an eighteen-year-old farm servant, was also returning from the feeing market. He was in the neighbouring compartment and heard Wilson's screams. He looked out of his window and saw Wilson's scared face, with her hair blowing in the wind and her eyes wide. Stephen asked why she was screaming and she told him there was a man in her compartment 'who will not let me go'. One of the other men in Stephen's compartment suggested that they go along the corridor to have a look, but in the event they sat tight.

When the train stopped at Johnshaven, George Milne, the train guard, came to see what all the fuss was about. Wilson was sitting crying and her hair was 'in disorder' with her hat lying on the floor of the compartment. Milne saw that there were two buttons ripped from her dress and one from her cape; Wilson told him that there was a button missing from her petticoat, which was also torn. She said that Bruce had 'meddled' with her. Milne escorted her onto the platform to go to a safer compartment. When she stepped outside, Stephen and his travelling companion, James Milne, thought she looked dishevelled, with Milne saying her hair was 'some ravelled like'.

George Milne locked Bruce in the compartment and when they reached Bervie he handed him over to the police.

At Bervie, Constable Adam Murray listened to Wilson's story and handed her to the care of a woman named Mrs Beattie. Wilson presented a pathetic picture: she was still crying, her clothes were torn and there were angry red marks on her knees and her neck; Mrs Beattie thought she looked as if she had been 'seized by the throat'. Murray asked Mrs Beattie to look after Wilson that night, rather than have her journey five miles home in the dark. Wilson cried all night, so that Mrs Beattie thought she was in 'real distress'. In the meantime, Murray charged Bruce with indecent assault.

The case came before the Circuit Court in January 1887. Bruce admitted he had put his hand up Wilson's skirt and pushed her against the seat, but said that was 'all I did'. As so often in cases of this nature, the defence tried to damage the victim's character. The defence concentrated on an earlier incident when Wilson had been in a carriage with a number of young men. A farm labourer named William Clark claimed that she had kissed him a number of times on that journey, much against his wishes. David Fairfoul, who was also present, said Wilson had conducted herself 'no verra weel' and she 'wouldna let be'.

Despite this counter-attack, the jury found Bruce guilty of indecent assault and he was sentenced to six months with hard labour.

Finally, railway stations themselves could also be targeted by criminals.

Station-breaking

As they were known to hold money paid for tickets, the lonely stations of the Great North of Scotland Railway could be targets for crime. The MacDuff and Turiff branch of the line was normally one of the quietest, with small stations divided by a mixture of farmland and moor, and one of its stations was Fyvie.

On Sunday night, 2 June 1876, the last train of the day rattled through the station at Fyvie and the stationmaster locked up. He returned at half past six the next morning to find that the place had been thoroughly ransacked. The burglar, or burglars, had broken the locks of the ticket office, and the ticket case, the desks and the cash drawer had all been smashed and the contents either stolen or scattered. It was obvious that there was no finesse in the attack; there had been no false keys used and probably a great deal of noise in the operation. The stationmaster found a small crowbar on the station veranda and believed that this was the tool used.

For all the effort, the burglar had not gained a great reward. From the office they extracted forty-one pounds of tobacco and about one shilling and sixpence in small change. They had also taken the key to the waiting room, where they had used the end of the crowbar to unscrew the locks of two trunks of clothes. Again, what they had not wanted had simply been thrown on the floor. From the waiting room they had moved to a trunk in the veranda, and another near the goods shed; finally they had taken a few parcels and left. In total, the value of the goods stolen was around £16, mostly in clothing, plus the tobacco.

The Aberdeenshire Police were not slow in chasing up the burglars. They had already noticed a couple of non-local men loitering around Fyvie, and the local people told them about a man who they had seen in the railway station. That was one advantage of small, tight communities: strangers were quickly noted and often watched. By asking around, the police traced the two men to Cuminestown. They had remained there until the Monday; one of them was alleged to have had an American accent. From Cuminestown the men went to Banff, but that was the end of their travels. Inspector McGregor was aware of the theft and of the suspects and he arrested them as soon as they arrived. The police found the tobacco hidden inside a bush just outside Fyvie Castle.

One of the men claimed to be a machine fitter named Philip Clark and the other said he was an engraver named Joseph Smith, sometimes known as 'Yankee Joe'. After some questioning by the police, Smith admitted two previous convictions in Aberdeen, where he had given his name as Thomas Edwards. Philip Clark also possessed a different name and an interesting history. When he was questioned more closely, his American accent and antecedents both disappeared and he admitted to being Peter Graham. He had been arrested for robbing the museum in Dundee, but had been released when the Lord Advocate heard that none other than the superintendent of police had bribed him into revealing where the stolen goods had been hidden.

Both men were placed in handcuffs and taken to Aberdeen, where Sheriff Comrie Thomson was pleased to meet them. However, despite their records and the deep suspicions of the Aberdeenshire police, both men were released. The case was not satisfactorily closed.

There were many cases of petty theft at railway stations in the area. For instance, in May 1877, a clerk named Colin MacIntyre and a labourer named Alexander Craib, both of whom worked at Fyvie station, were caught stealing whisky. They were fined £5 and £2 respectively. In December that same year, Peter Cassells, an Edinburgh publican, stole a quantity of tea and various other articles from the waiting room at the station and was sentenced to thirty days' hard labour.

Overall, the railway could be a magnet for crime, but usually they were the same, familiar types of crime, merely in a new setting. Other crimes were more high profile and some gave Aberdeenshire a place on the international stage.

11
The Fraudsters

The *Oxford Dictionary* defines fraud as 'criminal deception' or 'a dishonest artifice or trick', and Aberdeenshire seemed to spawn more than its share of fraudsters in the nineteenth century. Many of them were women, and some were expert in their chosen profession.

Alexandrina Grant

Alexandrina Grant, otherwise known as Jemima Mackenzie, was one such expert. Fate had been cruel to her: she was born in a prison around 1825, although she was not sure of the exact date, and both her parents were transported, leaving her to drag herself up in a world singularly devoid of sympathy or aid for the daughter of criminals.

Perhaps it was her genes, or just her circumstances, that guided her to a life of crime, but although fate had granted her few advantages, she made the most of those she had. She was good-looking, charming and possessed the ability to adapt her accent to ape those who believed themselves to be her betters. By the time Alexandrina Grant was in her mid teens she was experienced in playing the part of the daughter of an imaginary personage in order to gain the trust of gullible shopkeepers, or anybody else from whom she could wring money or goods.

After living in Inverness for a while, Grant ran out of people to defraud and moved into Aberdeen to try her skill there. In May 1843, she appeared at the lodging house of Mrs Lindsay in Huntly Street and asked to rent a room. She spun an interesting story: her father was a general in the army, she claimed, and had sent her up to Aberdeen to finish her education, as he believed the Scots had a better education system than that down south. Furthermore, Grant claimed that she had an uncle, a Mr Smith, in Aberdeen, who was a land surveyor, and she intended to visit him the moment she had finished her breakfast.

Mrs Lindsay swallowed the story, and in addition she gave Grant new gloves and a new collar. Asking Mrs Lindsay if she could borrow the servant boy to show her the way to her uncle's hotel, Grant left the lodgings. That was the last Mrs Lindsay saw of her. Grant lost the boy somewhere in the narrow streets of the town and vanished. It was not until much later that Mrs Lindsay realised she had been duped.

Grant disappeared from view for a month or so, but at the beginning of June she knocked on the door of Mrs McDonald, who ran a shop in Old Aberdeen's High Street. This time Grant was very chatty and claimed to be a daughter of General Cruickshank, who lived in the west, and that she was staying at the cottage of Mr Sutherland, between Old and New Aberdeen. She selected some goods from the shop, including napkins and some ribbon. As she chatted away to Mrs McDonald, she put the ribbon on her bonnet and suddenly realised that she had forgotten her purse.

Oh well, no matter, she would just have to come back later and pay for everything: Mrs McDonald would not mind, surely? Mrs McDonald was not quite as naive as to allow a total stranger, however charming and plausible, to waltz out of her shop with a sizeable collection of her stock. Instead, she retained most of the goods Grant had selected and watched as she left. When Grant did not return, Mrs McDonald proved that an Aberdeen shopkeeper could also make a good detective and traced her to a house in the Gallowgate. There were words spoken between the two, and Grant handed over a bonnet in part payment, plus a plethora of promises to pay the rest. Needless to say, she never returned to Mrs McDonald's shop.

That same month, Grant met with Mrs McKenzie in North Street on a Sunday evening. Mrs McKenzie was a broker's wife, and Grant told her it was too dark for her to walk to her lodgings at the Sutherlands' and asked where she could find lodgings for the night. Mrs McKenzie was a kindly woman and offered to show Grant where she could find a clean bed for the night. As they walked, Mrs McKenzie revealed that her husband came from Nairnshire, which seemed to please Grant, who said that her father was also a Nairnshire man: General Cruickshank of Pluscarden. Perhaps Mr McKenzie might know him?

Such a coincidence was as good as a calling card, and McKenzie took Grant in for the night, and gave her a bed and free breakfast and dinner. After that, Grant visited Mrs McKenzie's shop and dressed herself in some of the clothes that were there, posing happily and laughing with Mrs McKenzie and her young daughter. Grant suggested that she take the young girl with her to the Sutherlands', where she would hand over part of the £2 10s. for the clothes for the shop and a gown she thought the youngster would like. By now Mrs McKenzie was completely taken in and agreed, so Grant took the child by the hand and they walked to the Sutherlands' cottage. However, when they reached Mr Sutherland's gate, Grant told the child that she would meet her father on the Canal Bridge the next day. When the youngster went away, so did Grant, without entering the cottage. She walked towards Old Aberdeen.

Grant continued her career of fraud, always pretending to be the daughter of somebody in authority: twice it was Major Grant, who was the barrack master in Aberdeen. Grant used the major's name to get free accommodation at an inn near the Bridge of Don, telling the innkeeper, Mrs Ewing, that her father would be angry with her for staying at such a public place. When Mrs Ewing called on Major Grant to explain that his daughter was innocent of any sin, she found that he and his wife and family had been in the country for some weeks.

That was Grant's last attempt at deception in Aberdeen. She left the town and headed north, but by that time the authorities were looking for her. She was arrested about six miles north of Aberdeen and carried back to the jail. While she waited for her trial, she made two statements: she said she was the daughter of a Grantown farmer named Grant and of a Nairnshire farmer named McKenzie and had been in court twice in Inverness under the name of Jemima McKenzie. Whatever the truth, Grant was sentenced to seven years' transportation for falsehood, fraud and wilful imposition. Perhaps she met her parents in Australia.

The Female Midshipman

Some Aberdeenshire fraudsters became minor celebrities in their own right. One of these was a woman named Isabella Knowles, although she was also known by other names, including John Brown, Miss Danesbury and the Female Midshipman.

Isabella Knowles was a mysterious woman who could have been the victim of unfortunate circumstances rather than an out-and-out villain, despite the five criminal convictions she accrued in as many years. She was not known to the police at all until 1867, when she had a bad accident that put her in bed for eleven weeks. When she emerged, it seems that her entire personality had altered. From being the respectable daughter of decent parents, she became a thief, cross-dresser and confidence trickster. Knowles lived at Buxburn, then a small village but now known as Bucksburn, an area in north-west Aberdeen, and she had worked at the Stoneywood Paper Works. She was a tall, good-looking, intelligent young woman with a bit of a swagger, a lot of charm and a great deal of nerve.

On Wednesday, 24 January 1869, twenty-year-old Knowles was arrested for a series of thefts from drapers' shops in Aberdeen that had taken place in November and December 1868. By that time she already had been convicted twice at Greenock and knew that a further conviction could mean a long time in jail. While she was waiting for her trial, she noticed that the lock on the cell was loose, so rather than chance the decision of the judge, she broke the lock and ran. However, the Aberdeen police were not so easily eluded and picked her up before she had left the city. At her trial she was given six months in the East Jail.

Knowles obviously did not much enjoy prison life, for she decided very early on that she wanted to escape. On 4 February, she was helping a washerwoman in an outhouse of the prison at Lodge Walk, with her window overlooking the street below. Knowles did her best to look industrious, but the moment the attendant left her alone she slipped open the window and dropped down to Broad Street.

The distance was much further than Knowles realised and she landed with what she called a 'sair clyte' (a quick, stinging blow). She recovered and limped off, out of Aberdeen and all the way to Stonehaven in a single day. How Knowles travelled is a bit of a mystery, but it is known that she visited Glasgow, Edinburgh and the north-east of England, where she was employed in theatre work. She proved a natural actress and graced the stage disguised as a man. However, she must have been homesick, and, armed with her newfound talent as an actress, she altered her appearance to that of a young man, donned the clothes of a midshipman in the Royal Navy and called herself John Brown.

As John Brown, Knowles lived life to the full. She stayed at hotels and inns as Mr Midshipman Brown, passed policemen without a qualm and returned to one of her old stomping grounds of Woodside, where she remained undetected until either her funds ran out or she merely wanted to add some excitement to her life. After a while, Knowles began to steal clothing and stash it in the nearby quarry of Hilton. Unfortunately for her, the local people were not stupid, and when a shoemaker saw one of her bundles of clothing, he guessed it belonged to a thief and notified the police.

Sergeant Morrison of the Woodside Police brought a constable with him when he searched the area. Within a few moments they had located three bundles of stolen clothing hidden among the whins, and Morrison realised that the thief must use this as a storage area and would probably return for the goods. He whistled up Sergeant Findlay and a second constable from Aberdeen, and they took turns about to watch for the thief.

Sergeant Findlay was on watch in the dark of an evening when he saw a man with a bundle on his shoulders walking towards the quarry. Findlay wasted no time in arresting the man and took him to Woodside police office. The suspect told Sergeant Morrison that his name was John Brown and that he was a seaman from Stonehaven. He was dressed in a grey waistcoat and trousers and a long blue coat, fashionable but not of the best quality. The police estimated that he was around twenty, and he appeared to be exactly what he said: a shore-bound midshipman. Morrison locked Brown up safely and brought in all his booty.

There was around £30 worth of clothing, including a full riding costume, but when Brown was arrested he had also been carrying a pair of curtains. These had belonged to a commercial traveller who stayed at the Lemon Tree Hotel. The police were surprised to find that everything he stole thing was washed and clean.

When Sergeant Morrison told his wife all about the very handsome young midshipman who was in his cell, she immediately wanted to see him for herself. Obviously entertainment must have been in short supply in Woodside that year. Mrs Morrison took a turn to the cells, but no sooner did she meet John Brown than she laughed and informed her bemused husband that his prized midshipman was a woman. As Brown grinned at them, Morrison was in a bit of a quandary: he could hardly search Brown if he was a she, and Mrs Morrison would never search him in case he was the gender he claimed to be. However, Brown made it easier by admitting that he was in fact a woman. It was not long before Morrison worked out that Brown was Isabella Knowles, the escaped convict, and she was bundled off to Aberdeen in handcuffs. While some women had assumed a man's persona for a few hours to perform a particular act, Knowles had successfully passed herself off as John Brown for months, which either shows dedication to her role, or possibly a sheer love of play-acting that was proved by her time working in the theatre.

In late July 1869, Knowles appeared before Sheriff Comrie Thomson and the details of her theft came out. The majority of the goods had been in a single chest in a laundry room at her old workplace of the Stoneywood Paper Works. Mrs Pirie of Stoneywood House had left the trunk in the room but had not locked the door. Knowles had taken the box and floated it down the Don to near Hilton Quarry, and then carried the contents in easily manageable bundles to a place she thought it safe to hide. She was given a further fifteen months to add to her uncompleted six months' sentence.

However, Knowles either had not learned to control her impulse to steal or was incapable of doing so. She was released from jail about November 1870 and returned home as the prodigal daughter, full of promises to reform. However, at the beginning of February 1871, she was passing the Aberdeen and Leith Steam Shipping Company shed at Pocra Quay and she noticed an unattended carpet bag. The temptation was just too much, and she opened it, saw that it was full of clothes and took it away. Guessing that the owner would not be far away, Knowles handed the bag to the left-luggage office at the railway station, took the receipt and walked innocently away.

However, bad weather held back the steamboat and Alexander Stewart, a Leith blacksmith and the owner of the carpet bag decided to travel by the morning train instead. When he arrived to pick up his bag he was unhappy when he found it was missing. Concerned, but blaming himself for leaving it unattended, he hefted the remainder of his luggage to the left-luggage office, where it would be safer. He arrived there, noticed his missing carpet bag sitting in a corner of the room and asked for its return.

There was some confusion when Stewart tried to reclaim it, only to be told that it had been left by an immaculately dressed lady who called herself Miss Danesbury. Stewart informed the police, who were waiting when Knowles returned to claim the bag. A constable escorted her to the police office, but Knowles made a mad dash for freedom down St Catherine's Wynd. The policeman chased after her; he reached out to grab hold of her long skirt, whereupon she fell to the ground and rolled backwards so the officer tripped over her and fell headlong. Knowles lifted the hem of her skirt and ran, but the constable once more pursued her and this time he held her tight.

When Knowles was in the police office, she was searched again and a razor and razor case were found inside her clothes. Both were Stewart's property; he said that his bag had not been unlocked but forced open and the razor taken out. Knowles had no history of violence, so the razor could have been another example of her need for roleplay.

The case came to court in April 1871 and Knowles was found guilty of stealing the carpet bag. Lord Ardmillan recounted Knowles' criminal career, stating that she had already served sentences of thirty days, four months, six months and fifteen months, so he had to make it a longer sentence and gave her eighteen months.

On that occasion, Knowles seemed to have served her time without any attempt to escape, but she still had not fully learned that thieving was no longer a game, and in January 1874 she was in trouble again. The police caught her with a pair of male trousers and some poultry. The owner of the trousers came forward, but the hens remained unclaimed. However, this time Knowles was not treated leniently and was given seven years' penal servitude. That seems to have been enough to end her career of crime, but it is equally possible that she emerged, changed her name and continued with yet another different persona.

However clever the Female Midshipman was, her career pales into a faint shadow when compared to Mrs Gordon Baillie, surely one of the great deceivers of the nineteenth century.

'She Would Have Deceived the Devil Himself'

Very few people today will have heard of Mrs Gordon Baillie, yet in her time she created a sensation and caused consternation from Aberdeen to Port Arthur. She was perhaps one of the most successful fraudsters of the nineteenth century, fooling crofters, the aristocracy and even the most hard-headed of newspaper journalists with her subtle tongue and soft manners.

Throughout the 1880s, Mrs Gordon Baillie was frequently in the newspapers. She was known as a titled lady, a philanthropist and a lady of wealth and influence. However, that period came to a jarring close in the spring of 1888 when it was discovered that she was nothing of the sort. Taken to court for fraud, her amazing true life was gradually unravelled. In Scotland she had pretended to be a wealthy lady and a friend to the Hebridean crofters in their struggle for land rights and security of tenure. In Australia she had claimed to be the last of an old and distinguished family, with the Gordons on one side and the Baillies on the other, giving her name of Gordon Baillie. Unfortunately, she was neither one nor the other.

Mrs Gordon Baillie, aristocrat, philanthropist and the queen of fraudsters, had been born into poverty on Maiden Street, Peterhead, on 21 February 1848. She was the illegitimate daughter of a Peterhead woman, Catherine or Kate Beid, who was either a hawker or a servant, and was probably the daughter of a carter. Gordon Baillie's birth father was named John Newbond or John Newbone; he came from Inveraddie and was variously described as a farmer or a hawker of pork. Her stepfather, who may or may not have married her mother, was named Sutherland; he was a pew opener at a Dundee church. From Aberdeen, Gordon Baillie moved to Dundee, where she called herself Mary Ann Bruce Sutherland. She found a job as an evening teacher in the model (or good-quality) lodging house and preached evangelical Christianity. Ironically, in view of her later career, she spoke to many religious meetings back in Peterhead and she was well known for performing Christian missionary work.

Despite her lack of money, Gordon Baillie lived in a good-quality house in a respectable area and passed herself off as a teacher, so there was mystery about her even then. Her honesty was not unquestioned: she did not return underclothing that she borrowed from her elderly cleaner, while a local shoemaker gave her a pair of boots and was never paid. These early hints pointed to a future of fraud. Sometime around this period she met an Italian who taught her at least the rudiments of the language. By now she was living a life of fully fledged fraud, using her considerable charm to wheedle tradesmen and others into giving her things, for which she did not pay. Around 1869, with many people asking her for money, she left for London or perhaps Liverpool. There are hazy periods in her life, which is not surprising given the multitude of identities she used, but some dates and incidents stand out like islands of fact in a sea of duplicity.

She was certainly in Rome around 1872, for she was known in the one-room Scottish church. Here she used the name of Mrs Bruce Sutherland from Caithness. At that time she paraded herself in an open carriage, gave gentle orders to a servant and fawned over her younger brother, or half-brother, James. Gordon Baillie certainly lived the high life: she lived in a lovely villa just outside the city and claimed she was starting a Protestant school for Italian girls. Others thought she borrowed money very easily but was not so good at paying it back.

For a while Gordon Baillie mixed with the good and the great, took them for drives in her carriage and borrowed their money whenever she wished to make a purchase. She also borrowed substantial amounts from the bank, but when her creditors became too clamorous, she packed her bags and left for Florence and Turin. As well as changing her abode, she also changed her identity and nationality; now she claimed to be an American widow whose French husband, General de Boornian, had recently died. Without shame or conscience, Gordon Baillie charmed her way into the US Consulate and inveigled herself into the good graces of the local gentry until her luck ran out: the Italians sussed her deceit and banged her in prison for fraud.

Mrs Gordon Baillie did her time with a smile and was in Paris soon after, once more posing as Miss Bruce Sutherland. Here she persuaded a British doctor named Sir William Macormac to give his support in her philanthropic endeavours, including prison visiting. Gordon Baillie told Sir William that her mother in Scotland was ill, and graciously accepted his offer of his banker's card. Smiling, she drew money from his bank and neither he nor Paris saw her again.

Gordon Baillie was in Edinburgh for a while, and then in Whitfield Cottage, Dundee. She tried her old tricks in Scotland's fourth city, but rather than live the high life, she was dragged to the Sheriff and Jury Court and was jailed on 19 December 1872 for no less than seventeen charges of obtaining goods under false pretences. She got nine months with hard labour for that, but simultaneously, there was also talk of various wealthy people being asked to contribute to her scheme of a school in Switzerland. While in prison, Wanless of Dundee took her photograph and she was described as 'slightly pockmarked and bearing a mole on the left side of the neck'. Despite these minor imperfections, she was still beautiful and still game when she was discharged from Perth prison in September 1873.

Sometime between 1873 and 1876, Gordon Bailie was in Liverpool, but details are sketchy. She was in Edinburgh in 1876 as Miss Sutherland, but slipped south to London and found romance with an actor named Thomas Whyte. Using the name Annie Ogilvy Bruce, she married him. Her trousseau was valued at £300, but she had swindled it from the dressmaker so it did not cost her a penny. Whyte used the stage names of Knight Aston or Henry Lee Toller; the witnesses were Kate Miller and Lucy Murray, or they said they were. With Gordon Baillie it is doubtful if anything or anybody was what or who they seemed.

In January 1877, Westminster Police Court issued a warrant for her arrest for fraud, but that same month she boarded SS *Decolia* at Liverpool, bound for New York. Her exploits the next year are shaded, but she was in Greenock by 1878 and in London in 1879 at Grosvenor Square in London in 1879. That same year, a Miss Nelson of Portland Square claimed that Mrs Gordon Baillie had swindled her of a diamond and emerald necklace, but there does not seem to have been enough proof to make the charge stick.

Mrs Gordon Bailie changed addresses as often as she changed identities: Portsea Place, Cornwall Road and Walthamstow; she jumped from house to house, usually escaping the law by a whisker, always leaving a trail of unpaid bills and the memory of a charming smile. In 1882, her husband, Thomas Whyte, sailed for Australia, and she adopted the name of Gordon Murray.

She followed her husband to Australia and lived for on her wits and her charm. Flattered to have a real Scottish aristocrat living among them, the society of Melbourne welcomed her and Gordon Baillie mingled with the crème de la crème; she lived in fashionable Park Terrace, spent her time with the top echelon and probably spent their money as happily as she spent that of anybody else. While in

Melbourne, Mrs Gordon Bailie lived with a man named Percival Frost as husband and wife and was accompanied by two little girls who may, or may not, have been her daughters. What happened to Thomas Whyte? Did he mind his wife's shenanigans? Or perhaps they had an open marriage and he had his own paramours; some things may never be known. Mrs Whyte, Mrs Frost or Gordon Baillie was notoriously pushy and paraded in a fine carriage.

Gordon Baillie seemed to commute between Scotland and Australia that year. She was in Scotland and prominent during the agitation in Skye; she may even have had genuine sympathy for the plight of the crofters. There was no record of a Mrs Whyte, Frost or Gordon Baillie on any passenger steamer between Australia and the UK, but there were stories that she travelled with a man as Mr and Mrs Matthews on the steamer *Aurora*. Matthews may have been Frost under a different name. Gordon Baillie certainly leased a block of some 75,000 acres of land in Victoria and promised it to any dispossessed Hebridean crofter. It might have helped that the ex-mayor of Melbourne was a Perthshire man; she would understand what made him tick.

Posing as a literary gentlewoman of Bryanston Street, Portland Square, in London, Gordon Baillie was alleged to have given a sword to John Macpherson, the 'Glendale martyr' who sought rights for the crofters of Glendale. She later denied that act. However, she did visit Skye many times. 'Although I belong to, and have been reared among, the aristocracy, my sympathies are not with them. I think they have been guilty in too many cases of great injustice,' Mrs Gordon Baillie said.

During her travels in Skye she was described as 'young, of prepossessing appearance ... her features yet bore the stamp of mature womanhood'. She wore a crimson dressing gown, red silk stockings with 'natty high-heeled shoes with steel buckles ... the fourth and fifth fingers of her right hand were encrusted with jewelled rings ... large brown sanguine eyes beamed ... beneath fair hair falling in curls over her forehead'. In this personage, she visited the female crofter prisoners held at Calton jail in Edinburgh. Despite her philanthropic reputation, Gordon Baillie left Edinburgh without paying her bills, including the hire of a carriage and pair, and even duped Professor Blackie out of a guinea. Professor Blackie had vivid impressions of Mrs Gordon Baillie.

'She called upon me as a stranger and I received her politely, as I do all strangers,' he told the *Edinburgh Evening Dispatch*. He thought she talked 'good practical sense' and her 'manners were faultless and her appearance and bearing that of a lady a Highland proprietrix ... I verily believe she would have deceived the devil himself.'

A man who signed himself 'a country squire' was in full agreement; he wrote to the newspapers and said 'anyone coming within range of her fascinating personality might easily be deceived'.

Mrs Gordon Baillie had a vast number of aliases, depending on circumstances. At times she pretended to be a daughter of the Earl of Moray, stating that she was in fact the Countess of Moray but that because an ancestor had an irregular marriage she was barred from taking her proper place. Her husband, she said, had taken her name of Gordon Murray in order to keep the name intact. She called herself Annie Frost or Miss Ogilvie Bruce, Mrs Whyte or Miss Sutherland, but always her multiple characters shared a common link: they cheated those with whom they came into contact. As Mrs Whyte or White she was charged with defrauding a cabman, but did not turn up for the hearing at the Mansion House in London. In 1877, her Miss Ogilvy Bruce was accused of defrauding several people, including a silk merchant. In 1883, as Ann Whyte and acting with her husband, Thomas Whyte or Knight Aston, she was said to have defrauded a Walthamstow man named Harding of £300 worth of furniture. Harding claimed that there were many other people with accounts to settle with Mrs Gordon Baillie.

One wonders if Gordon Baillie saw the world as one huge stage and herself as the leading performer in a never-ending play. She certainly toyed with theatrical affairs. For a while she was known to have gone into partnership with a Captain Disney Roebuck to rent the Imperial Theatre, where she was going to perform as Lady Clancarty; however, she did not grace that particular stage and Roebuck was both let down and disappointed. Only his death at Cape Town prevented him from taking legal action against her. Mrs Gordon Baillie was also involved in a theatrical venture with Mr Gilbert Tait, when she proposed going on a Cape and Australian tour with her own company. That also did not transpire. In summer of 1885 at Bristol Summer Assizes, the dramatic author R. Palgrave demanded £50 she owed him for a manuscript, *Shadow and Sunshine*, he had given her; he won his case.

Mrs Gordon Baillie moved to the Isle of Wight and lived in seclusion with her four children. The quiet times were only relative: she was featured in the *Illustrated London News*, and she invested money in a Belgian banking company, but that venture failed. She lived at Herne Bay and Broadstairs and left debts in both places. She was also rumoured to have abandoned her children to the workhouse when life soured on her and her money supplies dried up. Her name changed again, this time to Mrs Maitland.

Around this time Gordon Baillie made the acquaintance of wealthy Sir Richard Duckworth King. He was elderly and deaf, she was young and demanding; he paid for her house in Brynston Square and financed her to the extent of as much as £15,000. Duckworth King went bankrupt: Mrs Gordon Baillie kissed him goodbye and went on her merry way to another fine house in Upper Brook Street, in London.

Still mobile, Gordon Baillie moved north to Barton Hall near Burton-on-Trent and acted the benevolent lady of the manor. In August 1886 she gave a picnic to local children and invited clergymen of different denominations to her house. It would be interesting to speculate that beneath her grasping shell, there was a heart that was genuinely interested in doing good deeds. She was again in Australia until Sir Richard Duckworth King died in 1887, and Gordon Baillie returned to England on SS *Orizaba*, still with Frost tagging on. The couple tried to claim some of King's properties but failed. As Mrs Seymour, and with Frost as her husband, she leased Marine House, in Broadstairs, and took back her children from the workhouse, yet left all but the youngest behind when she again donned the mantle of Gordon Baillie and resumed her campaign to help the crofters.

For all her faults, there were occasional flashes of what seemed to be genuine humanity. She seemed to care for her children, occasionally, and when one recovered from a serious illness she penned tender lines of poetry:

> *May heaven spare thee, bonny flower*
> *Long, long tae bloom*
> *An scent the sweet domestic bower*
> *Wi loves perfume*

However, in 1888 she was caught for fraud in London and prosecuted as Annie Frost, along with her supposed husband, Robert Percival Frost, and a second man, Robert Gidner, who was supposed to be their butler. They were charged with receiving goods by means of worthless cheques and conspiracy to cheat and defraud. It was alleged that Mrs Gordon Baillie had driven up to the banking company of Herries, Farquhar and Company on 18 June 1888 to get a chequebook. She stated that there was money to be paid in from Scotland, and although nothing was deposited, she wrote many cheques, all of which were dishonoured. The bank Smith, Payne and Smith of Lombard Street also claimed that Mrs Gordon Baillie had dishonoured cheques amounting to over £290. A butcher named Thomas Pogson chimed in and claimed that Mrs Gordon Baillie owed him money, but he had been offered a bribe not to offer evidence against her. The court found out that Mrs Gordon Baillie was not legally married to Robert Frost. A few details emerged about this man: he was a clergyman's son and had money through his mother. He and Gordon Baillie had met around 1885 and seemed to have clicked together for mutual financial and emotional gain.

However, Robert Percival Bodeley Frost challenged any allegations made against her, and Mrs Gordon Baillie also issued a statement in her defence, giving names and addresses of gentlemen with whom she was associated, including Sir Richard Duckworth King. Notwithstanding these attempts, the case proceeded with Mrs Gordon Baillie smartly dressed in black silk and with a fawn-coloured jacket: she was every inch the lady. To augment her charade of ladylike innocence, she had a bouquet of roses on her lap throughout the hearing and smelled them from time to time. Her age was estimated at thirty, when in reality she was ten years older. Frost himself was an undischarged bankrupt with debts estimated at over £130,000. Again they claimed to have been married, with Mrs Gordon Baillie saying they were married by a priest in Brussels in May 1886.

She was jailed: five years this time. Released in late 1893, she immediately returned to her old ways, and in early 1894 she tried to defraud a picture dealer in London, was caught again and sentenced to seven years' penal servitude, which was a harsh sentence by any standards and surely enough to crush all but the strongest spirit.

However, that was not the end of the amazing career of Mrs Gordon Baillie. She continued to change her name: Lady Campbell, Lady Cochrane, Lady Stewart, Lady Williams, Lady Dundonald . . . the list is long. The English police called her Scotch Ellen and she continued to appear in the courts and the newspapers from time to time.

By the early twentieth century she had once more crossed the Atlantic to relieve New York and Pittsburgh clergymen of their unused money. In October 1912 she was sentenced to six months in the Blackwell's Island Workhouse in Pittsburgh. By that time she was sixty-four, but still possessed exquisite manners. When Detective Sergeant Hayes arrested her, she wept and then, when that failed, put a curse on him: 'I pray God to curse you, waking and sleeping, standing and lying, eating and drinking as long as you live.' Mrs Gordon Baillie used a crutch on her way to the police station, but when that got her no sympathy she stuck it under her arm and strode along the street like a woman in her prime. Even at that date her career was a mystery: the American police believed that she had been married to Captain John Hill of the British Army, but that they later divorced.

So who and what was Mrs Gordon Baillie? A cold-hearted fraudster? A class warrior? A woman who lived by her wits? An actress who strutted her stuff across a worldwide stage? Or was she a genuinely compassionate person who merely enjoyed the high life? The evidence is mixed and confusing. It was said that she was illiterate, or at any rate a very poor writer; she had four or five children but may not have been married, or may have been married twice; she mingled with the richest in the land, but many thought her untrustworthy; she gave money to poor crofters and swindled anybody who crossed her path. Admire her or loathe her, there can be no doubt that Mrs Gordon Baillie, under any of her forty-plus aliases, was one of the most fascinating criminals of the nineteenth century. Peterhead may not be proud of her, but the town should certainly remember her.

Although Aberdeenshire produced these amazing, audacious women, some of the men could also create clever ploys to steal by fraud.

Husbands in Trouble

Detectives Wyness and Innes worked in Aberdeen in the 1880s. Most of their cases were routine: searching the pawnbrokers for stolen property or asking questions about simple theft or casual assaults, but occasionally they would come across an incident that had caused real distress, which made them keen to find the perpetrator. One such case occurred in June 1883.

Four people had been defrauded of all the ready cash they had, and in a manner calculated to cause two of them a great deal of worry. The first victim was Mrs Cooke of 8 Cotton Street, Aberdeen. At about half past ten on Friday, 1 June 1883, there was a rapid knock at her door. When she answered, a tall young man in the working clothes of Hall, Russell the shipbuilders stood there, obviously agitated. He did not say much, but handed Mrs Cooke a handwritten note and waited for an answer. The note stated:

> *Dear Wife – send me all the money that you have about you for i am in trouble i will tell you all about it when i come home poot the money into something so as not to let the man know what i have sent him for i do not want to let anyone know at present or i will be thrown into prison and i am sure you would not like that so send me all the money that you can spare at once or perhaps it will be too late from your husband JAMES COOKE.*

Cooke was a foreman moulder at Hall, Russell. Presumably Mrs Cooke was not used to seeing her husband's handwriting, for as soon as she saw the note she became agitated. She scoured the house and raised £6, which she handed over right away. She did not think to question the bearer or the accuracy of the content of the letter. The man took the money and vanished. He did not go far, however, for a few moments later he knocked at the door of Mrs Weatherspoon, a few houses away in the same street. He handed her another note with exactly the same message, except this one was signed 'your Husband A. Weatherspoon'.

Mrs Weatherspoon was equally upset and managed to raise thirty shillings. To encourage her search, the man said that 'Sandy is in the office wi' the maisters'.

When he had the money, the man vanished; both wives thought he would be hurrying back to the yard to secure the release of their husbands from whatever bother they had got themselves into. Both wives were relieved when their husbands came home for lunch at one o'clock, as they always did, but were very surprised to hear there had been no trouble at the work. The whole thing had been an elaborate fraud.

The Weatherspoons and the Cookes reported the incidents to the police, and then detectives Wyness and Innes were on the case. They wired a description of the fraudster to all the police stations in the area and as far south as Perth, in case he should take the train away. Alexander Weatherspoon thought the man could be a fellow labourer named James Stuart, a twenty-four-year-old ex-Scots Guard who had fought in the Egyptian campaign of 1882. The detectives found out that he lived in Schoolhill, but did not know the precise address. They made a house-to-house search of the area until they found his home in Donald's Court.

There was a young servant girl present when the police arrived. She said that Stuart lodged in the house with his brother and she took charge of it in their absence. She told the police that Stuart had sent her away while he changed from his working clothes into his Sunday-best suit. Armed with this information, Wyness and Innes asked if anybody had seen a well-dressed man in the area.

Somebody had seen such a man board a tram in George Street, heading for Kittybrewster. As he had alighted there, the detectives asked at the railway station, but no such man had boarded a train that day. The next logical step was to check the pubs, which the police did, asking questions in each one. They drew a blank, so returned to the tramway workers again. A conductor remembered a tall, well-dressed man having left his car at Woodside, so the detectives hurried there. They found that Stuart had boarded the three o'clock train for Peterhead. They checked the train times and found that the train was nearly due to arrive, so wired the police in Peterhead and warned them of Stuart's approach.

Inspector Richardson picked up Stuart as soon as he disembarked. Stuart claimed to be named Richard Harper, and when the police searched him they found £7 in his pockets. The police brought him into Aberdeen, where a number of workers from Hall, Russell waited at the station to see him arrive.

The case came before Sheriff Brown at the Aberdeen Sheriff Criminal Court on Wednesday, 4 July 1883. As well as defrauding the Cookes and Weatherspoons, Stuart had also stolen £1 from his brother before he left his home. Charles Buxton, appearing for his defence, said that as all the money had been recovered, nobody had suffered by the crime, and it had been a one-off and not a systematic fraud. He had been over six years in the Guards, where he had two good-conduct medals. The Sheriff gave him four months.

Although Aberdeenshire seemed to breed clever fraudsters, there were other types of people who committed more direct crimes.

12
Fishermen and Crime

The nineteenth century saw a tremendous expansion in the Scottish fishing industry. One major branch was the herring fishing, which saw boats from every port and creek in the country sail out to follow the great silver shoals that swam around the coasts of Britain. As well as creating major employment for the tens of thousands of fishermen, boat builders and the fishwives who gutted and packed the catch, the industry could create problems. Hundreds of boats and thousands of men would descend on some normally quiet coastal town, drink the pubs dry and sometimes hugely increase the crime rate.

The First Fraserburgh Riot

Usually fishermen ashore were more concerned with getting the boats and nets ready for sea, drinking and occasionally flirting with the younger fisherwomen, but occasionally there were outbreaks of violence. In August 1874, the visiting fishermen decided to riot in Fraserburgh. It was Saturday, 1 August, traditionally a day that the fishing boats did not go to sea, and the fishermen instead found their way to the public houses of the town.

By the evening there were hundreds of drunk or merry fishermen, and inevitably some were looking for trouble. The fishing had not been a success that week, which had led to some disgruntlement. Added to that was the high percentage of Highlanders among the fishermen, a fact that could lead to a culture clash with their Lowland hosts. In this case it was a tiny spark that started the trouble. A fisherman from Portmahomack named Walter Grant had been drinking and fighting in the brewery in Shore Street. The police picked him up and carried him to the cells as the other fishermen watched but did not interfere. At about twenty to eleven that night, the drink began to affect a twenty-five-year-old Stornoway fisherman named John Buchanan, and he attacked his companions. Sergeant Alexander Grant led six officers to the scene, but when he surveyed the situation he decided that an arrest might make things worse, so advised Buchanan's companions to take him home before he caused any more trouble.

However, as his friends were escorting him past the Saltoun Arms Hotel, Buchanan broke free and punched Grant to the ground. The other police closed on him, but Buchanan was tough and fighting mad. He felled Constable Dow next and kicked him evilly in the belly. When the other police grappled him, a crowd of around 400 fishermen came to Buchanan's rescue. As the police looked to be swamped by the mob, Inspector John Richardson arrived; he advised that they allow Buchanan to go free. Jubilant, the fishermen took hold of Buchanan and hustled him into his Back Street lodgings.

The fishermen were not yet finished. A few moments later there was renewed trouble on Back Street. Inspector Richardson sent his men to calm things down, but the mob was ugly and looking for trouble. The recently released Buchanan was prominent, as well as a man named Murdo McLean. Yelling in Gaelic, the mob attacked the police with fists, boots and cudgels. Constables Dow and Middleton were both involved in trying to quell the riot. Dow had the worst of it, being knocked down in a close and then having the fishermen crowd around him and stick the boot in. He got up, but the fishermen had taken a dislike to him and knocked him down again; when he got up he tried to escape to the police office, but when the crowd chased him he had to duck into the Saltoun Arms and stay there with the door bolted for safety. The police drew their batons and fought back, eventually quelling the trouble, if at the cost of a few broken heads among the Highlanders.

After that incident, Richardson split his force, with three men in Back Street and three in Broad Street. Only temporarily subdued, the mob charged over to the police office in the town house building in Broad Street, with three men – John McRae, James Innes and Ewan McKay – among the ringleaders. The police office and the cells were on the ground floor of the building, with stairs leading to the court house and the town house above. There were also some residential rooms on the first floor, where Sergeant Grant lived. The Hebrideans believed that Buchanan was being held inside and demanded his release. As the first missiles bounced from the walls, Richardson ordered Gaelic-speaking Constable Macpherson to inform the crowd that Buchanan was in his own house and not in a cell, but Macpherson's words were either not believed, unheeded or not heard above the hubbub.

Howling in anger, the crowd stoned the police office, smashed the window frames and -panes, and demanded the release of the prisoner. Sergeant Grant was next to try and inform them that Buchanan was not there, but they attacked him with punches and pushes. The Portmahomack man Walter Grant was in his cell, roaring the crowd on, but it seemed that the Hebridean fishermen were only interested in one of their own, not a man from the east coast.

The police who had been in Back Street were unable to get through the crowd and into the office so had to go round to a back entrance.

Unable to leave, the police prepared for a siege. They barricaded the door, drew their batons and waited for the inevitable charge. It came. The fishermen unshipped a mast from a fishing boat and used it as a battering ram to smash through the door. They milled about in the lobby, shouting and swearing as they broke the gas brackets and kicked in the door to the police office.

Hoping to assuage the anger of the crowd, Inspector Richardson told one of the English speakers that Buchanan had been released and was in his lodgings. He took some of the Hebrideans to Buchanan's lodgings to show them. When he returned to the office the crowd was completing the demolition of the building, urged on by a Fraserburgh carter named Innes. The fishermen wrecked the lower floor of the police office. The table, desk and two chairs were smashed and hurled out of the broken windows into the street below; uniforms were ripped to pieces; and the books were shredded. Even the cash box, complete with cash, was cheerfully tossed out into the street below. While some were rifling through everything, others banged on Grant's iron-lined cell door. When they saw Richardson, they threatened to murder him unless he released Grant.

Given that his headquarters were packed with drunken, shouting men, it is not surprising that Richardson agreed, on condition that the fishermen left the office. Although the men in the lobby believed him and began to file out, the mob outside had no idea what was happening and fought to get in, with blows and curses on both sides. In the meantime, Constable Macpherson again tried to shout sense into the rioters in their native Gaelic, but instead they tried to push him aside to reach the offices upstairs. He heard a Gaelic speaker say, 'We can do no more; we must set fire to it.'

The crowd knocked down a constable named Gray, kicked him and punched him, so he gradually forced to the fringes of the fracas. Together with Macpherson he drew his baton and laid about freely. He saw McLean in the thick of the crowd.

Sergeant Grant's wife and mother lived in the rooms directly above the police office, and Gray was not sure what would happen if the crowd got up there, so he bounded up the stairs, rescued them and, unable to press through the fishermen, opened a back window and handed them onto the slates of the roof. It was hardly an ideal place to be on a draughty night, but the women were safer there than amongst the crowd. By that time the gas was out, so there were no lights; the figures in the crowd were dim, and the noise levels were rising all the time.

When the crowd tried to get upstairs, Macpherson stepped onto the stairs, drew his baton and knocked the leading man to the ground, where he lay stunned and bleeding until his friends carried him away. He saw the recently released Walter Grant playing a leading part in the crowd, with a man named McRae as well.

Prudently, knowing he could not control the rioters, Inspector Richardson mentally noted faces and names, slipped out of the back window and searched the town for Major Ross, the chief constable. Limping from an injured knee and trying to disguise his uniform from the crowd, Sergeant Grant joined him.

Many of the Fraserburgh people watched the riot. Francis Davidson, a carter, saw the fishermen attacking the police and using spars from boats to try to break down the door of the police office. A saddler called James Murray saw McKay breaking windows of the police station with a long pole, while a carter called Alexander had seen the crowd attacking Constable Dow. A baker named George Ironside heard Innes shout 'down with the buggers'.

Shortly after the sacking of the police office, somebody began a rumour that the Volunteers had been called out, and the fishermen began to disperse. By now it was raining and the fishermen presented a miserable sight as they sloped home, wet, downcast and rapidly sobering up. They had left the police office with two outer doors and four inner doors smashed open, all the front windows shattered, the interior plasterwork damaged, the chandeliers half ripped from the ceiling and damaged by thrown stones, and the interior wrecked. All the police had suffered some sort of injury, but none serious.

As the riot subsided, Major Ross, the Aberdeenshire Chief Constable, appeared alongside Mr Anderson, the police magistrate. Ross enrolled two-dozen special constables and instituted patrols on the streets until about three in the morning, but there was no further trouble. Fifty soldiers of the 92nd and 93rd Highlanders arrived from Aberdeen, and when fifteen police constables reinforced Fraserburgh's small force the authorities felt strong enough to make two arrests. John Masson, a cooper from Stornoway, and James Innes, a local carter, were placed in the cells. The police wanted other Stornoway men, but were not immediately successful in arresting them. It was believed they sailed back to the Hebrides. The soldiers only remained one day and returned to Aberdeen.

Six men were eventually arrested: John Masson and Innes; plus John McRae, a twenty-four-year-old cooper from Stornoway; twenty-six-year-old Ewan Mackay from Tongue, in Sutherland; John Buchanan, a twenty-five-year-old fisherman from Stornoway; and Murdoch McLean, a twenty-four-year-old and also a Stornoway fisherman. They were tried at the Circuit Court in Aberdeen on 16 September. McLean and Buchanan did not turn up and were outlawed; the others pleaded not guilty. The charges against McRae were found not proven; James Innes was given nine months and Ewan Mackay twelve months in jail. The supposed ringleader, Colin McLean, was hauled before Sheriff Comrie Thomson in February 1875. McLean claimed he had suffered sunstroke that day, but Thomson gave him fifteen months in jail.

The Second Fraserburgh Riot

Sail-powered fishing boats were heavily dependent on the weather: too little or too much wind meant they could not be put to sea. The night of Thursday, 21 July 1881 was wild and wet and windy, so the hundreds of boats that were in Fraserburgh harbour remained there, while the crews were idle. However, shore-bound fishermen with money usually graduated to the nearest public house, and these men were no exception.

There were between two and three thousand Highland, or 'stranger', fishermen in the port and at just after eleven o'clock they realised that most of the pubs were shut. A large crowd gathered outside the Saltoun Hotel and shouted for admission. The handful of local police watched warily, hoping there would be no repeat of the 1874 riot. When the innkeeper refused to open up, the fishermen lost patience and launched a volley of stones at the windows. After a while they grew tired of that and debouched along Broad Street and Seaforth Street to the Station Hotel.

Once again they began hammering at the door and demanding entrance to get whisky; they complained that the people inside the hotel would give them neither whisky nor money. However, when the door was opened to let a commercial traveller in, a group of fishermen also pushed through. They demanded a bottle of whisky and threw two shillings on the table. A handful of local police including Inspector Hendry handed the money back and told the fishermen it was after hours, so it was illegal for the hotel to sell them whisky.

The fishermen left, but one said that unless he got proper justice he would 'burn the place down and smash every policeman in the burgh'. The police arrested him and were dragging him along Broad Street to the police office when a crowd of around 100 fishermen stopped them.

In a scenario that must have been familiar to the veterans of the previous riot, the crowd attempted to rescue the prisoner. One of the fishermen yelled out what witnesses thought was 'evidently a war cry', followed by a concerted rush at the police. Somebody cracked Hendry over the head and he fell to the ground. He got up and tried to clear a path to get the prisoner to the police office, with the prisoner being co-operative but the crowd getting in the way. Hendry shoved ahead and opened the office door to bring the prisoner in, but when he looked back he saw the crowd had dragged the prisoner about ten yards away.

The police drew their batons and lunged into the mob to retrieve him. The prisoner grabbed hold of a man's leg and refused to let go, so both were arrested and dragged inside the police office. More fishermen gathered and began to throw stones, bottles and sticks at the office. They threatened to 'take down the office', saying it had been done before and they would do it again. The police told the fishermen that if they went home, the prisoners would be released on bail, as the only charge against them was breach of the peace.

Hendry brought in a fisherman, John McLeod of Lochbroom, to the office and let him watch as the prisoner was set free; he also left the door open so the crowd knew what was happening, but the stones and sticks continued to fly. Constable Lamont was cut on the back of the neck and Constable Mathieson was cut on the mouth. They tried to send the fishermen away again, and when that failed they resorted once more to their batons.

By now it was half past eleven. Ironically, it was the two released prisoners who were most vociferous in urging the crowd to destroy the office. Two fishermen named McIver and McDougal led a number of charges on the police, and in return Hendry gave orders to use the batons on anybody who refused to go away.

Around midnight, McDougal grabbed Constable Rankine's uniform jacket and tried to drag him deeper into the crowd, saying, 'If I had you there' – pointing to the yelling mob behind him – 'you would not take or assist in taking a Highlandman into that office for the next two or three months.' Rankine struggled free, taking many kicks and knocks in the process.

Francis Thomson was a hired fisherman and he saw the crowd outside the inn as the police made the first arrest. He thought it was McIver, who he called 'the black fellow', rather than McDougal who tried to drag Rankine into the crowd. Eventually the crowd began to drift away, in ones and twos and then all together, and the streets of Fraserburgh were left to the wind and rain.

When the case came to Aberdeen Sheriff Court in July 1881, both McIver and McDougal got a £10 fine and three months' hard labour.

It was not only Hebridean fishermen who could cause trouble in Aberdeenshire; sometimes the locals were every bit as capable of creating their own mayhem.

A Violent Family

Alexander Gowl was a forty-six-year-old Aberdeen fisherman with a bad attitude and an unhappy marriage. In September 1894, he was living in Stronach's Close and staying apart from his forty-five-year-old wife, Isabella. She had taken a fancy to drink and a married Dyce cabinetmaker named John Grant. Gowl was not particularly happy with this situation, so when he saw Grant with Isabella he attacked the cabinetmaker. Gowl made such a good job of the matter that he was placed in prison for seven days to cool his temper.

On 14 September 1894, he came out of the cells and returned home to Isabella, who was probably waiting for him with some trepidation. There was some dispute as to exactly what was said next, but no arguing about the end result. According to Gowl, Isabella told him that she had spent the entire week of his incarceration drinking, while Isabella denied she had said any such thing. Gowl also accused her of 'carrying on with a married man', which she also denied.

There is also some dispute about what Gowl said next. A neighbour claimed that Gowl had said he 'would give her as much as she would be of no use to any man', while Gowl denied that. He claimed he had merely said that 'a woman like her ought to be kicked to death'. Apparently that was a lesser penalty. Either way he did his best to carry out both threats, repeatedly kicking his wife in her abdomen with his heavy boots. It seems that Isabella was drunk at the time while Gowl was sober, but the result was that Isabella's lower abdomen was swollen and, according to a neighbour, Mrs Walker, 'as black as a pot'.

Constable Barclay, who came to the scene, thought that Isabella possibly had been cheating on Gowl. When Gowl accused one of the neighbours of helping Isabella with her affairs, he was counter-accused of having an affair himself with a young girl the previous summer.

The case came to trial in the Police Court in September. Isabella was unable to attend on the first date as her injuries kept her in bed, and as some of her wounds had festered, she was still in pain when she eventually did appear. The prosecutor advised that Gowl had a duty 'to get rid' of his wife, for if he continued to 'harbour the same thoughts and intentions' it might lead to murder. Bailie Henderson sent Gowl to prison for twenty-one days.

There was a postscript. The couple split up and Isabella moved to 149 George Street with her cabinetmaker lover, but the quarrel between Grant and Gowl was not yet resolved. In July 1895, Gowl moved back in with Isabella and Grant found himself unwanted and out of the house. On 20 July, Grant came to the George Street house to pick up the clothes he had left there, but he met Gowl in the lobby. Gowl acted first, barging into Grant and pushing him down the first flight of steps in the common stair. When Grant tried to get up, Gowl grabbed him again, but Grant pulled out his pocketknife and rammed it into Gowl's left shoulder. This time it was Grant who appeared before the court and was given three months' hard labour.

Isabella Gowl was certainly no shy innocent; she was quite capable of domestic violence herself. In August 1891, the family was living by the curing station at Point Law, Aberdeen harbour, where both she and her seventeen-year-old daughter Christina were employed at the herring gutting. That month Isabella Gowl was taken to court for assaulting her two daughters, Christina and eight-year-old Isabella.

She was particularly unpleasant to Christina, for after slapping her about the room, she grabbed the girl by the hair and dragged her around the house. A few moments after the assault, Christina fled screaming out of the door, ran to the end of a wooden jetty and threw herself into the sea in an apparent attempt to commit suicide. Two Newhaven fishermen, Henry Rutherford and Charles Wilson, saw her jump in and swam out to rescue her.

Altogether, the Gowl family were probably best left in peace, but they were not alone. In the nineteenth century, Scottish fishermen could be a rough bunch.

Sea Versus Land

On the night of Saturday, 19 July 1881, at Portlethen, eight miles from Stonehaven, there was a stand-up fight between fishermen from Downies and farm lads from the landward districts. The original motive was unclear, but possibly was nothing more than rivalry between young men who worked at sea and their opposite numbers who worked on the land. Three fishermen had attacked some young rural lads and were beating them up when three farm labourers happened to be passing by. The labourers tried to help the youngsters, but the fishermen drew knives and attacked the farm workers, wounding them quite badly. Two of the landsmen, John Kelman and John Bridgeford, worked at Causeyport, near Banchory, and the third, William Wilson, was the foreman at Mains of Portlethen, where the fight took place. One of the Causeyport men was badly hurt with an artery in his arm cut, while the other two landsmen had deep gashes on their arms. The fishermen had aimed at the bodies, but the servants had managed to deflect the knives.

The landsmen reported what happened to Robert Walker, the farmer at Mains of Portlethen, who telegraphed Dr Michie at Cove, who hurried up to help. Walker told the police the next day and three fishermen, Alexander 'Derry' Leiper, aged twenty-six, with George and William Main, were arrested at Downies village and placed in Stonehaven prison.

Overall, it was best not to cross Scottish fisherfolk in the nineteenth century. Men and women were eminently capable of looking after themselves.

13
Prostitution

Nineteenth-century Britain has a reputation for sexual repression and high morals, with 'Victorian Values' a byword for all that is upstanding and correct in society. However, the reality revealed by the scrape of a prostitute's painted nails would curl the hair of the most respectable Victorian. Every city and probably most towns were home to a thriving population of prostitutes.

There were many types of prostitutes, from those who serviced gentlemen and lived in comfort to those who frequented the dockside alleys and dark closes and spent their lives in squalor. Sometimes a woman could start at the top, but as her looks faded she would end up pressing her back against some festering wall while a drunken seaman expended the pent-up lust of a long voyage in a few panting moments. Nevertheless, most prostitutes were not full-time professionals, but women with no option; prostitution was a hard necessity rather than a career choice at a time when most work open to women was low paid, repetitive and harsh.

The Victorians were as concerned about prostitution and its attendant evils of disease as they were about juvenile crime and drunkenness. In June 1857, the Aberdeen police commissioners discussed what powers they possessed to put down brothels and prostitution. At that time there were an estimated 500 prostitutes living in Aberdeen, working in about 100 licensed premises. There was some disagreement about the best course to take, as a few years before there had been an attempt to clean up the streets by arresting any woman found on them after a certain time: in other words, subjecting women to a curfew. That attempt had failed, as the many innocent women who had been swept into the police office had strongly objected. The police had quickly scrapped the system. With that recent memory to embarrass them, the commissioners decided that it was the job of the Kirk to control vice, not the police.

However, others were equally concerned and even heavier-handed. In 1864, Parliament passed the Contagious Diseases Act, which gave the police sweeping powers to arrest prostitutes and have them inspected for venereal diseases. This Act only applied to some ports and towns where there was a large military presence. Once again, completely innocent women were swept into the net along with hardened streetwalkers, with the additional humiliation and genuine trauma of an internal examination. It was not the police's job to prove the women's guilt; the women had to try to prove their innocence. Those women who were found to be diseased were secured in a locked hospital until they were judged clean enough to be released to the hordes of innocent men who waited their attentions. The men were not subject to any such restrictive act. Not surprisingly, there was a hurricane of protest against this draconian Act, which was repealed in 1886.

According to the American historian Judith Walkowitz in *Prostitution and Victorian Society*, any British city could have one prostitute for every thirty-six people. It was also believed that up to one third of the soldiers in Queen Victoria's army carried venereal disease, but as marriage was not encouraged for private soldiers, nor for officers under a certain rank, sexual licence was hardly surprising among healthy young men. As late as 1898, Kitchener ordered that every soldier be warned about sexual disease.

In Aberdeen, the police targeted brothels when the neighbours complained about them, and arrested women for 'loitering' on the streets. Women seemed to run most of the city's brothels or 'disorderly houses', but some were run by a partnership of a woman and a man. For example, in August 1829 Elizabeth Birnie and John Hay were each sent to Bridewell for fourteen days and then banished from Aberdeen for a year for keeping a brothel.

The brothels were not concentrated in any one place but were scattered all over the centre of Aberdeen. In the 1850s one of the most notorious was in Frederick Street, but they could be virtually anywhere. In August 1879, fifty-eight-year-old Margaret Macdonald was charged with keeping a brothel in Flourmill Lane. Thirteen prostitutes were found in her house. Detectives Innes and Wyness said the house had been a brothel for years. When they raided the place, the detectives said she was keeping thieves and prostitutes; Macdonald said she had 'no thieves but I can't deny harbouring prostitutes'. Alex Badenoch, a tailor, said he often passed the house, especially on a Sunday, and it was a notorious brothel, particularly when the militia were around. He had not heard much foul language, but the girls had sometimes accosted him and he had seen many young girls standing with soldiers about the place. Macdonald was fined £10 with the option of sixty days in prison.

On 12 October 1880, the Police Court heard a case against William Kirton, who kept a public house at Green. He was accused of allowing women of 'notoriously bad fame' to assemble in his pub. The police had heard rumours, and on 21 September 1880 Inspector Ewan and Detectives Wyness and Innes held a snap inspection. In one room the police found one man in the company of two women, in another two women and two men, and in a third room tucked away in the back they found two women and three men. The rooms had no doors, but were separated by curtains. All the seven women were known to the police as prostitutes.

Kirton claimed he had not known that the women had bad characters and anyway there was no assembling or meeting in the accepted sense of the words. He also said he was entitled to serve anybody he liked at an open bar. Detective Innes returned three days later, on 24 September, and again found the place full of women of the same profession. Mrs Kirton told Innes that a businessman had assured her that she was legally permitted to serve such women. That statement proved that Kirton knew exactly what line of business the women were in. Bailie Alexander Duffus fined Kirton twenty-five shillings with expenses or fourteen days in prison.

There was another well-known brothel in Shiprow in 1880 where Robert Bennison harboured five known prostitutes. In November the following year, Elizabeth Christie denied she had kept prostitutes at her house at 46 Netherkirkgate. However, the police brought forward evidence that the neighbours had complained that her house was used as a brothel, with numerous men and women of 'bad character' being frequent visitors. At least two of the women who had been acting as prostitutes were only fifteen years old, and they testified that their customers paid Christie for their services. When Christie appeared at the Police Court, Bailie Walker said it was a very aggravated case as not only was the house used for immoral purposes but Christie had also used it to train up girls for immoral purposes, thereby ruining their body and soul. He imposed a fine of £10 or sixty days in jail.

In the spring and summer of 1893, Mary Reid kept a brothel in Burnett's Close. She pleaded not guilty at the Police Court, but the police had frequent complaints from people about money being stolen from them in the house: a ship's officer had had a gold ring stolen from him there. She was sent to prison for two months. These examples were just the tip of the iceberg as the police struggled to remove prostitution from the city. For instance, in 1863 alone upwards of twenty brothels were closed down and the number of females known to be prostitutes reduced from more than 400 to just 200.

The second prong of the police assault on prostitution targeted the streetwalkers. These women would loiter in certain places and approach men who looked as if they were lonely or perhaps too drunk to realise what was happening. The campaign against these women was relentless. For example, at the Police Court on 9 February 1830, two streetwalkers, Mary Moir and Elizabeth Henry, were given thirty and sixty days respectively in Bridewell for 'conducting themselves in a riotous and disorderly manner' on Broad Street.

The late 1870s and the 1880s saw the police inject more vigour into their campaign against streetwalking. For example, in 1879, twenty-seven-year-old Margaret Duthie of Flourmill Lane and thirty-year-old Barbara Watt were both fined ten shillings for loitering. The same crime cost Cecilia Scorgie and Margaret Grant of Flourmill Lane ten shillings each on 23 September 1880, while in October 1880 Elspeth Robb, Helen Mann and Ann Low were fined twenty-one shillings for loitering in Shiprow. There were many others.

Sometimes the same woman would appear on numerous occasions. Ann Burke of Exchequer Court, described as a 'young woman', was one such. On 11 September 1880, she was fined twenty-one shillings for loitering, only to be picked up again in Union Street eleven days later and fined another twenty shillings and again in St Nicholas Street on 18 October and fined twenty-one shillings again, with an alternative of a jail sentence. If she was able to pay these fines, then she must have made enough money by selling herself. It is unlikely that any factory or mill worker could have pocketed sufficient wages to avoid prison, which is a pointer to the reason so many women fell into prostitution. If the authorities had targeted the cause – starvation wages for women – rather than the effects, they may have had more success.

14
Juvenile Crime

Authorities of the nineteenth century had two major preoccupations: drunkenness and juvenile crime. The respectable majority of the country was concerned that a whole new generation of lawbreakers, a criminal class, could emerge among them, unless the youth of the day were steered towards a regular lifestyle of hard work and religion.

Speaking in September 1878, the Circuit Judge Lord Deas said he 'could quite well remember when there were a great many more criminals and much more crime in Aberdeen than there is now … there were persons in this town of the female sex whose whole business was to train up young thieves, and consequently there existed what was properly called a criminal population; but it appears to me that there was now no criminal class – no criminal class properly speaking as compared with what there was in former years.'

It is possible that His Lordship was referring to youths such as the gang of pickpockets that haunted the city in the early winter of 1848. The police caught at least two, Peter Martin and George Steven, in January, but it is unlikely that the sixty-day sentence they each received would be much of a deterrent.

Lord Deas thought the improvement since his young days was due to the attention paid to the education and moral teaching of the young. If they were not trained when young they would never be honest. He claimed that in all his experience he never yet knew an old thief reform. His motto seemed to be 'catch them young' and that was what the Victorians tried to do, with a combination of education, Christianity and removing the vulnerable from temptation.

Juvenile Plunderers

In the early decades of the century, Aberdeen, in common with other urban centres, was frequently plagued by what the *Aberdeen Journal* of 21 December 1831 termed 'juvenile plunderers who are continually prowling about our streets'.

One example of this was on the evening of Saturday, 1 November 1834, when the Justice Street watchman saw a prostitute offering a new pair of boots for sale to any passers-by. The watchman took her to the watch house and asked from where she had got the boots. She said that a group of young boys had sold them very cheaply to her, and when the watchman asked the boys' names, she mentioned one called James Sangster. The watchman knew that boy as a habitual thief. He arrested Sangster and two of his friends. Sangster was jailed for forty days and the others for thirty days. They had stolen the boots from Birse the shoemaker in George Street, who had been unaware of their loss.

Sometimes these juvenile thieves struck out alone. One such was Robert McAndrew. Fagin would have been proud of Robert McAndrew. He was a bright, intelligent boy with sparkling eyes and the ability to learn new skills in a short time. Unfortunately he was also vicious, bad-tempered and a habitual thief. He was born in Banff around 1838, with his father working on the railways. Railway work was not always the safest, and when his father was badly injured his working days ended. Young Robert was left to himself and he chose the left-hand path.

He first came to the notice of the court, if not the police, on 10 August 1848 when he was given sixty days for theft. That was a hefty sentence for a ten-year-old and gives rise to the suspicion that he was already a known face. At that period it was normal for very young boys to be working, but McAndrew did not have a job of any description.

On 26 December that same year, McAndrew was caught picking the pocket of a too-wary lady and the next day he again appeared before the Police Court. He was again given sixty days in jail to think over his misdeeds. The imprisonment was so effective that it prevented McAndrew from being caught for just over a week after his release. On 7 March 1849, he was again arrested and appeared for the third time at the Police Court.

This time McAndrew's two months' free lodging was for stealing money from a shop. He may have been a habitual thief, but he was not a very efficient one, to judge by the number of times he was caught. He was out again on 6 May and ready to haunt the streets in search of prey. In the middle of June he was again caught, but because of his previous convictions he was at the Sheriff Court this time, for stealing a cravat from outside a shop.

Perhaps McAndrew expected a longer sentence than those he had previously been given, but the fifteen months he was handed may have come as a bit of a shock. In September 1850, he was free and in Aberdeen, and already a hardened convict who was not yet in his teen years. For a few months his life altered as he was taken in by an experimental industrial school in Lech Street. In the three months or so that he was there, McAndrew proved his intelligence by learning to read and polishing up his rough attitude. However, fate stepped in to block his progress, as the finance for the school dried up and McAndrew joined the other unfortunates of society back on the streets and bereft of hope and opportunity.

From shoplifting and pickpocketing, McAndrew moved on to burglary, and on 18 January 1851 he broke into a house in the Green and took away a gold ring. There was a key left lying in the house, and that gave McAndrew access to a lockfast chest, where he found a purse, two seals and another gold ring. Again he was caught and this time was hauled before the High Court. He was sent away to prison for two years. He was just thirteen years old.

Transportation

Sometimes the punishment seemed extraordinarily harsh for the crime. In April 1844, two boys named George Crerar and John Sievewright were hauled before the Circuit Court and charged with theft. The evidence against them was quite clear. On 13 September 1843 they had broken into a shop in King Street and stolen a pilot coat (a heavy coat used by seamen), and followed that by breaking into the house of Mr Clark in Clark's Court, Upperkirkgate. They stole two silk umbrellas. Witnesses saw both boys outside the shop, and also outside Clark's house.

Sievewright pawned the coat the same day, using his own name on the pawn ticket, and was also seen carrying two umbrellas. Crerar pawned an umbrella, and was seen carrying another on the following day. As both boys were known thieves they were tried at the Circuit Court, where Crerar pleaded guilty to stealing the umbrella and Sievewright denied both thefts.

Not surprisingly, both boys were found guilty. Crerar was given eighteen months in jail and Sievewright seven years' transportation. He sailed on the convict ship *Ratcliffe* for Van Diemen's Land in July 1848.

Stealing From the Army

Girls could be just as bad as boys. In the first week of October 1845, a young girl named Jane Lynch broke into the sergeants' mess of the 87th regiment and stole all the knives and forks, which she pawned through the town. She was traced by the pawn tickets and taken to the Police Court, where she was sent to prison for ten days.

Forgery by a Child

Although petty thieving and general mischief were common, children were capable of all sorts of crime. On 1 March 1883, a young man passed a cheque for £49 18s. However, the teller was a bit dubious that the youngster was indeed A. Bowman, as the signature on the cheque claimed, and he called his manager. The police arrived and took the supposed A. Bowman away for questioning.

His name was John Wyness Thomson and he was just fourteen years old. When the case came to court his defending solicitor, Mr Burnett, said he was of 'extreme youth' and he 'did not belong to the class with which they were familiar'. Apparently the better 'class' of the culprit was 'a case for the leniency of the court'. Lord Craighill gave him six months.

Children in Prison

For much of the nineteenth century, children were imprisoned very much like their elders, often mixing with hardened criminals three and four times their age. However, there were many adults who did not agree with putting children into jail. One such was the Reverend Daniel Baxter, Chaplain of Aberdeen prisons. In his quarterly report of December 1848, Baxter spoke of one boy, whom he did not name. This boy was 'imprisoned for the first time' and 'though only twelve years old has been known to some of the police officers for the last year and a half as habit and repute a thief . . . seems a hardened little fellow'.

Rather than sympathise with the boy, Baxter stated that while 'in prison he had better milk better broth more porridge and a warmer bed than at home . . . another important difference between his father's house and the prison – that in the former he had often been beaten – in the latter never. In his case the prison is no longer an object of terror and reformation in sixty days is out of the question.'

Baxter argued for corporal punishment for such boys, or perhaps a harsher regime in the prison. Alexander Thomson, Convenor of the Committee on Juvenile Delinquency, spoke at Banchory House in November that same year. He said that every large town had 'a certain youthful criminal population growing up from infancy in idleness'. Thomson believed that short prison sentences were useless and recommended that sentences of a year as 'the minimum in which time there might be a reasonable hope of making salutary impressions and conveying useful instructions'.

However, Thomson was not advocating an altogether sterner approach. He believed that a combination of education and Christianity would save most children from the miseries of a life of crime. He hoped to see 'a great deal done with the youthful criminal and for him before recourse is had to prison at all'. Thomson advocated that rather than order a child to prison, a magistrate should send any recalcitrant child to school. The children were to be given 'abundant religious instruction . . . secular knowledge suited to future prospects . . . train them up in honest industry to enable them to be independent in future life'. In common with general practice of the period, Thomson recommended that they be encouraged to attend by 'the perfect certainty of receiving a whipping at school . . . on each occasion of wilful desertion'. There were limits, though, as girls older than twelve and boys older than fourteen were to be free from the threat of corporal punishment.

Once properly educated and disciplined to the system, the majority of these boys and girls were not expected to be received into the mainstream of society. Instead they were to be 'fitted for emigration to our colonies'. It would be interesting to know what process of logic led to that conclusion.

School Break

The idea of industrial schools was to bring in boys who had a poor home life and train them up to be useful members of society. However, they were also places where boys who had criminal tendencies could meet and trade ideas. In the summer of 1878, two teenage boys were among the many incarcerated inside the Skene Square Industrial School in Aberdeen. These boys were Alexander Mitchell Berry and Neil Smith, both aged fourteen. Neither was happy in the school, and in the middle of July they broke out and planned to put as much distance as possible between themselves and Aberdeen. However, to do that they needed money and neither boy had any, so they had to either earn some, which would be a slow process, or steal some, which was far quicker and probably their preferred option.

The inmates of the school were allowed a modicum of freedom, so both boys knew their way around the immediate locality. They had found Coutt's grocer's shop in Crown Street and thought they knew how to break in. Rather than enter by the door or the window, they opened the cover of a coal chute in the pavement above, pulled the cover shut behind them and squeezed along the narrow tunnel that led to the cellar below. A wall separated them from the cellar of the grocer's shop next door, but there was a boy-sized hole high up. They slipped through, scurried up a handy ladder to the shop above, and found a whole assortment of delights, from boiled sweets to sherbet. However, neither of the boys wasted time over such things but made straight to the till.

Berry took the £4 that was there – equivalent to a month's wages for a skilled man and the boys made their way back out. They were very careful to put everything back in its proper place so there was no evidence that they had ever been there. When they reached the bottom of the coal chute, Smith pushed Berry in front and he negotiated the slippery slide and lifted the cover that gave access to the street. Unfortunately, his timing could hardly have been worse.

Just as the cover opened, a man passed by. He saw the cover lift and a coal-smeared face peer out; the cover closed again, only to reopen. Berry climbed out, glanced around and stretched down to help Smith, but saw he was being watched, yelled for Smith not to come out yet and ran for his life. The man opened the hatch, hauled Smith out and handed him to the police. The Police Court gave him ten days in jail and five years at Old Mills Reformatory.

Berry was more fortunate and eluded capture. He escaped Aberdeen and found sanctuary with an aunt in Collieston, a fishing village fifteen miles north of the city. He was there for a while, but left the day before the police came looking for him. He departed with twenty-five shillings that belonged to a lodger of his aunt; Berry had picked the man's pocket when the two were out swimming. Berry used the money, or other funds he had stolen, to take a train to London. After a few days there, he returned to Scotland and stayed with friends at Glassel, by Banchory, in Kincardineshire, but somebody whispered his where-abouts to the police and Sergeant Macpherson arrested him. He was also sent to prison for ten days followed by five years in Old Mills.

Reform School Riot

Reformatories were intended to reform the minds and habits of those young people who were sent there. They imposed a strict regime of learning and discipline that was intended to prepare the youngsters for life outside, but naturally many of the inmates were not happy at having their lives restricted. By their very nature, reformatories were intended for youngsters who had either failed to conform to mainstream life or those who the authorities thought might follow a life of crime. Youngsters who had already committed an offence were sent to reformatories, while those who were deemed neglected at home were sent to an industrial school. The normal procedure was that children convicted of a crime would be sent to prison for a few days, then ordered to the reformatory for a period of two years or more.

With all these factors taken into consideration, it is not surprising that some of these establishments should be powder kegs of tension, just waiting for the right spark to explode. The Old Mills Reformatory for Boys had been founded in 1857. It taught a range of skills, including agriculture, weaving, tailoring and shoemaking. Under its long-serving governor, Robert Simpson, Old Mills was reckoned to be one of the most successful reformatories in Scotland, and was largely self-funding through its inmates' labours. However, on 4 May 1882, some of the boys mutinied, set fire to the weaving shop and then absconded.

The outbreak happened when Simpson was absent in Aberdeen and George Bain, the reformatory farm manager, was in charge. The boys had a morning break that ended at quarter to twelve, and Bain was near the weaver's shed to ensure everything ran smoothly. He heard somebody shout out 'fire' and saw smoke rising from the shed roof. The workshops for shoemaking, tailoring and weaving were in a block at the back of the main building, so there was little chance of a fire spreading down to the main establishment, but it was still dangerous to have scores of wild young boys running around. Bain sent a farm worker named Florence to warn the authorities in Aberdeen. Florence must have stuck in his spurs, for he covered the two and a half miles by noon.

The flames spread even quicker than news of the mutiny, and three of the workshops were in flames by the time the police and fire brigade arrived. There were 136 boys at the institution and they crowded round to watch the fun. The staff tried to fight the flames, with the matron, Mrs Campbell, fetching buckets while Bain unrolled the reformatory's hose. The water gushed out for a few seconds and then abruptly halted: one of the boys had cut the hose. When Mrs Campbell saw a group of boys charging upstairs 'where they had no business to be' she threatened to set the dog on them. Moments later a second fire started in the loft above the weaver's shop. There was chaos for a while as one of the boys threw a stool at the head of a teacher named John Jeffrey.

Major Ross, the police superintendent, brought a brace of sergeants and a number of constables to see what all the fuss was about. The fire brigade also arrived and pushed through the boys; some of the inmates helped, some refused to help, but only when the flames were quelled did the staff call the roll: ten of the inmates had vanished. Bain ordered the remaining boys into the schoolroom and the police guarded the exits in case any more inmates decided they had experienced enough education. The search for the escapees and the enquiry into the circumstances behind the trouble began simultaneously. Simpson must have been an unhappy man when the Lord Provost Esslemont and a gaggle of assorted councillors also arrived to see what had happened.

There had been a riot in the Duke Street Reformatory in Glasgow in January, and ever since the boys heard the news they had been restless. Some of the older boys had gathered in small knots to whisper together, with the staff afraid they were planning trouble. Robert Simpson described the atmosphere in the reformatory as 'uneasy' at this time. He had spoken to the boys individually and in groups to try and calm the place down, but the underlying tension continued. On 4 May, three days before the fire, the first outbreak had occurred. At seven in the evening the boys had gathered in the main hall for supper. There were nine long tables in the room, each numbered, and Simpson stood at the end of table number four.

Alexander Donald was one of the older boys. He was sixteen years old and originally from Dundee. He sat at the number two table, about three metres away from Simpson. While Simpson's back was turned, Donald lifted his porridge tin and threw it. It struck Simpson a glancing blow on the side of the head and the lukewarm porridge ran down his face and body. A second later, a two-foot-long iron bar also whirled through the air. It grazed Simpson's head and clattered onto the ground behind him. Simpson turned around and saw Donald advancing towards him, yelling and holding an iron divider. When Simpson met him halfway, Donald grabbed the ladle from the porridge tureen and smashed it against his elbow, following that by throwing the tureen against Simpson's legs. Simpson grappled with him, held him tight and shouted for somebody to help take him away. John Jeffrey joined in and wrestled Donald to a bedroom, where he was locked in for the night. Simpson was left with a cut forehead and a bruised and throbbing arm.

The next morning a boy named Johnstone reported that some of the inmates had attempted to set the west dormitory on fire. An inspection found that a blanket had been thrust into the roof space above the water closet and set on fire. Fortunately the flames had only scorched one of the joists and had not spread further. Simpson travelled into Aberdeen on the Monday to report all that had happened, and when he got back to the reformatory shortly after half past twelve he found the shoemaker's shop, carpet-shoe shop and weaving shop ablaze.

In the meantime, the ten runaways fled to the woods near the reformatory and quickly changed into clothes they had stolen, and then headed south, possibly intending to catch a train to Dundee or Edinburgh. Sergeants Brandie and Adam, with Constable Middleton of the Aberdeenshire Constabulary, removed their uniforms and disguised themselves as cattle dealers before they began to track them down. Other policemen and volunteers scoured the local woods and farmland in case the boys were merely lying low.

The escapees made it relatively easy for the police by leaving a trail of discarded reformatory clothing. They also left their footprints in ploughed fields, stole a number of minor items, remained together and carried heavy cudgels. Not surprisingly, the local people were more than willing to help the police trace this formidable group of youths. The youngest of the boys, fifteen-year-old James Bell, was unable to keep pace with the rest, so they abandoned him. The police scooped him up, barefoot and disconsolate, as he ploughed through a bog near Hazelhead. In 1877, Bell had been convicted for stealing a bottle of wine and was sentenced to ten days in prison and five years in Old Mills.

The other runaways came to a toll bridge across the River Dee at Park, near Crathes. Without a penny between them, the boys charged across in a body, leaving the toll keeper staring, but about a mile and a half later Sergeants Brandie and Adam caught them at Durrie, on the south bank of the river. The three ringleaders of the escapees were James McKenzie, Alexander Berry and John Sutherland. When Brandie bundled them onto the train at Park and brought them back to Aberdeen, handcuffed in pairs, Berry admitted, 'I got no sleep last night thinking of the fire we would have today.' Adam told Sutherland he was being taken back to Aberdeen, and Sutherland said that if they were taken back to Old Mills they would 'burn the whole place down'.

Crowds gathered at Aberdeen railway station to watch the boys be escorted from the train and loaded into cabs for the short hop to the police station.

James McKenzie was a seventeen-year-old Aberdonian and one of those blamed with starting the fire. He was not the best-behaved inmate at the reformatory, being a poor worker and frequently in trouble. He had already absconded from the school and had been brought back and belted, which he resented. The rules of the reformatory allowed for 'moderate physical correction', but Simpson admitted to having given sixteen strokes of the belt on some occasions, while some of the inmates claimed he had once given thirty strokes for smoking.

Both the case of assault against Donald and the fire-raising came to court in June 1882. Five boys stood before the judge: Alexander Donald was accused of assault, and Sutherland, William Robb, McKenzie and Alexander Berry of wilful fire-raising. All pleaded not guilty. Some of the many witnesses gave contradictory evidence.

Fifteen-year-old John Gordon said that Donald threw a spoon and a tin at Simpson, and had held a metal bar in his hand. On the day of the fire James McKenzie had told Gordon they 'were going to have a row' but gave no details except to say the place was to be 'set on fire'. McKenzie also said he 'would have nothing to do with it'.

William McConnachie, a thirteen-year-old inmate, told the court that at about eleven o'clock on the day of the fire a boy called Alexander Anderson had asked him to find matches. He got them from an inmate called John Macdonald and gave them to Anderson, who in turn handed them to a boy named Robb. George Reid, another inmate, told the court that he heard a number of the boys, including Robb, discussing the fire some three hours before it happened. Sixteen-year-old Robert Clover said that the attack on Simpson had been planned in advance and he saw Donald throw the tin of porridge, the piece of iron and a divider. A boy called Thomas Ross told the court that Berry and a boy named McInally spoke about the fire before it broke out while John Sutherland kicked in the panel of the clothes-store door and stole the clothes.

William Robb said he did not see Donald throw anything and thought that he was the first to give the alarm of the fire. Eighteen-year-old James Brown saw John Sutherland smash the window of the shoemaker's shop and kick in the door of the tailor's shop. Brown also said that it was Sutherland who threw the stool at Jeffrey; he said that Sutherland emptied two pails of water onto the fire but then threw the pails into the flames afterwards. However, Brown also admitted that it was he who had cut the hose. Stewart Clark also incriminated Sutherland, and added that Sutherland had also threatened to break Simpson's legs with a stick, and led the runaways.

Donald told the court that he threw the tin and spoon at Simpson because he was not getting fair treatment. He said he had to work despite having an abscess in his breast, but disclaimed any knowledge about a plan to set fire to anything.

Sutherland said he had not known about Donald's attack on Simpson until it happened, but he had known of a different plan that had not taken place. He claimed that he had learned about the fire-raising plot shortly before the fire began and agreed he would not help douse the flames. Sutherland said the reason for the conspiracy was that Simpson made them work fourteen-hour days.

McKenzie said there had been a proposal to give Simpson 'a thrashing', as he was cruel to them and gave out too many punishments. Berry also knew of a previous abortive plan to attack Simpson. It had been Berry's idea to set fire to the blankets in the dormitory, but he denied setting fire to the workshops. He also had a grudge against Simpson, who had apparently broken a promise to free him after half his sentence, and had not allowed him to work in the farm.

When he summed up, the Advocate General said that out of the 140 or so boys in the Reformatory, twenty had been in a state of wilful insubordination. The fire had been caused to help these boys escape, but it was 'a great peculiarity' that the boy who had been accused of lighting the fire was the youngest. Lord Deas, the judge, said the question was 'was there an actual combination to set fire to a certain part of the building' and whether these boys were involved.

The jury found Alexander Donald guilty of assault, and Sutherland, Robb, McKenzie and Berry guilty of wilful fire-raising. Lord Deas sentenced Donald to nine months with hard labour and the others to twelve months with hard labour.

The Pattern of Crime

The following tables show the number of juvenile arrests in various decades. The first table is from 1845 to 1851.

Children under twelve years old who were arrested and who appeared in court

Year	Male	Female	Total
1845	42	7	49
1846	25	3	28
1847	25	2	27
1848	13	6	19
1849	11	5	16
1850	14	8	22
1851	6	2	8

The second table shows the number of arrests from 1883 to 1899. The total number has escalated, showing that either the police were more vigilant or the methods of preventing child crime did not work.

Children of twelve years and under who were arrested and who appeared in court

Year	Boys	Girls	Total
1883	60	2	62
1884	75	14	89
1885	86	8	94
1886	77	16	93
1887	90	17	107
1888	135	22	157
1889	113	15	128
1890	91	16	107
1891	153	12	165

1892	109	17	126
1893	157	14	171
1894	230	19	249
1895	241	9	250
1896	277	15	292
1897	291	16	307
1898	288	32	320
1899	482	22	504

These figures show an erratic but steadily upward climb in the number of arrests for juvenile crime. What is most noticeable is the increasing gulf between male and female arrests. Whatever the cause, it is obvious that juvenile crime remained a problem in Aberdeen right to the end of the nineteenth century.

15
Brutal Assaults

Along with petty theft and drunkenness, assault was one of the most common crimes, and a crime that could happen to anybody. However, there were many types and levels of assault, from a simple punch in the nose to attacks of sickening brutality. This chapter shows a selection of the many different types of assaults that Aberdeen experienced in the nineteenth century.

Assaulting the Girlfriend

Shortly after midnight on Sunday, 4 August 1871, Andrew Adamson came home to his attic flat and his sweetheart, Jane Noble. He had spent the night drinking and was anything but sober. Noble was in bed, but notwithstanding, Adamson ordered her to get up and make his supper.

'You might have come home earlier,' Noble grumbled, but that casual remark seems to have annoyed Adamson. Grabbing Noble by the hair of her head, he dragged her out of bed, tied her hair to the bedpost and began to beat her up. He used his fists and perhaps a blunt instrument, cutting her face and head badly, inflicting wounds up to nine and a half centimetres long and laying bare part of her skull.

Tearing herself free at the expense of losing some hair, Noble ran out of the house and, still in her nightdress, ran for help. Despite the time of night, the shop next door was open and she staggered inside and collapsed on the floor with her head and face smeared with blood. The shopkeeper called for the police, who paid a visit to Adamson and sent Dr Ogston to care for Noble.

The police found the floor and furniture of Adamson's flat smeared with blood, despite his clumsy attempts to clean it, but he was relatively sober when they arrested him. He ended up in jail for sixty days.

Assaulting the Old Friend

Sixty-two-year-old saddler Adam Cruickshank and seventy-two-year-old labourer Peter Leonard had been friends for years. They shared an address at 16 Princes Street, but lived in different rooms, and while Cruickshank lived alone, Leonard shared his house with his daughter, Margaret.

At ten at night on Saturday, 1 January 1881, Margaret Leonard left her father sitting beside the fire in his nightclothes while she visited her friend Mary Mearns at 14 Princes Street. About quarter of an hour later she heard a noise coming from her house; her father shouted 'murder' and 'oh me!' Margaret dropped everything and rushed next door, with Mearns close at her heels. She met Adam Cruickshank in the lobby outside, leaving the house and hurrying in the opposite direction.

'What have you done to my father?' Margaret asked, in a mild panic.

Cruickshank swore at her and hurried away. Margaret ran into her house.

Mary Mearns lingered a little longer. 'What is this you have done, you villain?' she asked. Cruickshank swore again and held up something shiny in his hand. Mearns did not know what it was, but later she thought it might have been an awl.

When Margaret entered her house, her father was walking around the room with both hands pressed to his stomach and obviously in pain. Margaret asked what had happened and Leonard sat down slowly. He said that 'the saddler struck me'. Then Leonard fainted. All the noise had attracted a number of neighbours, and they manoeuvred Leonard into his bed and called the police.

Sergeant Presslie, a bevy of constables and Dr Ogston arrived shortly afterwards. Ogston found a narrow but deep wound in Leonard's stomach, and thought it had been made with a saddler's awl. Leonard had lost a great deal of blood and Ogston believed he was in danger of dying. As it happened, Leonard made a full recovery. The police took Leonard's statement and shortly afterwards crossed the lobby to Cruickshank's house. Cruickshank was lying in bed, drunk and with his clothes over his face. He mumbled that the Leonards had stolen his beef and his bread, even though both were on the table in his own house. The police arrested him and searched the house; they found Cruickshank's toolbox open and two awls on top. When they combined Leonard's statement to the police and the knowledge that Cruickshank had been convicted of three previous acts of violence, they had no doubt they had found their man.

The case came to the Sheriff Court on 21 February 1881. Leonard said that he had answered a knock at the door and Cruickshank had been there, 'raging drunk'. Leonard had invited him in and was in the act of getting a chair when Cruickshank had said 'take that, you bastard' and had stabbed him with no warning or motive. Cruickshank could give no defence except a brief mumble about his bread, so the jury had an easy task to find him guilty of stabbing Leonard. Sheriff Dove Wilson sentenced him to nine months in prison.

Assaulting the Wife

In the nineteenth century, sport was as important to the people of Scotland as it is today. There were waves of interest in different types of sports, from horse racing to curling to pugilism and football. In the middle of the 1880s, a sport called pedestrianism crossed the country, as men and women strived to take part in walking competitions, either against each other or simply in an attempt to walk long distances in short times. Margaret McPhee of Seamount Place in Aberdeen was smitten by this sport and spent much of her time travelling to various meetings to test her walking prowess.

In March 1886 she had taken part in a sixteen-hour pedestrian competition in Dundee, and her scavenger (or street cleaner) husband, William McPhee, met her at the railway station when she arrived back in Aberdeen. They returned home side by side, but there had been some resentment building up between them and that night it boiled over into harsh words and violence. Mrs McPhee had gone to bed, tired after her exertions, and her husband began to forcibly make his point.

William McPhee was annoyed that his wife spent so much time engaged in her hobby that he had not only to work long hours making money, but he also had to care for the children and ensure the house was in order and the food purchased and cooked. When Mrs McPhee did not seem to care about his position and said she was too tired to work in their house or even argue, he came to their bed, knelt on top of her and grabbed her by the throat.

'I'll make sure you're never tired again,' McPhee said, and threatened to murder her there and then.

The children began to scream, which alerted the neighbours, who called the police. William McPhee was bundled away and appeared before the Police Court on 2 May. Unfortunately for him, the magistrates did not consider his wife's neglect sufficient cause for assault and fined McPhee ten shillings and sixpence with an alternative of five days in prison.

Other sports could also lead to assault.

Pugilism

Prizefighting was the forerunner of boxing, but was a much more brutal affair. The men fought without gloves or fixed rounds. A round ended when one man was felled, and he was allowed thirty seconds to recover and get back to 'scratch' – the centre of the ring. Many of the spectators bet money on the outcome of the fight, which could last for hours.

In 1830, there was a prizefight between twenty-six-year-old Alexander 'Sandy' Mackay and an Irishman named Simon Byrne for the Championship of England. The Irishman won the fight after forty-seven rounds and the Glasgow man, Mackay, literally fought to the death. There were rumours that the supporters of Byrne had drugged his water bottle. Whatever the reason, the fatal outcome created riots in Glasgow between Irish and Scots and resulted in many arrests, injuries and three reported deaths. In Aberdeen the outcome was less dramatic, but did see an upsurge in interest in prizefighting, or pugilism, as it was also known.

In the summer of 1830, the streets of Aberdeen became the scene of scores of minor impromptu encounters between would-be prizefighters. Most were over in minutes, but on Monday, 14 June, two blacksmiths met to fight in what was then known as a 'regular go'. The two men did not meet purely for the love of fighting; they were also fighting for the sake of love. Both men had fallen for the same woman and believed that the only way to win her affection was to batter his rival into bloody submission. The woman was obviously of a like mind and said she would favour the victor, whoever he was.

The two men met on the Links, with a large crowd there to watch and bet on the outcome. They battled bravely for three or four rounds. However, the police had also been alerted and the fighters disappeared as soon as the police appeared. There is no record of the woman picking either man.

Female Fighters

The Links in Aberdeen could present some interesting sports. It was the venue for the horse racing, but there were also some less legal encounters there. On Friday, 4 September 1835, two women argued and decided to settle their differences with a fist fight. They did not want a scrappy contest but a fully fledged bare-knuckle prizefight complete with rounds and seconds. They met on the Links, near the Bannermill, with a gaggle of boys as seconds and witnesses.

The girls stripped to their shifts and petticoats, which in itself must have been enough to attract a crowd, and battled gamely. Following the accredited rules of prizefighting, every time one was knocked down, the round ended. One of the boys provided a knee for the combatants to recover on, then stood her up and propelled her forwards for the next round.

The fight took place near the bathing machines, and when one of the men who worked there tried to interfere, he was promptly punched in the eye. The police eventually arrived and arrested the girls, but the boys were not having that and attacked them to effect a rescue, and so they were arrested as well. One of the female pugilists got forty days and the other thirty days in jail, the same as the boys who had tried to effect a rescue.

Assaulting the Workmate

Young David Smith lived at Upper Balfour, Durris, in Kincardineshire. He had recently been employed as a storekeeper for the Aberdeen

Lime Company, which meant he moved around the area quite a lot to collect payments for various accounts. On Thursday, 27 February 1889, Smith had collected a large sum of money at Dunnet; he arrived at Crathes Station and began the two-and-a-half-mile walk back to his home. A local farmer accompanied him as far as the bridge over the Dee, but then he was alone as darkness crowded in. There was a man standing in the middle of the bridge; Smith did not recognise him in the dark but bid him a 'fine evening' and walked on.

The man replied that it was, and then followed a few steps behind. About five minutes later he pulled out a hammer and smashed Smith over the head three times. Smith staggered, but he recovered, and rather than run away, he grappled with the man and the two wrestled on the ground. Smith grabbed hold of the hammer and returned the blows, thumping his attacker in exactly the same manner in which he had been attacked. After a few blows, the handle of the hammer broke and the other man shouted out 'murder!' and ran away, holding his head.

Rather than let his attacker escape, Smith followed and again grabbed hold of him, but the man slipped free and dashed off again. By now Smith was exhausted and in considerable pain from the hammer blows to his head. He staggered to the nearby farmhouse of Brigton, where Mr Gray brought him in and sent a messenger to Smith's father and to Dr McHardy to come and treat Smith's wounds.

When Smith got home, his father contacted Sergeant Thompson of the Banchory police. Smith could not give a detailed description, but his rough outline was all Thompson needed to gain an idea of who to look for. Thompson called at all the local lodging houses in the belief that the attacker may have been a tramp; however, the description Smith gave tallied with a man named William Forbes, who lived at Abendie, near Banchory. It was strange that Smith did not recognise the man, as the two had a history.

Forbes had been the previous storekeeper for the Aberdeen Lime

Company. After two years in the job, he had been sacked, but in a curious piece of mismanagement, he had trained up David Smith as his replacement. Forbes was a man in his forties, married with a family of five, and was now unemployed. Obviously he had borne a grudge against young Smith. Sergeant Thompson tried to track Forbes down. He had been home at about nine on the Thursday night and on the Friday morning had been drinking in the Burnett Arms Hotel, later visiting Mr Lunan's druggist shop in Banchory to buy two ounces of laudanum. Lunan had asked what it was for and Forbes had said it was 'to dose a cow'.

When the police failed to find Forbes at his house on the Friday morning, they returned later that day. He was still absent, but his wife told them he had intended to go to the Craigton Quarries to look for work. The police did not find him there, or anywhere nearby, so Thompson sent a telegraph to Aberdeen in case Forbes had taken the train to the city. Thompson also arranged to have the local railway stations watched. In the meantime, he asked around Banchory and found out that Forbes had been seen going to nearby Tillybrek Wood. The police gathered a search party and on Saturday morning Constable Gauld found Forbes' dead body sitting in the centre of the wood. He had bandaged the hammer wounds on his head and had poisoned himself with laudanum.

The case has a few points that will never be cleared up: did Forbes attack Smith out of frustration at losing his job? Why did Smith not recognise a man he had worked closely with for two weeks? And did Forbes commit suicide out of shame or because he was unemployed? The full truth will never be known.

Assault by a Soldier

In the Victorian period, the army had a mixed bag of publicity. Kipling was exactly right when he said they were lauded as heroes when involved in any of the innumerable small wars of Empire, but were not always treated well when they were at home in barracks. Sometimes, however, they were the authors of their own misfortune.

Such a situation arose in Aberdeen in September 1880 when the 92nd Regiment, the Gordon Highlanders, were the resident garrison. George Noble Taylor was a visiting mariner. He was a Fraserburgh man and, like many seamen ashore, he visited some of the local pubs. He was no longer sober when he met two soldiers, Private John Martin and Private John McGhone. The three of them continued on the circuit of Aberdeen public houses, including Grant's in Sugar Lane, where Mrs Ann Grant served them. By the time they staggered into a pub called Dempsey's, Taylor was a little befuddled; he met a third soldier and thought his name was McGuiness. At a pub named Hick's, Taylor dropped a sixpenny piece, and had a small argument with the supposed McGuiness, who stepped on the coin to claim it for himself. Perhaps because of the disagreement, McGuiness left and Taylor and the remaining two soldiers went to a pub named Duncan's. The binge ended in a pie shop run by a Mrs Hopper.

Mary Jane Barron served the threesome in the pie shop. She thought that Taylor was 'pretty well on' and 'could not have moved along by himself; he required assistance'. So by that time Taylor was hardly fit to stand, let alone walk, but he was happy in his inebriation. Once they left the pie shop, the two soldiers linked arms with Taylor and led him into a passageway that stretched as far as the City Board Parochial Offices.

As soon as they were deep in the gloom of the close, the soldiers asked Taylor if he would like to swap jackets with them as a sign of their deep friendship. Before Taylor could reply, McGhone lifted his walking cane and cracked him over the head. At the same time, Martin grabbed his shoulders and held tight. Too drunk to put up much resistance, Taylor struggled as best he could, but the two Gordon Highlanders knocked him down and hauled off his jacket, his waistcoat and his trousers. They rifled through his pockets and found over £6 in notes and coins, his seaman's indentures and thirteen certificates of discharge, which were documents that proved his experience at sea and his good character. When they were satisfied they had everything of value, they threw away his clothes and fled, leaving Taylor lying, dazed, stripped and robbed, on the ground.

Mrs Rachel Spence kept the Aberdeen City Parochial Board Office, which was situated at the head of the close in which Taylor had been attacked. She noticed the three men coming up the close but did not pay any particular attention to them until she heard sounds of a struggle. She peered into the gloom and saw Taylor, drunk and undressed, staggering up the close and complaining that he had just been robbed. Without a second thought, Mrs Spence immediately came to help. She found Taylor's clothes and helped him dress, then cast around and found most of his certificates of discharge and his indentures. She did not find his money.

Mrs Grant, who had served Taylor in her pub earlier, saw Mrs Spence helping dress Taylor and came out to assist him to the police office. Next day Detective James Wyness brought Taylor to the barracks to try to identify his attackers. Taylor eventually picked out the two privates he claimed had assaulted him.

When the case came to trial at the High Court it was pointed out that McGuiness was unavailable, as he was dead. That confused the court, as there had been nobody of that name involved in the assault. The other two privates, McGhone and Martin, pleaded not guilty. Their defence solicitor said that Taylor had been too drunk to know who had attacked him and that the two soldiers had only been in Aberdeen for a couple of weeks and could not have known where the closes were. However, the jury found both guilty and they were sentenced to a year in jail.

Assault at the Aikey Fair

Fair days were often marked by an increase in crime, usually drink-induced brawls and petty theft, but occasionally there were more serious consequences. The Aikey Fair was no exception. Held at Old Deer, in Buchan, it was the largest fair in the north of Scotland and was traditionally held on the first Wednesday after 19 July. At its peak in the nineteenth century, the fair covered some sixty acres of land as up to 10,000 people converged on it to trade livestock, meet acquaintances or view and buy everything and anything that might be of use on a farm.

James Cruikshank was a crofter at Middlemuir, Belhelvie, a few miles north of Aberdeen. He had been at the fair in July 1878 and had returned his horse to the stable at the Aden Arms, New Deer, at about nine at night. He was not altogether sober at the time, but certainly not drunk. There were two men standing talking together, but save for a casual glance, Cruikshank did not pay them much attention. He brushed his horse down, fed and watered it, sat down for a rest and promptly fell asleep. As he slept, two men entered the stables, saw him and decided that he was worth robbing. They threw Cruikshank off his seat, and while one man clamped a hand over his mouth to keep him quiet, the other went through his pockets for anything worth stealing.

'Have you got it yet?' one of the men asked.

The other grabbed Cruikshank's pocketbook with £8 in it. 'Yes,' he said.

They left hurriedly, but not before Cruikshank had had time to look up and recognise one as George Dickson, one of the men who had been outside the stable. The other he was not sure about.

When the local policeman, Constable James Birnie, was informed, he visited the local inns and two days later saw Dickson with a man named Alexander Thom at the bar of the inn at Old Deer. He arrested them both and demanded the return of the stolen money, but Dickson pointed to the bar and said, 'Go find it there but you are too late.' As he spoke he made a lunge for the door, but Birnie followed and caught him only a few yards outside.

'I am a real Cowgate boy,' Dickson boasted.

The case came to the Circuit Court in September and a fifteen-year-old lad named Alexander Mackie was called as a witness. He had seen the whole thing and he recognised George Dickson and Alexander Thom. He said he had seen them enter the stable where Cruikshank was sleeping. He saw them knock him to the floor and hold him down and rob him and then leave. A labourer named Alexander Melvin was first to enter the stable and found Cruikshank lying on the ground bleeding and with his shirt and waistcoat open; he also saw the two men who were at the bar.

Thom was a known thief with two previous convictions at Peterhead and one in Glasgow, but Dickson was unknown to the police. Lord Deas summed up the case and said that he was going to be lenient. The case was one of robbery with violence, but there was little violence used so he was going to treat it as theft. Robbery with violence meant seven years' penal servitude, which he thought harsh, so instead he sentenced both to eighteen months' imprisonment.

Assaulting Another Wife

William Tawse was an elderly man with a respectable, even jaunty air. At seventy-four years old he had been married for years, and walked around Aberdeen dressed in a black suit. To the outside world he appeared a figure to be trusted and looked up to, but appearances were very deceptive: William Tawse was a singularly unpleasant man with a history of violence and three convictions for assault.

Tawse's wife, Anne Tawse, worked in a public house in Adelphi Lane, but no longer lived with him. On the 18 May 1860, Tawse entered the pub and drank a little with her. They did not argue and he left quite sober, to return again a short while later. It was about nine at night and he approached Anne and asked her if they could talk at the door of the pub.

She agreed and walked with him to the door. 'What's this now?' Tawse asked and immediately threw some vitriol – sulphuric acid – in her face. Anne screamed as the corrosive liquid splashed into her eyes and skin. She covered her face with her hands, screaming as the pain intensified. Obviously the noise attracted her customers and somebody escorted her to the police watch house. Dr Ogston, the police surgeon, found that her face and hands were burned and red and tried his best to treat her, but unfortunately Anne's eye subsequently burst because of the acid. She was in the infirmary for more than five weeks as the doctors tried to repair the damage. She lost the sight in her left eye and her hands were also burned where she had put them up to protect her face. The upper part of Anne's dress was also burned through where the acid dripped down from her face.

In the meantime, Tawse spread the news that Anne constantly led him on, promising that they would get back together but gathering money until the time of the Lothian harvest, when she would head south and he would never see her again. Tawse boasted that he had 'put a stop to that'. He said he would never lift a hand to his wife, even though she had sworn she would rather die than live with him again, but he would 'blind her' and 'she would never see to go' to the Lothians.

Tawse was arrested and brought to the Circuit Court on 8 October 1860. There was no difficulty in finding him guilty and the Lord Justice Clerk sentenced him to five years' penal servitude.

Strange Assault

Sometimes even the most experienced of magistrates could find it hard to unravel the truth behind the stories they heard from the other side of the bench. Such a case occurred at the Police Court in late December 1888. Joseph Cochrane, an apparently inoffensive labourer, appeared as the primary witness in front of Bailies Crombie and Gordon. His face was cut and scratched and he appeared very nervous to be in such a place, but he straightened his back and spoke up manfully as he related his story.

Cochrane said that on the night of 15 December 1888 he and his wife had been out for a quiet drink together. They had been coming home in the early morning of the 16th, when they passed the shop of Jane Allen in Guestrow. Allen had come to the door and invited Cochrane inside. When Cochrane declined, Mrs Allen grabbed hold of him and dragged him into the shop. She locked the door so Mrs Cochrane could not get in and immediately began to rant and swear.

A mild man, Cochrane did not retaliate in the slightest, even when Mrs Allen smashed him on the head with a bottle and called for her friends to come and help her. Mary Brown and a shepherd named Joseph Burnett immediately appeared from the back of the shop and joined in the unprovoked assault on Cochrane, who still refused to retaliate. Mrs Brown raked her fingernails down his face, but when she lifted a poker and threw it at him that was too much and he shouted 'murder!' at the top of his voice.

The first witness called to the court was a man who had happened to be passing and heard Jane Allen call out, 'This is your man,' and threaten to keep him inside the shop until she 'got satisfaction'. He heard Cochrane shouting 'murder' and saw Mrs Cochrane running around searching for a policeman. When Mrs Cochrane gave the same story, nearly word for word, the defence were suspicious that there was corroboration and no motive for the attack, but the policeman who arrived avowed that Cochrane was indeed locked inside the shop and his face was newly scratched, so the accused were found guilty and fined £1 each. An explanation for Mrs Allen's actions was neither sought nor given.

Assault by Stabbing

Sometimes an assault occurred with the escalation of a simple argument. Such a case happened in Dyce, a few miles west of Aberdeen, on the night of 27 June 1896. John Riach and Andrew Mathieson, both quarry workers, were guests in the cottage of Mrs Paul. Mathieson had been drinking at the Prince of Wales Hotel but he was not drunk, although he did have a reputation for becoming quarrelsome after only a few pints of beer. Riach and Mathieson knew each other well, but were not the best of friends. Riach accused Mathieson of spreading ugly rumours about him, and then they began to argue about their respective wages, which ended in the classic Scottish situation of Riach challenging Mathieson to a fight. Not wanting to be thought a coward, Mathieson agreed, and they barged outside to settle their differences man to man and fist to fist.

They traded punches for a few moments, then grappled and tumbled into a ditch. A labourer named Andrew Ross separated them and Riach walked away, while Mathieson returned to the cottage. There was peace for a while, but Riach returned after a while and again challenged Mathieson to step outside and fight. Mathieson again agreed and left the house. By this time it was nearly dark, but Riach did not give him time to get ready.

Riach was outside first, and as soon as Mathieson stepped out of the door, he leaped from the side of the cottage and stabbed him in the forehead. The blade passed through Mathieson's hat and into his right temple, so blood poured out, temporarily blinding him. This type of attack was quite common in the nineteenth century: men would slash a knife across the forehead of the victim so blood blinded them and they were made vulnerable to a robber. (Scandinavian seamen were expert at this manoeuvre.) He staggered for a while and then collapsed on the ground.

There was no doubt of Riach's guilt, so the judge sent him to jail for two months.

Assault by Mugging

On the evening of Monday, 28 July 1894, a carter named William Wright walked up Burnett's Close on his way home. He had been shopping and had a bottle of rum in his hand, so was quite pleased with life at that moment. However, he was being stalked. Four men surrounded him, punched him in the face, knocked him on the back of the head and threw him to the ground. While three held him there, the fourth went through his pockets and took the rum. Then they landed a couple of final kicks and ran away, leaving Wright lying, shaken and robbed, on the ground.

Eventually Wright got up and reported the assault to the police. From his description, the beat policeman recognised one of the men as John Gow, an old offender, and visited his known haunts. Within a few hours he arrested Gow and three of his companions; all four appeared before the Police Court on Wednesday. John Gow had already served six months for assault, so was sent down for nine months; William Roy was given three months; and John Learmont, a tool grinder, and James Stopper, a millworker, both of whom seemed to have fallen into bad company, were given fourteen days each.

Assault by Garrotting

Despite the reputation of Jack the Ripper and the worries about riots and disturbance, probably the crime that was most feared in the nineteenth century was garrotting. It was a simple enough crime: the perpetrator, or more often perpetrators, would entice their victim to a lonely corner or just creep up behind him, then strangle him to unconsciousness and rob him. Sometimes the assailants merely used their hands, but on other occasions they looped a wire or a piece of rope around his throat. The procedure seems to have started in Glasgow, but it spread rapidly and eventually created such consternation throughout the country that new laws were created to curb it.

Aberdeen was not immune. On Monday, 23 February 1852, a young man left a concert in the County Rooms and was walking through the centre of town. He entered the small lane that took him from Diamond Square to Union Terrace when a man approached him silently from behind. Somebody wrapped strong arms around him so he could not move, while a noose was flung around his throat and tightened so he choked. After a few moments he passed out, and when he awoke he was bleeding from the mouth and nose. He had also been robbed of his silver watch, his keys and all the money he carried with him. The police searched, but the assailants were never found.

Assault in a Temperance Hotel

Drink was often a factor in assault cases, and it may have been involved when Mrs Margaret MacGregor attacked Jane Lamont in August 1880. Unusually, the assault took place in a temperance hotel and Mrs MacGregor was sober at the time. Mrs MacGregor and her husband, James MacGregor, ran the Crown Hotel at 4 and 5 Crown Terrace in Aberdeen, while Jane Lamont had been a general servant there for about six weeks.

At about half past five in the evening of Wednesday, 2 August 1880, James and Margaret MacGregor were discussing business with a customer in the hotel's smoking room when Lamont came in. It was immediately obvious that Lamont had been drinking. Mrs MacGregor lost no time in telling Lamont that drink was not appropriate in a temperance hotel, and added a few personal insults for good measure.

Lamont began to cry, which angered the MacGregors further, and Mr MacGregor told her to get to bed to sleep it off. As it was not yet six in the evening, Lamont refused to go, so James MacGregor hauled her out of the smoking room and down the stairs to her room. He threw her on the bed, with Margaret MacGregor following and adding her voice. 'You go away now,' Margaret MacGregor said to her husband, 'and I will see to the matter myself.'

Once James MacGregor had left, Margaret MacGregor continued her verbal assault on Lamont, shouting that she was 'making a fool of my house' and 'I will do for you now', and attacked her with her fists and nails. Lamont screamed so loudly that people in the street outside heard, as did three children in the house next door. MacGregor punched and slapped her face, then clawed at her, drawing deep scratches on her lips and tongue and inside her mouth. After a few moments the frenzied assault ended and sanity returned. MacGregor scurried to get water to bathe the bruises and wash away the blood, but Lamont did not wait.

Still screaming, she ran up the stairs to the back door, out of the house and into the street. She saw a cab at the corner of Bridge Street, jumped in and, speaking through her tears, asked to be taken to the police office. Inspector Lewis Gordon was in charge at the time and he saw Lamont come in visibly upset and with her face all swollen and bruised. He knew at once that she had been drinking but that she was a long way from being drunk; her speech was coherent and she spoke as sensibly as anybody could who had just been beaten up by her employer.

When the case came to the Police Court, Margaret MacGregor protested her innocence, but Bailie Esslemont pointed out that she and Lamont had been the only people in the room and nobody had injured Lamont outside the hotel so he had no doubt that MacGregor was guilty. He dismissed an attempt by Mr MacGregor to give evidence on his wife's behalf and sentenced Mrs MacGregor to forty days in jail or a forty-shilling fine.

However savage an assault could be, the victim was usually an adult who was in the wrong place at the wrong time. The nineteenth-century public were more inclined to be sympathetic when a child was the victim.

16
Cruelty to Children

Although the century was rife with the fear of juvenile crime, children were as likely to be victims as aggressors. One crime that decreased during the century was child-stripping, where adults decoyed children into lonely places and stripped them of their clothes, which would be pawned for a few pennies. For example, in the summer of 1829 there was a 'set of wretches' who infested Guestrow and Union Street preying on children. However, another, possibly more insidious crime was the failure of parents to look after their children. The absent fathers of illegitimate children were particularly guilty of this crime, but the courts tried to help the mothers. For example, in July 1829 a butcher who refused to give the mother of his illegitimate child financial help was sentenced to sixty days with hard labour.

Indecent Assault in a School

Thirty-one-year-old Henry Boyd was a schoolmaster from Fintry, near Turriff. However, he was also guilty of indecent acts towards some of the young girls to whom he had a duty of trust and care. The known cases started in October 1878 and continued until September 1882. It seemed that Boyd had started with nearly innocent actions and continued with each instance becoming more serious. The school was unaware of his behaviour, but eventually one of the girls involved told her parents and then Boyd was hauled before the Circuit Court, where Lord Craighill gave him eighteen months.

Assault on Her Daughter

It is often distressing to read of children sent to Victorian industrial schools, with their strict regime of hard work and discipline. Yet there are other occasions when the original home life of the children is illuminated, and the schools must have been an oasis of order and hope in a blighted life. Jessie Reid of 19 Berry Lane, Aberdeen, may have been one of these latter inmates.

Jessie's mother was Mary Reid, who already had fifteen convictions for assault and drunken behaviour when she came to visit Jessie in Whitehall Industrial School on 28 July 1883. However, only a few moments later she attacked Jessie, punching her on the head and then on the back. She grabbed Jessie's hair, punched her again and again, knocked her down and would have continued had the staff not stopped her. Mary Reid claimed that Jessie had stolen her shawl and was impudent, but Sheriff Brown sided with the daughter and gave Mary ten days in jail.

What Shall We Do with the Drunken Father?

James Johnstone was a pedlar, which was a precarious occupation even for a single man with no family to support. He was an Irishman, but his journeys took him to Aberdeen; en route he found a wife and started a family. In 1885, the parish authorities stepped in to help with money and advice and for a while the family existed inside the poorhouse. However, James Johnstone was not happy with the strict regulations and he refused to leave his family behind, so they all left together and struggled along in a welter of neglect and pauperism, with babies arriving at regular intervals.

The family jogged along until Johnstone's wife died, and then their world fell apart. Johnstone exchanged his affection for his wife for his love of the contents of a bottle. By 1899 the eldest daughter, Catherine, was fifteen and working in a mill, but her entire five-shilling weekly wages went to her father, who spent it in the nearest pub. Neighbours of his Gardner's Lane house complained to the police that the children were neglected, so they called around.

The house was empty of everything except a shakedown bed (a rough-and-ready, makeshift pile of blankets rather than a real bed). Four of the five children were crowded together, unwashed, unkempt, nearly unclad and wholly uneducated. Johnstone was drunk, and the only food in the house was a single slice of stale bread. In April 1899, Sheriff Robertson sent him to jail for two months and ordered the children into the workhouse, where they would be better fed, washed, educated and dressed than they were with their father.

The Cruel Schoolteacher

David Robertson was both a preacher and a schoolmaster in the parish of Rayne, in Aberdeenshire. He was also known as a man of uncertain temper who could take his frustrations out on those under his authority. On Thursday, 5 November 1829, some of his pupils thought he had overstepped the mark. He was accused of inflicting 'excessive and outrageous bodily correction' on eleven-year-old James Morran 'to the danger of his life'.

When the case came to the Sheriff Court in December 1829, Robertson's defence lawyer tried to get it thrown out. He claimed it was not assault, as 'personal chastisement of a pupil by a schoolmaster, however violent' was not illegal 'unless maliciously administered and productive of permanent personal injury.' In other words, the school-master had virtually unlimited powers to inflict corporal punishment on his pupils in the name of education. However, the sheriff did not agree and allowed the case to continue, but the phrase 'to the danger of his life' was deleted from the charge.

Young James Morran gave his own version of what happened to the court. He must have been nervous facing a panel of stern-faced men, but he seems to have given his evidence steadily enough. He admitted that he had not learned his lesson properly. Robertson was rightly irritated and ordered Morran to hold out his hand. Morran did so, but pulled it back as Robertson lashed down, so the tawse (or school belt) missed its target completely. That minor misdemeanour was enough to rouse Robertson's temper. Instead of ordering the boy to hold out his hand a second time, Robertson whacked him on the head and back with the tawse. Not surprisingly, Morran tried to escape, but Robertson chased after him, grabbed him and dragged him along the floor to a bench. He thrust Morran's head between his knees so the boy was held in a bending position, and then began to unfasten Morran's trousers. Again, Morran struggled free. He ran towards the door but tripped and fell on his hands and knees.

Robertson lunged forwards and grabbed him. 'Take down your trousers,' Robertson ordered. This time Morran complied. By now, according to Morran, Robertson was 'in a passion'; he grabbed him by the collar and dragged him along the floor, before throwing him face down over a form. While Morran was in that position, Robertson 'lickit' him with the tawse on the head, back and bottom. Afterwards, Morran had great pains in his side and his breast. He felt sick that night and could not eat.

Morran was in pain for days, with his nose bleeding and occasional bouts of fever when he became delirious and threw himself around on the bed. He was confined to bed for weeks, which was unusual for a boy who was quite familiar with the tawse. His mother called Dr Duncan Campbell, who noted lumps on his head and ugly stripes and bruises on various parts of him. A second doctor named Beatty also examined Morran, but did not see anything untoward at all except some marks on his knees. As a precaution, a third doctor, Alexander Robertson examined Morran and, except for some marks inflicted by the tawse, found nothing wrong with him.

A near neighbour, Christian Allan, said she heard 'louder screams than usual' that day, which suggests that Robertson was in the habit of inflicting severe punishment on his charges. Mary Robertson, a ten-year-old pupil at the school, would confirm this as she gave evidence that she had seen boys flogged over a seat in the class before. In 1825 Robertson had appeared before the Presbytery accused of cruelty to boys in his school, but it seemed that the lesson had not been learned.

The case was found not proven by a majority of eight to seven, but the sheriff reminded everybody that not proven was not the same as not guilty, and he warned Robertson to 'govern his passion while administering correction to his pupils'.

That case was a reminder that children could be vulnerable even when they were in an environment that had been designed to keep them safe. There were some places in Aberdeen where nobody was safe, child or adult. One such place was Shuttle Lane.

17

A Century of Crime

Every city in the world has its less salubrious areas: streets where crime is common and criminals congregate. In the nineteenth century, these were often in the oldest parts of the cities, those left behind by rampant progress. Aberdeen had its share of small streets where crime flourished. For example, there was Justice Street, where in one sitting of the Police Court in November 1835 the town sergeants had brought in five shopkeepers charged with harbouring prostitutes in their back shops. Bailie Milne thought that the ironically named Justice Street had more complaints about it than all the other parts of Aberdeen combined. There was also Burnett's Close, which in the 1880s began to have a reputation for sordid misery and drunken violence.

Shuttle Lane

However, over the course of the century, for its size and population, Shuttle Lane was perhaps the equal of any street in the city for long-standing criminality. In 1848, there was a public house and a penny theatre for every ten families in the area, and even at the end of the century, after city improvements had removed many of the worst slums from Aberdeen, Shuttle Lane remained bare, bleak and crowded. Any visitor, even at this late date, would see unfriendly faces at the windows and women blocking the entrance to every close, challenging the intruder with chilling eyes and harsh voices, with the occasional wild screech of laughter to raise the hairs on the back of the stranger's neck. The laughter was as false as any pretended hope in this street of despair, poverty and crime.

The tenements were low, red-bricked, dirty and stinking with rot and mould, ranked on either side of a passageway that was only thirteen feet wide for most of its length but widened to seventeen feet where it terminated at a cul de sac at the west. Ragged children played in the filth and drunken men reeled past the haunts of ten-a-penny prostitutes. The name Shuttle Lane implies that handloom weavers plied their trade there when they were the kings of industry before the factory system swept them down destitution's drain. As the century wore on, years of neglect began to tell on the fabric of the street, so on Sunday, 2 September 1849, one of the old houses, then fortunately used as a stable rather than a residence, suddenly collapsed into a pile of dust and rubble.

Hundreds of people crammed into those buildings as the landlords looked for the maximum profit for the minimum outlay, and the desperate hoped only for shelter from the weather. For example, in October 1851 a house of one room, twelve feet by six feet, held a family of seven tinkers, or 'cairds' in the local terminology. They were related by marriage or blood, as were their ten children, while the woman who lodged with them was unrelated but uncomplaining. Of the eighteen people, the seven adult tinkers were arrested for breach of the peace and assault that month, and six of these seven were given ten days in prison. The cell would have seemed luxurious and spacious in comparison to their Shuttle Lane home.

Thieves' Kitchen

At the beginning of the century there was a notorious thieves' kitchen at the east end of Shuttle Lane. In the summer of 1829, the denizens of this place created a simple trick. One or other of them would enter a spirit shop and ask the shopkeeper to fill up a bottle with whisky. When this was done, the woman would ask for another small item, and when the shopkeeper went to get it, she would run away with the whisky. However, in June one female shopkeeper refused to be a passive victim and chased the women right into Shuttle Lane and into their home, where she was immediately surrounded by two women and three men. The shopkeeper courageously demanded payment for the whisky, but instead two of the men held her while her pocket was cut from her side. Luckily, her husband had followed: he pulled his wife free and held the door against the thieves until the police arrived and arrested the whole gang.

Robbing the Gullible

Another Shuttle Lane speciality was for a smiling woman to entice a gullible man into a dark room to be robbed. One example was in 6 January 1854, when James Gruer visited Aberdeen. He was not used to town life, being a farm servant from Tominrau, near the Castleton of Braemar, and he did not expect the friendliness of the people to be quite so extreme. In particular, he was impressed by the smiling face and swinging hips of a girl he met in the town centre. She was a genuine charmer who held him in the palm of her warm, soft hand and promised him all the delights of her warm, soft body. He listened and believed, so walked willingly with her to a house in Shuttle Lane. Only then did he experience the hard heart beneath the silky exterior as she left him alone in a dark room and John Baillie, a twenty-seven-year-old man, loomed out of the shadows and attacked him.

Baillie thumped Gruer, knocked him down and robbed him of his pocketbook and seventeen shillings, all the money he had with him. Gruer complained to the police, and Baillie was arrested and charged, eventually being sent on penal servitude for six years.

There was a similar occurrence in November 1886 when three young women, Harriet Thompson, Ann Paterson and Helen Newlands, enticed a Drumoaks farmer named George Forbes into their house in Shuttle Lane and robbed him of two £5 notes. It is impossible to know the full extent of this type of robbery, as very often the victim would be too embarrassed to admit that he followed the sway of a shapely hip into such a foolish trap.

Pickpockets and Thieves

Anybody walking through the lane was obviously counted as fair game and catching the many pickpockets and footpads was not easy. For example, on Friday, 1 April 1829, a visitor from the country had his pocket picked in Justice Street. He followed the female thief to Shuttle Lane, but she dived into the first house, out the back window and escaped.

Shuttle Lane was the home of scores of thieves, many of who appeared before the courts in Aberdeen. For example, there was Mary Kennedy, who was a habitual thief. By November 1848 she had already had three convictions for theft, and that month she appeared in the Sheriff Criminal Court. She was charged with four separate acts of theft, mostly of clothes but also of a silver watch, from various houses in Aberdeen. She pleaded guilty and was sent to jail for eighteen months.

Listing all the known thieves of Shuttle Lane would make tedious reading, but the following are some minor examples. There was David Wales, who broke into Ogg's Bottlers on John Street on 10 April 1878 by climbing an eleven-foot-high wall and opening a back door. He forced a desk and took £10 from a cash box. Mary Maclean was a habitual thief, given twenty days for picking a pair of gloves from a mason's pocket in December 1878 and forty days for picking a labourer's pocket in April 1880. Then there was seventeen-year-old John Innes, who was given twenty days in November 1877 for stealing poultry, and twenty-four-year-old John Robertson, a comb maker who was given twenty days for stealing a carpet bag from a Castle Street spirit dealer. Duncan Ferguson really ought to have known better: he was convicted for theft at least twelve times, and was arrested again in June 1878 and charged with stealing clothes, which was not quite the behaviour expected from a schoolteacher.

Other thefts were slightly different. Alexander Russell was nineteen and teamed up with three other teenagers to scout out the fishing boats at Point Law and decide if there was anything worth stealing. There were no valuables in the cabins, so the thieves grabbed a basket of herring instead and ran off with it. There was method in Russell's madness, as his sister was a fisherwoman and bought the fish from him, but he had been seen in the boat and was given thirty days in jail to think of a more clever way to steal.

Other denizens of Shuttle Lane also liked to steal fish. At dawn of 19 May 1900, the police found two men, including Robert McHaffie of Shuttle Lane, on the Bridge of Don with three young salmon. The poachers appeared at the Sheriff Court in June and McHaffie continually interrupted the proceedings with insults and questions directly sharply at Sheriff Robertson. When Sheriff Robertson warned him to behave, McHaffie became violent; the sheriff ordered him removed 'until he became sober', but McHaffie insisted he had 'not tasted drink that day'. To add to his case, he winked at the audience and jabbed a pointing finger at Robertson, who fined him five shillings, with sixteen shillings and ninepence in expenses.

Eleven-year-old Alexander Russell was perhaps less fortunate. In July 1871 he was arrested for pick pocketing a purse containing £2, but was only found guilty of reset. That cost him ten days in jail and five years in a reform school.

A Haven of Sin

There were prostitutes as well as thieves and muggers. In 1829, three men, a seaman named George Keith, a labourer named Peter Skinner, and a flesher named David Adams, helped Elizabeth Thom run a brothel in Shuttle Lane. The police pounced and on Wednesday, 22 July all four appeared in court accused of 'harbouring thieves and vagrants'. They were each given three months with hard labour in Bridewell then banished from Aberdeen for a year. There were many others, such as Isabella Pringle and Robert Proctor, who were fined £10 for harbouring prostitutes in November 1886, and 39-year-old Janet Horne, who failed to turn up for her trial in September 1887. Other prostitutes lived in Shuttle Lane but plied their trade elsewhere, such as Mary Ann McLean, who was fined ten shillings for loitering in East North Street in July 1879; Jane Smith, who loitered on Castle Street in March 1880; and Elspet Robb and Margaret Grey, who also worked in East North Street in July 1880.

Casual Violence

Augmenting the theft and prostitution of Shuttle Lane was the casual violence as the inhabitants assaulted each other, or anybody else they happened to fall out with when they were walking the streets of Aberdeen. Catherine Handlings was one woman who knew about casual violence. She had a dog, while her neighbour, a man named Stewart, owned a cat. When Handling's dog attacked Stewart's cat, Stewart had dived in to the rescue of his pet, but in doing so had kicked the dog. Handling grabbed the poker from the fireplace and rushed to the rescue of her dog, smashing Stewart over the head 'to the effusion of blood'. The police had been called and the case came to the Police Court on 1 September 1850. Handling, an old offender, was fined seven shillings and sixpence.

Husbands and wives were also liable to disagree in Shuttle Lane. At about half past three on Saturday, 18 August 1883, thirty-eight-year-old Duncan Davidson came home and found his wife was having a party with some of her friends. He had stopped off at a pub on the way home for a glass but was sober, or so he believed, while many of the people in his house were roaring drunk and the whisky was flowing free.

One of the visitors was Margaret Cadman. She agreed that there was a group of women in the house and they were 'real happy together'. She claimed they had only three pints of porter and a gill of whisky between the lot of them. Duncan Davidson put the women out of the house, and a few moments later Cadman heard Ann Davidson, Duncan's wife, 'give a skirl' and she rushed back to see what had happened. Ann was lying flat out 'in a pool of blood'. When Cadman helped Ann to her feet, she was told Duncan had given her a 'skelp'. The other women also returned to the house, but Duncan Davidson threatened that if they did not leave he would 'give them as much'.

Somebody called the police and the case came before the Sheriff on 24 September that year. Duncan Davidson was arrested and charged with stabbing Ann on the nose with a screwdriver. Duncan pleaded not guilty, claiming that Ann had been holding a screwdriver: he had tried to get it from her and she had been stabbed by accident.

Ann told a similar story. She said that once he had cleared the house of her friends, Duncan had wanted to go out, but she was 'determined to keep him in'. Ann had got angry. The lock on the door was broken and she had taken the screwdriver to try to fix it, but when Duncan tried to take it, she had got hurt. Ann said that there was 'nothing the matter with my face in the world' as she tried to defend her husband, but the sheriff disagreed and sent him to jail for thirty days.

Wife-beating

It was horribly common for men to knock about their wives or partners. In 1890, John Bolton, a fisherman of 22 Shuttle Lane, was not much of a drinking man, but his partner, Ann Moir, was. Bolton's pet vice was his vicious temper, which he took out on her from time to time, leaving her with sundry bruises. He was at home on the evening of Wednesday, 12 February, but at about eleven at night Moir staggered in 'beastly drunk' and began to abuse and shout at Bolton. He put her out of the house. When she protested and tried to get back inside, Bolton knocked her down and kicked her where she lay.

However, Moir had no intention of staying outside on a freezing winter's night, so got back up and barged straight back inside, screaming abuse. Bolton put her outside again, and Moir returned again, still attacking him verbally. Bolton threw her outside a second time, but when she crashed in again, he lost his temper. He smacked her in the face, knocked her head against a pail and kicked her in the belly. Moir staggered to her feet and ran to the police for help. Dr Matthew Hay examined her and thought her injuries were serious, while one of her female friends reported that next morning she was still bleeding 'about the body'. The police arrested Bolton, who was fined £2.

Various Disputes

Brothers could also fall out. On Thursday, 2 November 1848, Shaw and David Mackenzie had a stand-up fist-to-fist fight in the middle of Shuttle Lane. They made such a noise about settling their fraternal differences that the police were called. Shaw, with eight previous convictions for assault, breach of the peace and theft, was sent to prison for sixty days, and David, with a mere four convictions, was given forty days.

These were only examples of the seething unrest of Shuttle Lane:

there was also Mark McAllister, who was fined thirty shillings in April 1876 for attacking a woman, and William McKay, who in August 1884 assaulted Constable John Laing, as well as breaching the peace, obstructing a police officer in the course of his duty and trying to rescue a prisoner. He was given a lenient £5 fine. There was also Ann Walker, who assaulted a woman at her home in Shuttle Lane in July 1877 and was fined twenty shillings, but was herself attacked in August 1879 and again in August 1884. There were many more.

Hiding the Loot

Shuttle Lane could also be used as a place to conceal stolen goods. In October 1856, John Brunton was released from an eighteen-month spell in Perth Penitentiary and returned to his native Aberdeen. He immediately teamed up with John Clark, another experienced thief, and went on the prowl. They visited a house in Queen Street and stole a large copper boiler that they touted around the city, but without success. They were left with a piece of potentially valuable merchandise, but no buyer. Rather than merely abandon it, they dug a large hole in a piece of waste ground north of the city poor house and buried it there until the market improved. However, Brunton and Clark were not the only thieves in Aberdeen, and somebody stole their boiler and hid it near the powder magazine, but a third set of thieves had also been watching, and grabbed the boiler and carried it to the back of Shuttle Lane, where the police found it. The police also picked up Brunton and Clark and put them back in prison where they belonged.

Thefts in the Lane

Shuttle Lane was a target as well as a home for thieves. In autumn 1861, two thieves, Mark Grant and Andrew McGruer, broke into the house of a Shuttle Lane rat-catcher named Donald McAllister. They stole a selection of clothes, a glass decanter and a watch. The two were caught and in December they were convicted at the Sheriff Court. Grant was a young boy but already a convicted thief and was given fourteen days in jail and five years in the reformatory, while McGruer was given three months in jail.

Sentencing for theft seemed erratic: when Mary Inch stole a blanket from a house in Shuttle Lane in November 1853, she was sentenced to four years' penal servitude.

Breaches of the Peace

The most common crime was breach of the peace, which in the nineteenth century usually meant making a drunken racket outside somebody's house. For example, on 20 November 1850 Jane Annand received her eighth conviction for breach of the peace. She had walked along Shuttle Lane screaming foul-mouthed vituperation at everybody she saw. Annand was fined ten shillings and sixpence with a twenty-day alternative. On 4 December that same year, Isabella Murdoch was provoked by verbal abuse until she retaliated by smashing several panes of glass in a Shuttle Lane window. Because of the extenuating circumstances, the magistrate only fined her sixpence. That magistrate must have been feeling very lenient: on 14 November 1888, Margaret Lawrence was fined fifteen shillings, or about a week's wages, for using obscene language.

Married couples were very prone to arguing: on 1 November 1883, forty-year-old Robert Hendry and his twenty-four-year-old wife Jane disturbed what passed for peace in Shuttle Lane by fighting and quarrelling with each other. They appeared at the Police Court the next day: it was Robert's fourth appearance and Jane's eighth. She tried to take all the blame, but Bailie Donald thought they were both equally at fault and fined each fifteen shillings, with the alternative of seven days in jail.

Some people obviously could not help themselves: on 12 July 1877, a carter named William Maitland was fined ten shillings on his tenth conviction for creating a disturbance. His record was beaten in October 1876 when sixty-year-old Margaret Mitchell was fined ten shillings for her eleventh conviction, but Mary O'Rourke outshone them both. In November 1868 she appeared before the Police Court for her nineteenth time, mainly for breach of the peace but also for theft and malicious mischief.

A Collection of Petty Criminals

There were other crimes, year after year. In August 1856 at the Sheriff Court, William Doyle, a labourer, was given six months for reset of stolen goods. In July 1872, a cab driver named George Fyfe was fined fifteen shillings for getting drunk and indecently assaulting two thirteen-year-old girls in West North Street and a married woman in Shuttle Lane. In September 1888, Christina Allan was given three months for perjury. She had been a witness in the Police Court on 31 August and had stated she had seen a man attack the school-board officer, James Geddes. Allan had sworn on oath that the attacker was not John McNamee the pedlar, although she was well aware that it had been. In her defence she stated that the night before the trial McNamee's wife had threatened her with serious injury if she had identified her husband.

In May 1886, Elizabeth Humphrey was charged with neglecting to send her thirteen-year-old daughter Elizabeth to school. Humphrey denied it, but she was known as a woman with a very bad character. Indeed, the school-board officer thought that Humphrey was keeping her daughter off school to use her as a prostitute. 'I beg your pardon,' Humphrey replied, 'allow me to call you a liar.' All the same there was no doubt that young Elizabeth had not been to school, so Humphrey was fined five shillings, with another five shillings' expenses.

The Sad Side

There were also tragedies: on Saturday, 1 November 1834, a mother left her four-year-old son in the care of her friend, who was less than attentive and left him alone in a room with an open fire. The boy strayed too close to the flames and his clothes caught fire. He was too small to open the door, so grabbed a poker and lifted the latch, but even when adults reached him it was too late and he died the next morning. Then in July 1861, marital troubles caused a Mrs McIntosh to leave her Shuttle Lane house and go to a friend in King Street, where she took a razor and tried to cut her own throat. Fortunately, she was rescued before she succeeded.

Overall, Shuttle Lane was a sad, sordid street. At one time it had thrived, but as industrialisation bit, the street descended into poverty and the inhabitants scrabbled for survival, using every resource they could, from pick pocketing to theft and assault. It was not a place for the faint-hearted.

18
Later Police

As the century rolled on, the police of Aberdeen and Aberdeenshire progressed in efficiency and technique. It was a dynamic force that frequently altered to meet new challenges, and had its manpower in a constant state of flux. A landmark year was 1868, with John Swanson of Edinburgh taking the reins as superintendent. He presided over a uniform change, as helmets replaced the old-style top hats and watchmen were given whistles but lost their long staffs.

Swanson inherited the old bugbear of early Victorian policing: the problem of pickpockets. This was a particular nuisance during major events such as fairs or shows. The Aberdeen races were no different, so in September 1876 Superintendent Swanson sent most of his detectives to the races, while the remainder did a pre-emptive strike on the known haunts of the pickpockets. They hauled in all they could find, with the result that there were no reported cases of pick pocketing at the races.

Swanson was in charge until 1880, when Thomas Wyness took over. Improvements and alterations came thick and fast in the latter decades of the century, with the first telephone arriving in the police headquarters in 1882 and the town boundaries expanding to include Old Aberdeen and Torry. With the larger responsibilities came a demand for more men on the beat and a number of sub police stations as well. That same year saw a prison van provided, with bicycles and tram passes for the constables, while the superintendent was given a dog cart and horse to give him dignified mobility around his charge. In September 1884, the Aberdeen police were given a wage rise: after five years as a first-class constable the pay rose by twopence a week. Even so, Aberdeen police earned less than their counterparts in other cities, so that after they were trained, many Aberdeen policemen left to work in Edinburgh or Glasgow.

Attacking the Police

Even late in the century, when respectable people accepted the police as part of life, disgruntled or drunken civilians could take their frustrations out on lone constables. For example, at about one in the morning of Sunday, 1 July 1877, Constable Johnstone was in duty on King Street when James Leiper, a fisherman of Water Lane, roared along the street, 'making a great noise' and threatening to commit suicide. When Johnstone warned him to keep quiet, Leiper punched him in the face. It was Leiper's ninth conviction and his third for assault: it cost him forty days in jail.

Another example was on Thursday, 30 April 1878, when forty-two-year-old confectioner William Cooper argued with his wife and daughter. He was a bad-tempered man at best, with two previous convictions for assault, but this time he went a bit far. It was late at night and he was at home in Justice Street, but he made so much noise arguing with his wife that the neighbours called the police. No sooner had a constable appeared to quieten things down than Cooper lunged at him with a knife. The policeman had to struggle hard to defend himself, and Cooper ripped his uniform with the blade. Eventually the policeman was successful, but not before his wrist was sprained. He arrested Cooper for assault.

Possibly the discontented attacked the police because they were winning the war on crime. In 1887, there were sixteen attacks on policemen. That was a typical year, which can be used as an example of the duties the Aberdeen police performed. That year, the Aberdeen police arrested 3,046 people, of whom 3,004 were dealt with in the Police Court for minor offences and forty-two at higher courts. The actual number of offenders was less than the number of arrests, as many were arrested on multiple occasions. There were 1,515 males and 714 females arrested, with one case of culpable homicide, one 'lewd and libidinous' assault, two arrests for indecent exposure, and ten assaults, including one by stabbing, and one woman arrested for neglecting her child. There were eight cases of robbery, 284 cases of simple theft, and 166 arrests for using obscene language.

Of the offenders, 634 men and 491 women were imprisoned, including 107 children under twelve years old. Compared with 509 women, 1,140 men were found drunk on the street. The worst street for crime was Castle Street, with 192 arrests, followed by Union Street, with 122. Shuttle Lane, for all its small length, had thirty-seven arrests. Of the 126 men in the police force that year, one died, eleven voluntarily resigned and two were encouraged to resign rather than be discharged.

By May 1893, the Aberdeen force amounted to one chief constable and one superintendent, eight inspectors, six sergeants, two detective officers and seventy-nine constables. Peterhead had a sergeant and seven constables, Cults had two constables, and Fraserburgh a sergeant and three constables, but in the herring-fishing season a further four men were recruited. All in all, the police coped well. In order to give a picture of these men, a short sketch of the careers of three long-serving officers is given.

Inspector John Hendry

One of these policemen was John Hendry. He was born in Newmachar on 7 October 1832 and had no immediate inclination to join the police. He worked at a blacksmith's forge until he was twenty, when he signed up with the Royal Artillery. Although he volunteered to fight in the Crimean War (1854–56), he was not selected so spent his time in England and the Mediterranean, before he left the army and returned to a blacksmith's forge at Cuminestown. After a while he began to give drill lessons to the local police, but the lure of a uniform drew him to Aberdeen and enlistment.

After a spell working in the weights and measures department, in 1864 Hendry was posted to Inverurie, just in time to become involved in a murder case. On Sunday, 31 December, fourteen-year-old George Cruickshank had found a badly injured woman named Ann Forbes in a wood at Thainstone House. Somebody had battered her around the head with something heavy and sharp. In the folds of her clothes was a letter to a sixty-two-year-old wood merchant named George Stephen. The two had been more than friends twenty-seven years previously and Forbes had wanted to renew their relationship. The two had met and walked into the woods, where Stephen had smacked her on the back of the head with an axe.

Stephen had just come through some traumatic times that may have altered his personality. He had been very ill and his business had suffered. Constable Hendry escorted Stephen into the room where Forbes lay bleeding. Hendry's intention may have been to persuade the victim to identify her attacker, but she died without saying a word. However, Hendry found an axe covered in blood and hair that belonged to the now dead woman. There was no doubt about Stephen's guilt, but his motive was unclear. He was found guilty and sentenced to penal servitude.

Hendry's next posting was Newmachar, where there was one

interesting incident. There was a theft of clothes from the trunk of a farm servant at Hill of Middleton, near Disblair. Hendry investigated and asked questions: a woman from the nearby Hatton of Fintry said she had seen a large man carrying a bundle past her house. Hendry inspected the moorland and found footprints: they were about fourteen inches long and with unusually narrow toes. He followed the trail to Hatton of Fintry, where they vanished in a patch of hard ground, but by then he knew the direction in which the thief had gone.

The next day, Hendry travelled into Aberdeen and asked the town police for help. A Sergeant Matthew helped him tour the pawnbrokers, where eventually they found the stolen clothes. Hendry must have been a very lucky or a very observant man: he was walking along Broad Street and St Paul Street when he saw a tall man. He followed his police instincts and looked at the man's feet: they were long and thin. He told Sergeant Matthew that he thought that was their man, and they placed the tall man under arrest. The man denied everything, but the pawnbroker recognised him and he got sixty days in jail for the theft.

Hendry was posted to Old Aberdeen next, but there was only one notable arrest there. There was a theft at Restock's Mill, and Hendry arrested the thief in Guestrow; the man was a habitual thief and got ten years.

After promotion to sergeant and then inspector, in 1874 Hendry was posted to Fraserburgh. He played a prominent role in trying to quell the fisherman's riot there (see Chapter 12 for more details).

From Fraserburgh, Inspector Hendry moved to Inverurie and was involved in the Dunecht mystery (see Chapter 2), but that was the last major incident in his long career. He retired in 1898 after forty years' service. His career had taken him from the city to the country and the coast, so he had experienced much of Aberdeenshire's crime and policing.

Inspector William McHardy

Unlike Hendry, William McHardy was from a police family, although his own immediate background was not in the force. In common with many of the best Aberdeenshire policemen, William McHardy was a countryman: he was born in Glenluie, near Ben MacDhui, with his father a gamekeeper. His uncle was Inspector Cran; his brother Alister joined the police and rose to become Chief Constable of Invernessshire; his second brother, Charles, became Chief Constable of Dunbartonshire; and a third brother, Peter, was also a policeman for a while. To keep the family connection, two of his sons also joined the service.

William McHardy's first job was as a ghillie, an attendant for a sportsman in the hills, an occupation whose tracking skills came in handy during his career. When he was nine, the family moved to Linn of Quoich, close to Braemar, and in June 1854 he joined the Aberdeenshire Police. His first few years saw him at Cruden, then Affleck, near Huntly, and then in 1859, as a sergeant, he was sent to Ellon.

It was in Ellon that McHardy had the first major incident of his career, but it was not connected to any crime. In 1861, the three-arched railway bridge over the River Ythan collapsed in an avalanche of falling stone and lime. McHardy had to help clear up the confusion. There was a small consolation for the locals in that the lime poisoned a number of salmon, which meant free food for those fortunate enough to pick them up. There was another accident on the railway later when a number of ballast wagons ran off the rails and killed one man and hurt another fourteen people. McHardy was there to help the injured and care for the family of the deceased.

After another couple of moves, McHardy was promoted to an inspector at Aboyne. He was involved with the security of Queen Victoria and also with the shooting of Peter Gerrie at Torphins, in Deeside, which created a sensation at the time. Gerrie was a young man, the foreman of a banker and grain merchant named William McPetrie. He was shot twice, once in the head and the second time on the body, but his heavy winter coat – it was February 1878 – helped break the force of the shot and Gerrie survived. The fact that two shots were fired made it obvious that it was a deliberate attack and not merely a sporting accident.

McHardy's investigations found a shotgun that had been thrown away in dense woodland, while the local gunmaker said it had only been fired once since he had sold it to McPetrie. McHardy also found footprints in the mud that exactly matched McPetrie's boots and a place in McPetrie's bank where a shotgun could have been hidden. Just as significant, McPetrie had taken out an insurance policy on Gerrie's life. McPetrie and Gerrie had been friends since they were apprenticed together, but they had only recently become business partners. When Gerrie found some irregularities in the books, he wanted to pull out, but McPetrie objected. Newly married and a new father, McPetrie was in dire need of money, which seems to have been the motive for the murder. When William McPetrie appeared before the Circuit Court, he was awarded twenty years' penal servitude, while Gerrie eventually recovered.

At nearly the same time as the shooting of Gerrie, Alexander Duncan, aged sixty-three, and John Moir, a fifty-eight-year-old local Torphins farmer, were attacked. The attacker came behind and cracked Moir brutally over the head with a heavy stick. Moir had ten separate injuries and died not long after.

Duncan managed to run to safety, losing his hat in the process. Shortly afterwards, a cattle dealer named George Nicol also claimed to have been attacked and robbed. His clothes and face were heavily bloodstained, and sympathetic locals called the police. McHardy arrived, but noticed that Nicol wore a hat very similar to the one that Duncan had lost. Nicol immediately blamed the injured Moir for stealing his hat, pretended that he was badly hurt and feigned sleep.

McHardy was not fooled and arrested him. Nicol was given two years in jail.

McHardy was also connected to the case of an Elgin horse thief named John McLean. In that case, McHardy used all his old ghillie's skills in a sixty-mile trail over the hills to find McLean.

McLean had stolen a horse and gig at Crathes and hid it at the back of Queen's Hill, behind Aboyne Castle. He tucked the gig into the shadow of the hill flank and waited for the dark hours to pass, before driving the mile or so to the farm of Heughhead. In the dim dawn, McLean sneaked into the stable and attempted to swap his stolen horse for one less recognisable. However, the horse was a good judge of character and bit him. Leaving the horse safely in its stall, McLean broke into the servants' quarters and stole a new suit of clothes instead.

By that time, McHardy was on the trail of the stolen gig. He asked at the farms and cottages and followed the trail. He found the gig and its horse on a quiet track in the middle of the hills, but there was no sign of McLean. McHardy called up the constable from Ballater, and together they traced McLean over the wind-cropped heights to Tomintoul and Avonside, but without grabbing hold of him. When he reached Tomintoul, McHardy sent the Ballater policeman home, recruited the Tomintoul officer and traced McLean all the way to Ballindalloch, where he placed him under arrest. McLean was given six years' penal servitude.

McHardy's next posting was to Aberdeen and then to Inverurie. He was married to Eliza Robertson of Fyvie and they had ten children, of whom eight survived. He retired to Braemar in 1898 after a career of unwavering success.

Inspector Alexander Morrison

The last of the trio of later Victorian police officers was Inspector Alexander Morrison. He was also a countryman, born in the parish of

Forgue and educated at the small local school of Drumblade. After a childhood and early youth spent working in agriculture, in 1856 he joined the Aberdeenshire Police. He began his career at Cruden, where he helped catch a serial thief named Mackie. That was a change from his more normal duties of patrolling the coast to stop the widespread practice of shooting sea birds for sport. He then moved to Aboyne, where his routine duties were interrupted when the railway navvies murdered the Lumphanan blacksmith Fenton Petrie, but the culprit was never discovered (see Chapter 10).

His next station was Murtle, between Banchory and Aberdeen, and then he went to New Pitsligo, which was then terrorised by a group of youths and young men known as 'the Black Band' who came out with the dark to cause mayhem. After periods at Ellon and Peterhead, the now Sergeant Morrison was promoted to inspector at Alford. In 1882, he transferred to Fraserburgh and things livened up in his life. There was a major riot with the fishermen and a drunken scramash at the railway station in September when the Highland fishermen crammed into trains to return home. Drunken fishermen were crawling through the carriage windows and embracing each other publicly, much to the amusement of the local men.

There was also an elopement, where a pedlar named Michael Reilly absconded with the clothes of James Johnston, a Fraserburgh labourer, as well as his wife and eight-year-old daughter. Morrison traced the trio to Aberdeen Links, where Morrison was found wearing Johnston's clothes and with his wife at his side. Morrison brought all three back to Fraserburgh, but the wife refused to return to her husband, and the daughter seemed to prefer Reilly to her father.

That was followed by a nasty outbreak of cattle killing in the farms around Aberdour. The killer crept into the byres at night and stabbed the animals as they stood helpless in their confined spaces.

Morrison made a number of enquiries and found out that on each farm where a cow had been murdered, a local butcher named Strachan had miraculously appeared the next morning to buy hay and had ended up buying the dead animal for a song. He was arrested and fined £40, but absconded to America rather than pay it and was outlawed instead.

A more serious crime occurred in Crimond, where a farmer named Pirie had sold his sheep for a good sum, but the same night he was burgled and had £279 stolen. Even worse, there was evidence that somebody had tried to set fire to the house. Again, Morrison made enquiries and found out that a few weeks before a joiner named George Chalmers had repaired the locks in the house, and that same man had been seen boarding a train at Lonmay Station for Aberdeen. Chalmers had been a respectable workman until recently, when he had begun drinking. Morrison telegraphed Aberdeen and the police waited in the station until Chalmers appeared for the return train to his home in Crimond. He was arrested and ended up in the jail.

In 1889, Morrison was involved in an assault at Whitehill, near New Deer, when a farmer named Urquhart was attacked, knocked unconscious and thrown down a well. Luckily a young girl found him before he drowned. Two years later, Morrison was once more standing between fishermen and trouble when trawler crews landed their catch at Fraserburgh and the local Broadsea men gathered to protest. There was no love lost between trawlermen and the local long-liners, who believed that trawls damaged the seabed and would ruin fishing in the long term. On this occasion there was lots of shouting, but only a handful of men were arrested for breach of the peace.

In addition to his routine duties, Morrison also helped look after the queen at Balmoral during the Fenian troubles in the 1860s, and was sent to Blairgowrie and Thurso when there were election riots.

In 1898, Morrison retired after a career that had seen riots, thefts, poaching and assaults: he was a pretty typical Victorian police officer.

Overall, the later Aberdeen and Aberdeenshire police had all the usual city crimes, plus those habitual to the countryside, and coped with everything that the criminal element threw at them. The three officers mentioned here were notable only in that they progressed to higher ranks. Their experiences could be mirrored a hundred times by the men who patrolled the highways and byways of the north-east in the later decades of the nineteenth century.

19
Hodgepodge of Crime

As well as the easily recognisable crimes such as theft and murder, there were many other methods of breaking the law. Some virtually defy description, while others are interesting for their own sake, or because they illustrate that however many years pass, crime continues in the same old way.

Grogging Casks

There are some crimes just would not be considered by ordinary people. The grogging of spirit casks is one. In the 1880s, James Brebner and Alexander Johnston were spirit dealers in Carnegie Brae in Aberdeen. Unfortunately, they neglected to tell Customs and Excise the nature of their business, so when the inspectors came to call they found a quantity of spirits on which no duty had been paid.

Brebner and Johnston pled ignorance that they had broken the law. They had a simple method of getting spirits. First they bought a large number of used whisky casks. They stored them in their premises, quite openly. Then they put water into the casks to make 'grog' as the spirits that the wood had absorbed came into the water. The process was illegal, but it happened. In May 1892, questions were asked in parliament, with an answer that the importation of spirit casks from abroad specifically to grog them was not widespread.

Brebner and Johnston grogged sufficient casks to produce ninety gallons of 'grog', which contained fifteen gallons of proof spirits; the duty payable amounted to over £7. With the excise laws being severe, there was a colossal fine of £300 payable. However, when the case reached the court, the judge reduced the fine to £75 and the forfeiture of the spirits.

Other cases were much worse.

A Creature in Human Form

Charles Jones, a seaman on HMS *Clyde*, was charged with what was euphemistically termed 'an unnatural crime'. He was found in a shed in Palmerston Road, Aberdeen, on 25 November 1886 with a young boy. The defence tried to create an alibi, but the jury had no difficulty in finding that Jones was guilty. The judge, Lord Young, did not try to hide his repulsion at 'having to address a creature in human form of whom such a charge is true'. Lord Young said, 'I fear you have been polluting boys here for some time … you are not to be hanged as a noxious animal as you might have been at no remote period but you must be shut up so that you shall have no opportunity to commit this crime again.' Jones was sentenced to penal servitude for fourteen years.

Rape

Proportionally, there was probably just as much sexual crime taking place in the nineteenth century as there is today. On 9 August 1876, William Mitchell of Fordoun, south of Aberdeen, decided he would go on a spree of ravishing. His first victim was ten-year-old Sarah Ann Stewart as she walked along the path between Auchinblae and Laurencekirk. She was passing Fordoun Kirk when Mitchell pounced. Despite her youth, he smacked her across the face first, and then smashed her across the back with a heavy bag of plumber's tools before he sexually assaulted her.

Mitchell's next victim was Ann Low, slightly older and the daughter of a blacksmith of Whitemyre. He grabbed her near Blackford House Wood. When he was finished with her he approached Betsy Cairncross, all of eleven years old, in a field near Crookieden in the same parish. Mitchell was only sixteen: he would have been twenty-three when he was released from the seven years' penal servitude to which he was sentenced.

Other crimes caught the most gullible of the population.

Fortune Telling

Even among a populace as notoriously hard-headed as the Aberdonians, there will be a certain number of credulous people who believe exactly what they are told. Ann Maria Smith and her husband Alfred Smith played on this credulity to make a living in the city during the late 1880s. Although the couple had probably been operating for some time, only a few victims were called on to give evidence at the Police Court. All were very young, impressionable servant girls whose one wish in life was to find a nice young man who would marry them.

On 16 February 1889, Ann Smith acted as a fortune teller in Beaconsfield Place. A string of servant girls came to her house, crossed her palm with silver that they could certainly not afford on their meagre wages, and were duly informed that they would soon marry a handsome man. Only the details varied. Ann Simpson was told that Smith could read her fortune by the marks on her hands and face; she was due to meet 'a very nice young man' in the near future. That piece of useless information cost sixpence. Jane Pearson entered the house on pure speculation and was told if she handed over silver her future would be revealed. Smith told her that she would not get married 'for a considerable time', which must have really raised her spirits.

Margaret Grant worked as a domestic servant at Fountainhall Road, but she had enough sense to keep her silver safe in its purse and walk away. On 26 February, the fortune tellers moved their base to Ashvale Place, but pulled the same scam. Jane Smith was one of their victims. She was a dressmaker from the Gallowgate and handed over the required sixpence to be told that her paramour would be fair-haired and they would marry in two years, by which time Ann Smith the fortune teller would be long gone and just a memory. Isabella Downie was also a dressmaker, and she was due a blond man as well. Smith spun her a long tale for her sixpence: her passage to love would not be smooth; they would argue; her man would run overseas; but it would be all right as he would return to marry her and they would live happily ever after.

Ann Smith may have run out of steam reading so many palms and faces, for her husband seems to have taken over the fortune-telling duties later that day. He checked the future of another dressmaker, Elizabeth Sutherland of Wales Street. Sutherland was also promised a fair-haired sweetheart who would leave the country but return to marry her, while young Helen Christie of Henry Place paid a shilling to be told exactly the same story.

When the police requested the fortune tellers to attend the Police Court, Ann Smith absconded while Albert revealed that his real job was as a horse dealer. He ended up in the jail, no doubt telling the fortunes of wardens and those in for many years.

There were other forms of deception.

Duping the Message Boy

Alexander Black came from South Mile End in Pitmuxton, a name that has now all but disappeared from Aberdeen, but which was between the Dee and Great Western Road. Black was a very young man with a good job and a fine career ahead of him. It was 10 December 1891 and he was employed by Ben Reid and Company as a messenger and apprentice clerk. He was an honest lad, and his manager sent him to the Market Branch of the North of Scotland Bank to hand over a cheque and collect the wages for the firm. Black picked up the money quite happily and was carrying them back to his work when one of the bank clerks hurried after him. Black had reached the junction of Windmill Brae and Bath Street when the clerk approached.

'Excuse me,' the clerk said, fiddling with the pen behind his ear, 'there is something wrong with the cheque; give me the money back and take this letter to your cashier.' The clerk handed a sealed envelope to the boy. 'The bank will be kept open for a quarter of an hour for your return.'

Faced with the voice and person of authority, Alexander Black did as he had been trained to since childhood: he obeyed orders and handed over the bag with the firm's wages – £77. He did not think to question the man with the pen behind his ear. Instead, he hurried back to his cashier with the letter. When the cashier opened the letter he found only a blank sheet of paper, and he immediately contacted the bank, who knew nothing about the matter. Black had been the victim of a clever theft.

The police believed that the thief would have taken the money and left the city right away, so they checked the railway station and alerted the police at other stations round about. At the same time they questioned Black and created a decent description of the supposed bank clerk. The police thought the description was similar to a tailor and known thief named Robert Kirkland. They also asked the bank tellers if they had seen anybody suspicious around the bank. The tellers said that two men had been lounging around at the same time as Black had exchanged his cheque for the wages. The police matched one of their descriptions with Kirkland, while the second was also familiar, a shoemaker named Charles Macpherson.

Armed with the names, the police began to search the streets and known haunts of the two suspects. They discovered that Macpherson had been in arrears with his rent but had suddenly found the cash, and had also hired cabs to travel around the town to various public houses. They had been enjoying themselves immensely, spreading money around with cheerful abandon. They had bought new watches and rings, clothes and fancy bedding. The police watched and then moved in, catching both men and two others who were their close companions.

Although all four were snatched, only Macpherson and Kirkland were charged with the theft. Kirkland was the actual thief while Macpherson was the brains behind the robbery. The trial was a long, drawn-out affair, as Kirkland failed to appear for the original trial, and a third man, a cab driver named Albert Freeman, was also charged. Kirkland was apprehended at Patrick and eventually and reluctantly gave evidence that saw his companions jailed.

Piracy on Land

There are many tales of piracy at sea, where a ship is forcibly boarded and stripped of everything of value. However, such things could also happen on land, and in the north-east of Scotland.

On 29 November 1810, the Pomeranian galliot *Vriendischap* was sailing across the Moray Firth bound from Hull to Gothenburg. Her home port was Bardit, then under Swedish control, and her master was Joachim Schmidt – Joe Smith – but she had a British licence and that was vitally important at a time when Europe was tearing itself apart with war. As is common in these waters, a storm blew up and *Vriendischap* keeled over; her ballast shifted and she was in considerable difficulties. The wind blasted her onto the beach slightly to the west of the burn of Tynet, near Banff.

The vessel was not damaged and none of the crew was injured, so no doubt Captain Schmidt would have sighed with relief and set about re-stowing the ballast and preparing to float *Vriendischap* off with the next tide. However, the local people had no intention of allowing a foreign vessel to sit on their beach unmolested.

Very soon after the ship came ashore, a great mob swarmed down to her. They ignored the pleading of Captain Schmidt that he had a British licence and plundered everything they could from *Vriendischap*. They entered the cabin and broke open all the cupboards and drawers to steal everything they could; they grabbed the ropes, rigging and tackle from the decks, pushed the crew aside and left, having harvested the galliot of everything portable.

When Schmidt complained to the authorities, a number of the local fishermen and others were rounded up. They included William Geddes, a white-fisher (a man who caught white fish with lines rather than herring with nets) from Port Gordon known as 'Whitey'; James Stewart, known as 'Lordie'; Alexander Clark, known as 'Sailor'; Peter Coull, known as 'Dumpie'; John Robertson, or 'young Cockie'; James Cowie, or 'Boggan's son'; Alexander Sclater; and James Innes. Only four were charged: Sclater, Innes, Clark and Coull were all sentenced to three months in the Banff Tolbooth as an example.

Dangerous Driving

At the Sheriff Court on 23 December 1829, a carter named George Fraser of Mounthcoly, Aberdeen, was accused of culpable homicide. On 24 August 1829 he had been driving his cart, fully loaded with stones, towards the yard of Joseph Munro, a stonecutter. Unfortunately, two-year-old Mary Tait was sitting on the kerb of the pavement at North Street and he ran over her. At the time, Fraser was driving on the wrong side of the road and was holding neither a rein nor a bridle as he walked a few paces behind the cart. The nearside wheels of the cart were within a foot of the edge of the road.

Fraser was found guilty and sentenced to two months in jail.

Reckless Driving

On Tuesday, 6 October 1829, a Highlander named John Stewart was driving the Star coach along the turnpike road between Huntly and Pitcaple. He was known as a careful driver and was nearing the farmhouse of Glenniestown in the parish of Gartly when the coach overturned and two women were severely injured. They had been outside passengers. Stewart was charged with driving in a reckless and culpable manner.

Margaret Skinner was married to James Skinner, an Aberdeen cooper. She had joined the coach at Huntly and clambered onto the seat beside James Brander, the guard, and John Stewart. She nodded a greeting to Mrs Anne Munro, the woman who sat on the other side of Stewart, and settled down for the journey. It should have been smooth, as the road was metalled. However, even before they left Huntly, she was alarmed as Stewart raced down Bogie Wynd; he drove so quickly and erratically that she wondered if he was drunk. She knew he had been drinking in Huntly.

Stewart did not slow down: he whipped the horses so they pulled the coach hard, even around the bends. There were four horses, with one of the leaders being livelier than the others. At the Brae of Glenniestown the road was gouged out of the side of a hill; the coach was on the right side of the road and only a few inches away from where the road ended abruptly at a steep downward and unguarded slope. Stewart was not only driving fast, he was also talking to Anne

Munro. Skinner yelled for Stewart to take care, and Brander, the guard, also asked him to slow down. Stewart replied, 'I know how to drive the horses myself.' He looked at the guard: 'Shall I walk the horses here?'

The guard said he should carry on. Immediately he said that, Stewart lifted the whip and slashed it across the haunches of the horses. They sprang forwards, and the coach tipped, ran off the road and slithered about fifty feet down the hill. As the passengers panicked, the coach and horses overturned and crashed down the side of the hill. Margaret Skinner was thrown off her seat, then one of the wheels of the coach smashed into her head and she was concussed. She had other injuries as well: bruises behind her ear, on her right arm and shoulder and her back, and some damaged ribs and internal damage. It was months before she could use the fingers of her right hand or even get out of bed without help.

Stewart and Brander urged the passengers to help drag the Star coach back onto the road and righted it. Despite their tumble, the horses were fit to continue and Stewart climbed back onto the driver's seat. Skinner immediately objected, saying that in her opinion he was not fit to drive. William Ammerson, another passenger, also objected, but rather more strenuously, so that a Glasgow shoemaker and self-appointed self-defence teacher named John Tracy had to break them apart as their dispute came to fisticuffs.

George Dunstan had also been a passenger on the Star coach. He sat beside the guard, driver and the two women on the outside. Stewart asked him to sit at the back of the coach to allow Mrs Munro to come up front so they could talk. However, in the event, Stewart did not continue to drive. By fortuitous happenstance, a second Star coach driver happened to come across the scene of the accident. He also believed that Stewart was unfit to drive and completed the journey. When the case came to the Sheriff Court, the sheriff ordered that Stewart be imprisoned for three months.

Concluding the Crime

Overall, Aberdeen and Aberdeenshire experienced a mixture of crime in the nineteenth century. There were brutal murders and fierce riots, careless seamanship and drunken driving, unruly youths and unscrupulous fraudsters. This knuckle of land, city, countryside, shore and sea was a microcosm of Scotland, with all its crime and all its kindness.

Looking back at the turbulent nineteenth century after the even more turbulent twentieth, it is hard to believe that some of these events took place. The female fraudsters still have the ability to astonish, the Kittybrewster murder sickens with its utter pointlessness, and the thefts and muggings are as familiar today as they were when Queen Victoria was on the throne, but other incidents are alien. Who could believe that 8,000 people would gather to watch a public hanging, or that an Aberdeen crowd would burn an anatomist's theatre to the ground, or that Aberdeen and Peterhead seamen would come to blows over ownership of a whale? Riots are very rare in Scotland now, and the possibility of thousands of fishermen rampaging through the streets of Stonehaven would raise a smile rather than a frown. The world has changed a lot in the past hundred-odd years, but one thing remains constant: the battle against crime.

Appendix

Convictions for selected crime in Aberdeen: odd years 1845–1859

Year	'45	'47	'49	'51	'53	'55	'57	'59
Murder				2	1	1	1	
Assault	165	152	196	174	170	121	107	124
Fire-raising				2	1	4	1	2
Malicious mischief	21	17	29	26	23	20	14	17
Rape					4			
Assault with intent			2	1				
Bigamy		1	2			1		
Robbery		2	1	6	4	6	3	
Cattle- and sheep-stealing	4	3	2	2	5	3	4	4
Housebreaking and opening lockfast places	23	24	15	9	12	21	23	4
Theft	315	381	297	318	349	319	283	262
Reset	12	12	7	6	5	9	11	5

Year	'45	'47	'49	'51	'53	'55	'57	'59
Forgery, uttering and coining	4	3	5	5	7	3	6	5
Fraud, breach of trust, embezzlement	20	31	54	25	27	19	23	28
Culpable homicide					2	3		
Child murder and concealment of pregnancy	1	3	2	2	1	3		
Breach of the peace and rioting	95	136	350	160	145	265	287	389
Breach of game laws	1	5	4	5	9	19	4	8

All data taken from the annual police reports.

Select Bibliography

Books

Aberdeen Journal

Archibald, Malcolm, *Whalehunters: Dundee and the Arctic Whalers* (Edinburgh: Mercat, 2004).

Barrie, David, *Police in the Age of Improvement: Police Development and the Civic Tradition in Scotland, 1775–1865* (Devon: Willan Publishing, 2008).

Burt, Edmund, *Burt's Letters from the North of Scotland* (Edinburgh: Birlinn, 1754/1998).

Burton, Anthony, *The Railway Builders* (London: John Murray, 1992).

Caledonian Mercury

Cameron, Joy, *Prisons and Punishment in Scotland from the Middle Ages to the Present* (Edinburgh: Canongate, 1983).

Cochrane, Lord, *Circuit Journeys* (Edinburgh, Hawick: Byways Publishing, 1888/1983).

——, *Memorials of His Time* (Edinburgh: Robert Grant & Son Ltd., 1856).

Coleman, Terry, *The Railway Navvies* (London: Penguin, 1965/1976).

Chesney, Kellow, *The Victorian Underworld* (London: Temple Smith, 1970).

Donnelly, Daniel and Scott, Kenneth (eds), *Policing Scotland* (Cullompten: Willan Publishing, 2005).

Fenton, Alexander, *Country Life in Scotland: Our Rural Past* (Edinburgh: John Donald, 1987).

Fraser, Derek, *Power and Authority in the Victorian City* (Oxford: Blackwell, 1979).

General Police Act 1862

Glen, A.E., Glen I.A. and Dunbar, A.G., *Great North of Scotland Railway Album* (London: Fraser Stewart Books, 1960).

Godfrey, Barry and Lawrence, Paul, *Crime and Justice 1750–1950* (Cullompten: Willan Publishing, 2005).

Glasgow Herald

Fraser, David, *The Christian Watt Papers* (Edinburgh: Paul Harris, 1983).

Haldane, A.R.B., *The Drove Roads of Scotland* (Edinburgh: Birlinn, 1997).

Hamilton, Judy, *Scottish Murders* (New Lanark: Waverley Books, 2006).

Hughes, Robert, *The Fatal Shore* (London: Colin Harvill, 1987).

Jackson, Gordon, *The British Whaling Trade* (London: A&C Black, 1978).

Jones, David, *Crime, Protest, Community and Police in Nineteenth-century Britain* (London: Routledge and Keegan Paul, 1982).

Keith, Alexander, *A Thousand Years of Aberdeen* (Aberdeen: Aberdeen University Press, 1972).

Knepper, Paul, *Criminology and Social Policy* (London: Sheffield University, 2007).

Livingstone, Sheila, Confess and be Hanged: Scottish Crime and Punishment Through the Ages (Edinburgh: Birlinn, 2000).

Lynch, Michael (ed.), *The Oxford Companion to Scottish History* (Oxford: Oxford University Press, 2001).

McLaren, Duncan, *The Rise and Progress of Whisky Drinking in Scotland and the Working of the Public Houses (Scotland) Act, commonly called the Forbes McKenzie Act* (Edinburgh, 1858).

Miller, James, *Salt in the Blood: Scotland's Fishing Communities Past and Present* (Edinburgh: Canongate, 1999).

Minto, C.S., *Victorian and Edwardian Scotland* (London: B. T. Batsford, 1970).

Murray, Patrick Joseph, *Not So Bad as They Seem: The Transportation, Ticket-of-leave, and Penal Servitude Questions* (Glasgow, 1857).

Rafter, Nicole, *The Origins of Criminology: A Reader* (Oxford: Routledge-Cavendish, 2009).

Ross-Shire Journal

Smout, T.C., *A History of the Scottish People, 1560–1830* (London: Fontana, 1969).

——, *A Century of the Scottish People, 1830–1950* (London: Fontana, 1987).

The Herald

Walkowitz, Judith, *Prostitution and Victorian Society* (Cambridge: Cambridge University Press, 1982).

Whitmore, Richard, *Victorian and Edwardian Crime and Punishment* (London: Batsford, 1978).

Whittington-Egan, Molly, *The Stockbridge Baby-farmer and Other Scottish Murder Stories* (Glasgow: Neil Wilson Publishing, 2001).

Selected Websites

Government records official website. http://hansard.millbanksystems.com/commons/1847/mar/04/riot-at-wick (accessed 20 November 2013).

Official site of Inveraray Jail. http://www.inverarayjail.co.uk/ (accessed 20 November 2013).

Queensland government site of convict history. http://www.slq.qld.gov.au/resources/family-history/info-guides/convicts (accessed 20 November 2013).

National Library of Scotland Digital Gallery. http://digital.nls.uk/ (accessed 20 November 2013).

Also by Malcolm Archibald

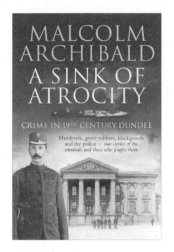

A Sink of Atrocity
RRP £9.99 – 978 1 84502 420 6

Dundee in the nineteenth century was a very dangerous place. Ever since the Circuit judge Lord Cockburn branded the city 'A Sink of Atrocity' in his memoirs, the image of old Dundee has been one of poverty and crime – but what was it really like to live in the streets and closes of Dundee at that time?

In *A Sink of Atrocity*, Malcolm Archibald reveals the real nineteenth-century Dundee and the ordinary and extraordinary crimes that took place. As well as the usual domestic violence, fighting and robberies, Dundee was also beset with a catalogue of different crimes during the century. There were the bodysnatchers and resurrection men who caused much panic in the 1820s and an epidemic of thieving in the 1860s. There were gang crimes, infamous murders and an astonishing outbreak of crimes committed by women, as well as the highly unusual theft of a whale at sea.

Poverty and drink played their part, and up against this tidal wave of crime stood men like Patrick Mackay, one of Dundee's Messengers-at-Arms, who was responsible for apprehending criminals before the advent of the police. It was not an easy job, but those who were caught faced the full force of the law, from fines to jail and from transportation to hanging, as the authorities fought to bring law and order to Dundee.

www.blackandwhitepublishing.com

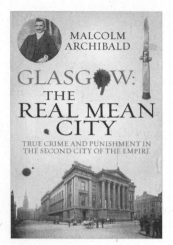

Glasgow: The Real Mean City
RRP £9.99 – 978 1 84502 536 6

There cannot be many cities where crime could mean anything from stealing a ship to singing a seditious song, but nineteenth-century Glasgow was a unique place with an amazing dynamism. Immigrants poured in from Ireland and the Highlands while the factories, shipyards and mills buzzed with innovation. However, underneath the bustle was a different world as an incredibly diverse criminal class worked for their own profit with total disregard for the law.

Robbers infested the highways and byways, a glut of garrotters gathered to jump on the unwary, drunken brawls disfigured the evening streets, prostitutes lured foolish men into dark corners, conmen connived clever schemes and perfidious poisoners plotted. There were dark and dangerous places such as the Tontine Close and there was always the possibility of a major riot – with religion the excuse – as a volatile population became angry at unjust poverty and poor housing.

It was perhaps not surprising that Glasgow formed Britain's first professional police force, and men such as Superintendent James Smart fought to stem the crime that at times seemed to overwhelm the city. The forces of law had to be mobile, with the robbery of the Paisley Bank involving a coach chase as far as London, while the robbery of Walter Baird's shop in the Argyll Arcade took Acting Superintendent George McKay over the sea to Belfast. The police had an often thankless task and *Glasgow: The Real Mean City* chronicles the century-long struggle of the forces of law and order to bring peace to a troubled city.

www.blackandwhitepublishing.com

Whisky Wars, Riots and Murder
RRP £9.99 – 978 1 84502 69 67

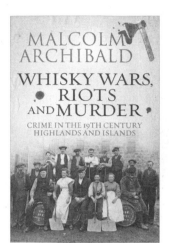

Although the nineteenth-century elite looked on the Highlands and Islands as a sporting paradise, for the indigenous population it was a turbulent place. Rather than a rural idyll, the glens and moors were home to poachers and whisky smugglers, while the towns were always ready to explode into riot and disorder. Even the Hebridean seas had their dangers while the islands seethed with discontent.

Whisky Wars, Riots and Murder reveals the reality behind the facade of romantic tartan and vast estates. Augmenting the usual quota of petty thefts and assaults, the Highlands had a coastal town where riots were endemic, an island rocked by a triple murder, a mob besieging the jail at Dornoch and religious troubles in the Black Isle. Add the charming thief who targeted tourist hotels and an exciseman who was hanged for forgery, and the hidden history of the Highlands is unearthed in all its unique detail.

www.blackandwhitepublishing.com

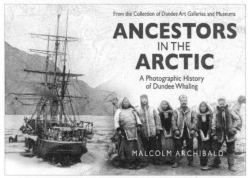

Ancestors in the Arctic
RRP £14.99 – 978 1 84502 715 5

For over 160 years, Dundee sent ships to the Arctic to hunt the whales. It was a brutal, dangerous business but one that was vital to the economy of the city. As well as providing baleen or whalebone, the whaling ships brought home skins for the leather industry and oil that was essential for the scores of jute mills and factories.

Ships built in Dundee became famous as possibly the best vessels for polar exploration of their time and Dundee seamen were sought for their experience and skill.

The McManus Museum in Dundee holds a whaling collection that is recognised as being of national importance. One of the most significant parts of the collection is the images of whaling ships, whaling men and the Inuit of the Arctic. This book shows some of the most evocative images, together with explanatory text. There is also a brief introduction that explains the importance of both the collection and the whaling industry to Dundee.

www.blackandwhitepublishing.com